| | Term-time opening hours: |
|---|---|
| _EGE | |
| _N | |

WITHDRAWN

# WORLD YEARBOOK
# OF EDUCATION 1997

# WORLD YEARBOOK
# OF EDUCATION 1997

# INTERCULTURAL
# EDUCATION

**Edited by**
**David Coulby, Jagdish Gundara and Crispin Jones**
Series editors: David Coulby and Crispin Jones

**KOGAN**
**PAGE**

London • Stirling (USA)

First published in 1997

Kogan Page Limited
120 Pentonville Road
London N1 9JN
and
22883 Quicksilver Drive
Stirling, VA 20166, USA

© David Coulby, Jagdish Gundara and Crispin Jones, 1997

**British Library Cataloguing in Publication Data**

A CIP record for this book is available from the British Library.

ISBN 0 7494 2114 2
ISSN 0084-2508

Typeset by Kogan Page
Printed in England by Clays Ltd, St Ives plc

# Contents

# Notes on the Contributors

**Sheila Aikman** is a Lecturer in Education and International Development at the Institute of Education, London, UK.

**Leslie Bash** is a Principal Lecturer in Education at Anglia University, UK.

**David Coulby** is Professor of Education and Dean of the Faculty of Education and Human Sciences at Bath College of Higher Education, UK.

**Robert Cowen** is a Senior Lecturer in Comparative Education in the Culture, Communication and Societies Group in the University of London Institute of Education, UK.

**Zubeida Desai** is a lecturer in the Education Faculty at the University of the Western Cape, specializing in language education.

**Jianhong Dong** is Deputy Director, Division of Education, Chinese National Commission for UNESCO, Beijing, People's Republic of China.

**Nigel Grant** is Professor Emeritus of Education at the University of Glasgow, UK.

**Jagdish Gundara** is Reader in Education in the Culture, Communication and Societies Group and Head of the International Centre for Intercultural Studies, University of London Institute of Education, UK.

**Olivier Hinton** was educated in France and is currently preparing a PhD at the Institute of Education, University of London, UK.

**Yasumasa Hirasawa** is Professor in the Faculty of Human Sciences, Osaka University, Japan.

**Crispin Jones** is a Senior Lecturer in Education in the Culture, Communication and Societies Group and is a member of the International Centre for Intercultural Studies at the Institute of Education, London University, UK.

**Tapas Majumdar** is Emeritus Professor of Economics at the Jawaharal Nehru University, New Delhi, India.

**John Mallea** is Professor and Past President of Brandon University, Manitoba, Canada.

**Kevin J Moran** is Research Assistant Professor in the School of Education, University of Pittsburgh, USA.

**Lisl Prendergast** is Assistant Principal at Hasting Girls' High School, Hawkes Bay, New Zealand.

**Euan Reid** is a Senior Lecturer at the Institute of Education, attached to the Culture, Communication and Societies Academic Group, University of London, UK.

**Nick Taylor** is Director of the Joint Education Trust, a development agency in Johannesburg, South Africa.

**Verena Taylor** works in the Directorate for Education, Culture and Sports at the Council of Europe, Strasbourg, where she is responsible for the Network for School Links and Exchanges and the Council of Europe's In-service Training Programme for Teachers.

**William B Thomas** is Professor of Education at the University of Pittsburgh, USA.

**Janusz Tomiak** was a Senior Lecturer in Comparative and East European Education at the Institute of Education and School of Slavonic and East European Studies in the University of London, UK, until his retirement in 1988.

**Jonathan Young** is a Full Professor in the Faculty of Education at the University of Manitoba, Canada, where he has just completed a term as Associate Dean.

# Preface

The collapse of Soviet-style communism has meant that the focus of concern in relation to societal diversity has once again shifted to the state. The European Union, the Confederation of Independent States, the North American Free Trade Area and the emergent grouping of the Pacific Rim point towards a trend for larger economic groupings that, perhaps paradoxically, may reawaken the aspirations of peoples previously contained within individual states. Yet the number of recognized states is small, while that of nations or of peoples is large. For example, of the 6,000 or so languages in the world, a mere 100 account for some 95% of the world's population: in other words, 5% of the world's population speak the remaining 5,900. Language is a powerful signifier of identity but many language groups, like other minority groups, are constantly having to assert their right to exist in the face of apathy/hostility from the states in which they live. This is because there are only some 200 or so states in the United Nations, most of which claim some form of putative unitary identity, as opposed to many thousands of linguistic and other powerful group identities.

The issues that arise for education from this situation are complex. Each state has an educational policy in regard to interculturalism, implicit or explicit. Within most states there is also an oppositional discourse or discourses, frequently advocating some form of pluralistic educational policy in response to societal diversity, or, more worryingly, asserting a fictitious monist state singularity. International organizations like the United Nations and the Council of Europe also have policy statements, mostly of a normative nature, supporting interculturalism; however, such statements often have little immediate effect on individual state educational policies.

This *Yearbook* attempts two things in relation to this state of affairs. First, it examines this broader context and attempts to assess the current state of play in relation to debates about interculturalism, state education and societal solidarity. Second, it looks at the policy debates, decisions and practices within specific national and international contexts in order to demonstrate the range that is currently extant. In doing this, the book will be an important marker in a crucial educational debate.

The book, therefore, falls into three sections. The first consists of a series of framing essays that look at key issues in relation to intercultural education.

Such issues include linguistic diversity, religious diversity and secularism, responses to diversity within the state and education and refugees. The second section consists of a series of regional studies, demonstrating that interculturalism should not be solely examined in individual state contexts. The third section is a series of national case studies. In addition to examining some or all of the issues raised in the first two sections, the case studies demonstrate the wide variety of perceptions of and responses to the issues involved.

As a whole, the book reveals the complexities of the issues involved under the broad heading of intercultural education. No state education system discussed in this book has met the range of aspirations of the various groups that make up their society. That is the pessimistic conclusion. The optimistic one is that all systems appear to take intercultural education seriously and most would claim that progress is slowly and painfully being made.

The editors would like to thank all the contributors for their hard work in preparing material for this *Yearbook*. In particular, they would like to thank Gail Edwards for being the administrative linchpin of the project. Thanks also to Robert Cowen for invaluable assistance in establishing the initial contacts.

*David Coulby, Jagdish Gundara and Crispin Jones*

# Section I:
# Issues in Intercultural Education

## 1. Nation, State and Diversity

Crispin Jones

States seldom go to war with one another as we reach the end of the century. It is a sort of progress, given the wars that filled the first half of the century. One reason is that so many modern states are involved in internal strife, even wars, that leave little energy for such external adventures. Thus, according to the Stockholm-based International Peace Research Institute, there were no inter-state wars but there were 30 internal civil wars in 1995 (Bellamy, 1996). In relation to individual state education systems, this means that curricula that are nationalist and ethnocentric, while still in full flourishing health, are now more concerned with the maintenance of some fictional state unity, best expressed in that modernist oxymoron, the 'nation state'. Of course, conscious or hidden demonizing of other states or a more general 'enemy without' (eg, 'capitalist running dogs', 'godless communism') is also a feature of most states' curricula but it is now matched by similar processes in connection with the 'enemy within'. At a simple level, words like 'foreigner', 'guest worker', 'immigrant' and even 'minority' and their non-English equivalents, can carry loaded and negative meanings in school classrooms as much as in the wider society outside the school.

As the need for the modernist state is put into question (Baumann, 1992; Hall *et al.*, 1992), the more its education system attempts to bolster its self-image of contented unity against the facts of demography and culture. A recent local and parochial example of this has been the debate in the English education system about the cultural responsibilities of schools, having as they do a culturally diverse student body. Dr Nicholas Tate, head of the British government's Schools Curriculum and Assessment Authority for England (SCAA), is arguing for a stronger sense of British identity to be inculcated by the schools. He wants a return to an Arnoldian 'best that is known and thought' high culture, where 'the curriculum needs to be firmly and proudly rooted in a cultural heritage with its roots in Greece and Rome, in Christianity and in

European civilisation' (Tate, 1996). Other traditions are recognized but not as 'British' and consequently are in a subordinate and unclear place within the curriculum of state schools in England. It is also revealing that Dr Tate tends to conflate British and English, much to the annoyance of Scots, Welsh and other British citizens who do not see themselves as English.

Tate's viewpoint or locally configured variations on it could well be accepted by certain powerful conservative or nationalistic educational groups in most state educational systems. In its European manifestations, the key elements are a belief in a common European heritage based on the Classics and Christianity. However, there is no objective agreement on where the boundaries of Europe are and who actually is a European (Coulby and Jones, 1995). In addition, such a view of a benevolent European civilization must bear in mind Ghandi's view of Western civilization, namely that it would be a good idea.

Confusion continues and is frequently compounded as 'Western', 'European' and 'civilization' are treated as synonyms in many school and college textbooks, as can be seen in Hollister's classic American college primer *Medieval Europe*, which shifts, in the space of one page, from 'Europe' to 'Western Europe' to 'Western Civilization', while describing the same area of scholarly concern (Hollister, 1964). As for the claims that European civilization has a unique cultivation and tolerance, a dispassionate view would be that other civilizations have an equal and perhaps equally spurious claim to the same attributes. In relation to Greece and Rome and Christianity, the so-called groundings of European civilization, Bernal has clearly demonstrated the problematic nature of the North European idealization of the Hellenic period (Bernal, 1987, 1991; Gundara, 1990). In relation to religion, Judaism has had a longer presence in Europe than its two related religions, Islam and Christianity. Christianity's domination of Europe has been the result of its repeated attempts to eliminate other religions through Crusades and pogroms, a process that continues to this day, as recent events in former Yugoslavia and the current wave of anti-Semitism across the European Union (EU) witness. Of course, Europe is not unique in terms of the educational struggles that have taken place in relation to the role of religion within the schooling system, an issue that is taken up in more detail in Chapter 3.

Mythologizing of their own antecedents is not confined to European education systems, despite the fact that many of the states they serve do have a longer history of group incorporation compared to other more recent states, such as settler states like Australia and the USA, the post-colonialist, cartographic states that are a feature of much of Africa and Asia, and the post-Soviet states. However, stressing state and national unity as coincident is a feature of most education systems and perhaps a necessary one. Thus, although all states discriminate against certain sections of their populations and this discrimination is frequently supported, tacitly or explicitly, by the education system, such discrimination is nearly always a dangerous balancing act. It can readily collapse, as has been recently seen in the CIS, Rwanda, Somalia, former Yugoslavia and Indonesia.

Yet the state's need for its education system to teach unity and loyalty to its idealized self is, on the surface, a sensible one, as it helps diminish potential inter-group conflict. As a consequence, the proponents of intercultural education are likely to be at variance with state education systems as the two may have conflicting aims. Stratton and Ang (1994) demonstrate this in their analysis of the critiques of multiculturalism in the USA and Australia from such liberal commentators as Schlesinger Jnr (1992). Recognition of the nature of this potential conflict is important for both sides. Intercultural education has to come to terms with the modern state; similarly, the modern state has to come to terms with its own diversity.

The dilemma is a real one for the modern state. The debate about subsidiarity apart, there are real dangers to peace if all groups, defining themselves and/or being defined by others, insist upon self-government. An illustration may help here. One symbol of group identity is language. If all language groups insisted on separate state status, there would be some 6,000 states, the vast majority very small but with one or two huge ones, such as the mainly Chinese-speaking state of the People's Republic of China (PRC). It is also salutary to remember that some of the national and/or linguistic minorities in the PRC are much larger than the total populations of many current UN states (Moseley and Asher, 1994). State constitutions and education systems have to compromise on this issue and, in doing so, are always open to criticism from one side of the debate or the other. Thus, as a typical example, the new, post-communist Bulgarian education system expounds the 'adoption of universal and national values, virtues and culture' in schools as well as supporting minority languages in an attempt to resolve some of these issues, but finds itself short of the actual resources to put such aspirations and policies into practice in an effective manner (Damianova-Ivanova, 1995).

Minorities, of course, can be of many types, not just linguistic, and to see them solely in terms of, say, an ethnic minority within a hostile state is too narrow a perspective. (Language issues are discussed in more detail in Chapter 4.) Consequently, the point about who actually does the defining is important. We can define ourselves and the groups to which we belong, in terms of language, history, culture, religion and so forth, but others may define us in different ways. They may only see our religious affiliations or our skin colour and define us in terms that suit their prejudices and stereotypes rather than our sense of ourselves and our group. This latter point is all-important in education, as it is often a minority, the economically and politically powerful, who define the nature of the education, particularly the curriculum, that the state is to provide for its future citizens. The list below (developed from Coulby and Jones, 1995) gives an indication of some of the complexities of this issue, showing some of the ways in which education can be organized and the student population divided up or differentiated:

By *age* – compulsory, post-compulsory; adult and continuing education; education for the elderly, University of the Third Age.

By *attainment* – elite educational institutions, such as grammar schools, lycées and gymnasia; low-status adult and technical education as against high-status universities.

By *attendance* – boarding/residential or day institutions; part-time/shift or full-time; daytime or evening.

By *behaviour* – separate educational institutions or classes for students seen as disruptive or separate provision for those convicted of crime, such as educational provision in prison.

By *citizenship* – asylum seekers and other refugee groups may have separate education provided, to make reintegration more easy.

By *contact* – classroom or correspondence/radio/TV, distance learning.

By *curricula* – educational institutions with an agricultural, technical or other vocational specialism, as opposed to those with a strongly academic orientation.

By *disability/special educational need* – separate educational institutions for students with disabilities that make it inappropriate, in the view of the education system's organizers, for them to be within mainstream educational institutions.

By *gender* – separate schools or different curricula for boys and girls. (No educational system currently takes on issues of sexual orientation in terms of provision.)

By *language* – state educational institutions using one or more national languages; other educational institutions in the same system using another national language or other languages.

By *location* – there are frequently differences between educational institutions in prosperous and poor areas, even though both are funded by the state; educational institutions in rural or urban areas are frequently different in their resourcing and curricula. As important, groups who are settled are frequently treated differently in education to groups who travel, eg the Roma.

By *nationality* – although often seen in terms of religion and/or language, this category could apply to those educational institutions set up to educate minority or subordinated peoples within or apart from the mainstream state system; schools on 'reservations'.

By *'race'* – segregated educational institutions, both *de facto* and *de jure*.

By *religion* – religious educational institutions/secular educational institutions; also, different educational institutions for different religions within the one system.

By *state* – or precisely, by being stateless or state-denied, the fate of refugee and asylum seeking students who frequently have schools, of a sort, set up in their refugee camps. It also refers to a large group of schools and other educational institutions set up by one state to educate a group claiming links with another, usually adjoining, state.

By *wealth* – private educational institutions for the wealthy.

This list sketches the potential range of differentiation; it does not attempt to be exhaustive. The categories also overlap without clear boundaries. With these caveats in mind, three issues arise from it.

The first is that, as has been stated earlier, the professional managers of all education systems feel the need to differentiate and that act, in itself, should not be seen as an axiomatic infringement of the educational aspirations, however defined, of the groups concerned. In addition, such differentiation has a curriculum element subject to a range of other pressures, a process that has been thought-provokingly examined by Denis Lawton in his book, *Education, Culture and the National Curriculum* (Lawton, 1989).

Another difficulty is the state's schooling system's dual role of instigating innovation and critical thinking, and passing on the culture or cultures of the state. The consequences of addressing these issues and attempting to resolve them in terms of curriculum practice in a manner that acknowledges such pluralism is still under-investigated. Certainly few state education systems currently address these issues in an open and systematic manner.

The second issue arises where the managers of an education system impose some form or forms of educational differentiation on a group without that group's permission or support. Educational and other inequalities are likely to result, sometimes leading to wider extra-educational protest. Decisions about languages and religions and their place in the educational system are an obvious example of this.

The other side of this particular argument, educational self-determination, has its difficulties as well. A minority group that insists on its children being given an education that contradicts official state policy, for example on religious matters or the responsibilities and loyalties the individual should have to the state, causes real dilemmas for a state education system, however well-intended it hopes to be. The reason is that if one of the purposes of a state's education system is to promote state unity and loyalty, as well as conformity to its laws, any group which refutes this view or wishes to provide an education system that does the opposite, for example, advocating some form of national independence, is likely to be seen as undesirable, at the very least. The dilemma is real for the providers of state education. Accept minority group separation in relation to education and the unity of the state may be threatened; enforce forms of differentiation that the same groups find alienating or destructive of their perceptions of identity and the unity of the state may also be threatened. There is no simple answer to this conundrum and the education system in each state usually attempts to resolve the issue in pragmatic ways which best secure the state's own stability, rather than the educational needs of the minorities concerned.

The third issue is that, although education and training systems often treat minorities as if they were a homogeneous group, minorities are themselves internally segmented, in education as in society generally. The questions of group versus individual human rights that arise from this are complex and difficult to resolve, as recent international conferences dealing with such issues well demonstrate. For educational systems and institutions, it can be difficult to locate an authentic voice for a community when various spokes-persons make different and indeed conflicting demands.

The chapters in this volume attempt to identify progressive practice in intercultural education and factors within states which can encourage or impede it. They seek to theorize the need for intercultural education in states which are increasingly aware both of their diversity and of the effects of globalization. They draw on a wide range of contexts and cover the many issues involved in educational provision in multicultural states.

## References

Baumann, Z (1992) *Intimations of Postmodernity*, London: Routledge.

Bellamy, C (1996) 'The end of war – and peace', *The Independent*, 14 June, p.1.

Bernal, M (1987) *Black Athena: The Afroasiatic Roots of Classical Civilisation, Volume I. The Fabrication of Ancient Greece 1785–1985*, London: Vintage.

Bernal, M (1991) *Black Athena: The Afroasiatic Roots of Classical Civilisation, Volume II. The Archaeological and Documentary Evidence*, London: Free Association Press.

Bremner, C (1996) 'Nation state's day is over, Britain told [by Kohl]', *The Times*, 3 February, p.1.

Coulby, D and Jones, C (1995) *Postmodernity and European Education Systems: Cultural Diversity and Centralist Knowledge*, Stoke-on-Trent: Trentham Books.

Damianova-Ivanova, A (1995) *Secondary Education in Bulgaria*, Strasbourg: Council of Europe Press.

Gundara, J (1990) 'Societal diversity and the issue of "the other"', *Oxford Review of Education*, 16, 1, 97–109.

Hall, S et al. (eds) (1992) *Modernity and its Futures*, Cambridge: Polity Press.

Hollister, C (1964) *Medieval Europe*, New York: John Wiley.

Lawson, M (1996) 'Turning time up and over', *The Guardian*, 30 April, pp.22–3.

Lawton, D (1989) *Education, Culture and the National Curriculum*, Sevenoaks: Hodder & Stoughton.

Moseley, C and Asher, R (eds) (1994) *Atlas of the World's Languages*, London: Routledge.

Schlesinger Jr, A (1992) *The Disuniting of America*, New York: Norton.

Stratton, J and Ang, I (1994) 'Multicultural imagined communities: cultural difference and national identity in Australia and the USA', *Continuum: The Australian Journal of Media & Culture*, 8, 2.

Tate, N (1996) 'Culture is not anarchy', *The Times*, 8 February, p.18.

# 2. Educational Responses to Diversity Within the State

David Coulby

## Segregation, stratification and naturalization

Education, along with immigration and citizenship legislation, is one of the main ways in which the state controls diversity and attempts to enforce homogeneity on its population. States differ in the extent to which the maintenance of homogeneity is an important policy objective – weak in South Africa and Hungary, stronger in China and France. Immigration, and increasingly asylum legislation, in many of the European Union states, for example, attempt to restrict the kinds of people who are allowed within their confines. Citizenship legislation, in states such as Germany as well as Latvia and Estonia (see Chapter 15), determines which components of a population are allowed to vote in the various levels of elections, who may carry what sort of a passport, and so on. Educational legislation and institutions segregate or integrate particular groups within a population (segregation), promote certain sections of them to academic and professional success (stratification) and instil within the population as a whole a myth concerning the history and identity of the state and of its citizens (naturalization).

This chapter examines these three processes of segregation, stratification and naturalization. While segregation and stratification are matters concerning the structure of educational systems and institutions, naturalization concerns the curricula of schools and universities.

## Segregation

There are a multitude of different criteria whereby educational institutions segregate pupils and students. These range from assessed educational performance to language or appearance (Coulby and Jones, 1995). The nature of segregated and differentiated provision is analysed in detail in Chapter 1. Examples include: the Magyar-speaking secondary schools of Transylvania, language classes for refugee children in the UK, the tripartite secondary system in Germany, and private universities in Bulgaria and Japan.

Segregation can lead to the separation of the school and/or university population, often for long periods of time. In a tripartite system where pupils are actually placed in different schools (as against France or the Netherlands where pupils can follow different curricula within the same institution) this separation can take on the illusion of being natural. Segregated special schools in the UK serve to enforce the difference and separation between their pupils and those in mainstream schools. By virtue (if that is the word) of being in a distinct institution, they come to view themselves as distinct kinds of people with different provision, aspirations and needs. In parallel, pupils in the mainstream or in the *gymnasium* do not have contact with other kinds of pupils and can, all the more easily, come to regard them as abnormal or intellectually inferior. Segregation is a process whereby educational institutions create and reinforce difference.

It is a sociological commonplace that this segregation frequently takes place along the lines of social class and that it functions overwhelmingly to reproduce it (Poulantzas, 1973; 1978a; 1978b). The lines of social class themselves are often very similar to those of language, religion or perceived ethnic identity. Thus disproportionate numbers of Afro-Caribbean children find themselves in segregated special education in the UK (Tomlinson, 1981) and very few Turkish children get through to the German gymnasium (Hoff, 1995a; 1995b). These segregated school placements obviously relate to the reproduction of the stratification of diversity discussed below. What is less commonly noted is that segregation may actually lead to the reinforcement of the sense of ethnic identity. The Romanian secondary school system with its Romanian, Magyar and (dwindling) German schools (each system in turn segregated according to perceived ability) functions to maintain and reproduce separation along the lines of language. Language classes and remedial provision may also serve to reinforce a sense of separateness, difference and possibly alienation among various groups. The state-language-speaking, non-remedial class groups are likely then to have their narrow parameters of state identity reinforced by not being educated alongside minority pupils and students and by being subjected to a curriculum in which the contribution of these groups is, in the main, remarkable by its absence. Segregation in school prepares for segregation in the workplace, the residential area and society.

To put this a different way: apparently non-racial, or more correctly apparently non-racist, segregations can have powerfully racist consequences. The example of Afro-Caribbean children in special schools in the UK is clear. Disproportionate numbers of these children are still referred to segregated Moderate Learning Difficulty or Emotionally or Behaviourally Disturbed schools. The consequences of this for the children concerned are examined in the following paragraphs, but there are many other sets of effects. Knowing this preponderance, are not teachers in mainstream schools more likely to expect unsatisfactory behaviour and/or performance from black children, and more likely to make a formal referral when they think they have found it and more likely to hope that this referral will lead to a psychologically legitimated exclusion from the mainstream? Will not the long-term cumulative consequences of this preponderance and these expectations be to justify racially stereotyped and negative ways of thinking about this whole group? The continued presence of racist psychology in the universities of both the UK (considered in Chapter 19) and the US is both a consequence of and a justification for these beliefs and practices. The children who remain in the mainstream will be in schools where a particular group has been disproportionately excluded. Some of the processes whereby this has occurred will be visible to them. Deprived of everyday interaction with this group, are they not likely to assume the negative attitudes of teachers and psychologists?

The point about segregated provision is that it is so rarely separate but equal. The very nature of the various pupil peer groups will mean that it cannot be equal. Frequently there are other inequalities built into systems: more elite provision often receives more resources per pupil or student, better qualified and motivated teachers and more active and committed parents. The curriculum taught in the elite or mainstream institution will be that geared towards preparation for the universities and/or the professions. This is clearly not the case of the Russian vocational school or the German *realschule*. In some cases the language of the school may actually discriminate against university entrance, as happened with the (now largely abandoned) Spanish-speaking schools of the USA or as, under the new Education Act (Government of Romania Public Information Department, 1995), is likely to happen with the Magyar schools of Romania. Unsurprisingly, the elite and mainstream schools turn out the professional and economic elite of a particular state.

The effect of segregation is to label pupils and students and to limit their aspirations. By being placed in inferior or lower status provision, children and young people inevitably reflect on their own performance and adjust their expectations for their future in education and the workplace. In some contexts this may serve to reinforce the solidarities which focus around linguistic, religious or ethnic identities. The Baltic languages attracted intensified loyalty under the Soviet regime. In other contexts this segregation may be correctly perceived by the group concerned as one of the manifestations of racism within the state's structures as a whole. Black children segregated into special schools is a good example here. In both these cases the danger that the children or young people accept the label which educational institutions are trying to place on them is mitigated. But this is clearly not the experience of all children and young people subjected to the stigmatizing processes often associated with placement in inferior provision.

Segregation and stratification are not entirely distinct processes. Segregation is in some ways the most extreme form of stratification. It entails the placement of particular groups quite away from the mainstream. It involves not only being judged and labelled as inferior but also cast out from the mainstream on the basis of this assessment.

## Stratification

It is the paraphernalia of assessment whereby schools and universities stratify populations of young people. This is not to put the responsibility for subsequent social stratification upon educational institutions. The process works the other way round. The workplace is stratified: in all states some jobs and functions (though not always the same ones) are perceived to be more important, or involve more scarce skills, than others and are rewarded with greater income and associated status. In order to maintain some rational or legitimatable process it is necessary to have a filtering system for these positions. A characteristic of modern states is that they often move away from sponsorship and ascription for such positions towards some mode of competition. Competition, in varying degrees of apparent fairness, gives the appearance of an open, egalitarian society. Those who succeed and those who fail are equally convinced of the justice of the process and, to an extent, of the stratification itself. The mechanism for this competition is the assessment processes of educational institutions. But if educational institutions were somehow to become so autonomous of their state and its economy as to be able to decide that assessment for stratification was not their business and either to cease competitive assessment or not to release the results, then some other competitive mechanism would have to be found immediately to ensure that the process of stratification maintained the illusion of legitimacy.

Unfortunately, even in apparently open and fair competitive examination systems such as those of the USA, Japan or many states in the European Union, certain groups tend to succeed and others to fail within this process. Various social indices can be predictors of success: parental income, parental education level, place of residence and language, as well as pseudo-scientific indices such as IQ. The same indicators may not apply between different states. Where the indicator is ethnic identity, however constructed, there can be marked contrasts: Hungarians are more successful in Hungary than in Slovakia; Afro-Caribbeans are more successful in Canada than in the UK. It is not that certain perceived ethnic groups constantly perform better or worse than others, as racist psychology would try to persuade. Rather it is that every group interacts with differential success according to the education system within which they are operating. It is the interaction between schools and universities in state systems and their particular modes of assessment on the one hand, and the varyingly constructed ethnic identities on the other, which leads to differential patterns of groups' achievement. It is the processes of assessment themselves as well as the other aspects of education which can lead to the differential performance between groups. Labov long ago showed how white assessment systems in the US advantaged white language and white knowledge and contributed substantially to black 'underachievement' (Labov, 1969). Gender may also be an important variable in these relative levels of success. Factors like these then enter conventional journalistic and educational wisdom. The level of success is not seen to be the responsibility of the interaction between the institution and the group but rather of the group alone. It can then become a negative stereotype which can be utilized in educational and political debate, for example the low achieving black male teenager stereotype found in the USA and the UK.

The result of the assessment conducted by educational institutions is a society stratified in terms of groups. The positions in the workplace with least access to wealth and power are disproportionately occupied by second generation immigrants in the countries of the European Union, by blacks and Hispanics in the US and so on. Educational institutions both operationalize this process of stratification and assist in giving it the appearance of legitimacy.

## Naturalization

As part of a massive exercise in self-perpetuation, states have, since the Enlightenment, increasingly attempted to identify themselves as nations. Rather than the multinational pre-modern states such as the Hapsburg Empire, the 20th century has been characterized by states with some claim to national self-determination – Austria, Hungary, Romania, for instance. These nationhoods have sometimes risen and fallen with political fortunes as is the case with Ireland, Latvia and Korea. They have sometimes emerged as historically new entities, such as India (see Chapter 12) and Indonesia. In all these cases, and indeed in that of those states which have apparently, historically aligned themselves successfully with a nation, such as France and Japan, there has been the need to create and reproduce loyalty to and acceptance of the state in its disguise as a nation. There are a range of institutions and processes that can be drawn on to this end, including the media, competitive sport, religious institutions and the jingoistic flag-waving of ceremonial, but it is probably schools and universities which are the most widely used and the most powerful.

Very few states indeed comprise one nation. They are actually characterized by immigrant groups in their large cities (urban diversity) and by distinct historical groups (national diversity). Thus, France, the country perhaps first to perceive itself as a 'nation state', has a highly diverse population including Maghrebians, Portuguese and Vietnamese in its large cities. It also has areas of historical nationalism such as Brittany, Languedoc and Corsica, which see themselves as distinct from and may indeed aspire to be separate from the state of France (see the discussion in Chapter 11). Only few European countries, notably Belgium and Finland, have taken full legal account of their national minorities. The highly progressive policies adopted in South Africa with the state's recognition of 11 official languages is an example of pluralism very rarely equalled elsewhere.

But the process of naturalization tends to be applied to all groups, not only those which constitute national and urban diversity. The insistence on the identity of the state as nation in the curriculum in Australia or the US functions to naturalize not least the white, Anglo-Saxon population. Similarly, the emphasis on the English 'heritage' in the National Curriculum of England and Wales operates to keep the state together. Were this pressure not to be maintained, why should English people raise any objections when the Welsh or the Scots demand independence from Westminster? (See the discussion of the confusions which are commonly held about the nature of the UK state in Chapter 19.) The self-perpetuation of the state is not the least function of educational institutions and it is through the way in which they handle the state as nation that this is, in the main, brought about.

The whole of the school and university curriculum is constructed around this function. It is most frequently demonstrated by examples from the history curriculum or from the teaching of the state language and literature. However, it is there also in the sponsored canons of philosophy as well as of music and art. It is also present in the identification and selection of science. Science too frequently presents itself as a neutral objective subject able to straddle loftily above forces of state nationalism. But the selection of western science and its pursuit, to the detriment of all other versions of science, nature and medicine in western schools and universities, is itself a manifestation of a narrow, nationalistic view of the nature of people and the nature of the world. Rather than attempt an exhaustive analysis of curricular systems, this chapter focuses on three examples of the way in which educational institutions implement the process of naturalization: the invention of a canon, Ancient Greece and asymmetrical bilingualism.

## The invention of a canon

The invention or reinvention of a canon is a phenomenon which stretches beyond school and university curricula. It is part of the trend towards the recommodification of the past which can be identified even in the fabric of cities themselves.

> Though putatively 'preserving' the past, the undertaking of historic preser-
> vationists and gentrifiers alike may be more accurately described as rewrit-
> ing or inventing the past since buildings and districts are 'renovated',
> 'restored' or 'rehabilitated' to correspond to ideal visions of the past and to
> satisfy contemporary needs and tastes by incorporating new technologies,
> floor plans and more. To give just one among a multitude of examples… the
> 'restoration' of the Old Town in Quebec City resulted in an assemblage of
> buildings which had never existed at the same time before (Ellin, 1996, p.65).

This recommodification, however, is not ideologically neutral. It tends to stress, even if, in terms of postmodern design, ironically, a version of heritage. Events, items and products of the past are pillaged to form a canon or a discourse which validates the power of the state-as-nation.

Recently or newly independent states need to write/rewrite their history to justify and glorify the nation with which they have chosen to identify themselves. They also need to locate a national canon of artistic achievement which can be propagated in educational institutions. This happened in older states as modernist forms of curriculum took over from traditionalist versions. It is less than a century since English established itself as a serious subject in the universities of the UK and brought about the gradual demise of the study of classical languages and literatures. New and resurgent states will certainly look for submerged literary traditions to bring into the light of day. If necessary, as in the case of Latvia, they will discover or virtually invent a literary canon which is congruent with state nationalist identities (Lieven, 1993). The example of Latvia also shows that the canon need not take conventionally western forms. This country has a very rich tradition of folk dance and folk music and these activities and associated values are stressed in the school curriculum. The canon then becomes a manifestation of the state's identity or its national greatness or, in the worst cases, as proof of national superiority. Leavis' literary criticism had a recurrent theme which, simply expressed, was that English literature is the best in the world and particularly superior to the French. (His work is punctuated by asides such as 'though I don't know that I wouldn't sooner read through again *Clarissa* than *A la recherche du temps perdu*' [Leavis, 1962, p.13].)

The nationalism which frequently underpins the creation or recreation of a canon can be seen in an extreme form in Serbia:

> the Serbian intellectual scene was, symbolically speaking, becoming the generator of the mass consumer items of ethnocentrism and war. Homilies by clergymen in churches and out in the streets, the songs of street balladeers (*guslars*), national poetry, national painting, literary evenings at Francuska #7, etc. Serbian intellectuals in the mid 1980s created a critical mass of prejudice, ethnocentrism and war-mongering that made possible Slobodan Milosevic's rise to power and which created the mass-psychological preconditions for aggression against Slovenes, Albanians, Croats and Muslims (Letica, 1996, p.102).

The 1995–96 exhibition, 'Art and Power: Images of the 1930s' seen in London, Barcelona and Berlin gave very clear examples of the relationship between art, the state and warfare (Hayward Gallery, 1995). The curricula of schools and universities can all too readily be incorporated in a warfare-prone canon (Coulby, 1996). This is exemplified, again in the case of the former Yugoslavia, by Pesic (1994).

It is not only the canon of their own states-as-nations that the schools and universities of western countries produce and reproduce. It is also the version of other states and other groups of people. Said (1995) has shown how Orientalism is 'a western style for dominating, restructuring and having authority over the Orient' (p.3). It is precisely this restructured and dominat-

ing version of the apparently remote and exotic east which is offered to
children whose families originate from these localities when they attend
western schools and universities. Orientalism is a selection of knowledge
which serves to continue the subordinate status of such groups:

> As a system of thought about the Orient, it always arose from the specifically
> human detail to the general transhuman one; an observation about a tenth
> century Arab poet multiplied itself into a policy towards (and about) the
> Oriental mentality in Egypt, Iraq, or Arabia. Similarly a verse from the Koran
> would be considered the best evidence of an ineradicable Muslim sensuality
> (Said, 1995, p.96).

The selection of a canon for others may be even more ideologically dangerous
than the selection of a state's own canon, though in the practice of school and
university curriculum definition the processes are often interconnected.

## Ancient Greece

Turning to the theme of Ancient Greece, there is an apparently more benevolent reconstruction of the culture of another. The version of Ancient Greece is
an important consideration in the school and university curricula of western
states and indeed of some others. Schools and universities in the west, not least
in Greece itself, have elaborated a version of world history which pays particular homage to Ancient Greece and especially to Athens in the fifth and
fourth centuries BC. Writing of contemporary Greece, Massialas and Flouris
(1994) comment:

> The emerging Greek identity is projected in part in terms of the heroic acts
> which began in classical Greece and continued until today. The modern
> Greek is the person who perpetuates the traditions of the warriors who
> fought at Marathon and Salamis (pp.3–4).

Massialas and Flouris provide further exemplification of the connections
between state knowledge and warfare, in this case underpinned by the
'heroic' classical period.

The celebrity of this period has in no way been diminished by the general
decline in the teaching of classical Greek. Rather it has become, if anything,
more general and has penetrated, as in the National Curriculum in England
and Wales, to the primary phase of schooling. The section on 'The creative
human being' in the Core Curriculum of Norway is illustrated by a Greek vase
and two pages of text apparently from Euclid (The Royal Ministry of Church,
Education and Research, 1994, p.13). This neo-classicism all too often tends to
imply that civilization, or at least European civilization, started with Ancient
Greece; that this is the one historical source for all that is true in philosophy,
science and mathematics and all that is beautiful in drama, poetry, architecture
and sculpture. Amplified by the tourist industry, this has become a taken-for-
granted western truth. Alongside this is the further historical notion that the

states of the west are somehow derived from and legitimated by Ancient Greece. There is seen to be a shining line of continuity from Greece, through Rome and the Renaissance to the Enlightenment and the modern states of the European Union and the US. The Greeks are seen through three simultaneous distortions: they were the originators; they were the best; we derive from them. A simplified and fallacious view of Ancient Greece underpins much of the petty nationalism and Eurocentrism within educational institutions and beyond.

## Asymmetrical bilingualism

With regard to asymmetrical bilingualism, Hobsbawm (1987) has identified the importance of language in the enterprise whereby states attempted to disguise themselves as nations (see also Hobsbawm 1962; 1975; 1994). He stresses how late this occurred in the cases of Gaelic, Basque, Macedonian and Hebrew (1987, p.146). Interestingly, in relation to the discussion of canons above, he also suggests that languages are themselves constructions and selections:

> the 'national languages' in which they discovered the essential character of their nations were, more often than not, artefacts, since they had to be compiled, standardised, homogenised and modernised for contemporary and literary use, out of the jigsaw puzzle of local or regional dialects which constituted non-literary languages as actually spoken (1987, p.147).

It is schools and universities which have had the task of promulgating and enforcing these codified national languages in the interest of the state. Even today, however, virtually no state has only one language.

Asymmetrical bilingualism operates in states where the population speaks more than one language but the state operates in and privileges only one. The more progressive policies of Belgium, Finland and South Africa have been mentioned above. It is difficult not to look to Eastern Europe and China (a trend which may itself be a manifestation of educational orientalism) for examples of the crudest asymmetry. The Russification of the former Soviet Union and much of Eastern Europe had a distinctly linguistic component (Haarmann, 1995). Latvian and Estonian speakers were moved in vast numbers out of their home areas. Large numbers of Russian speakers, often associated with the security or armed forces, moved in. The language of the state, the school and the university became Russian. Latvian and Estonian speakers saw the future of their languages in jeopardy. With independence the tables have been turned. The state and educational institutions now operate in the 'national' language. The large Russian-speaking minority (over half the population of Riga) has been stripped of its linguistic power along with its citizenship and its right to carry a passport. In secondary schools in Estonia and Latvia, Russian is being dropped as a subject in favour of English and German (for further details see Chapter 15). A not dissimilar policy is being pursued by the People's Republic of China in Tibet (see Chapter 17 for other aspects of Chinese policy with regard to minorities). Minority language is discouraged as part of the systematic discouragement of Buddhism. Even more effectively the immigration of Chinese workers is pressing Tibetan language, culture and religion to the oppressed margins. Asymmetric bilingualism is hardened through the curricula of schools and universities. It is often associated with other forms of curriculum chauvinism mentioned above. It takes a plurality which ought to give strength and diversity to a state and transforms it into a source of tension.

## Conclusion

In identifying the three processes of segregation, stratification and naturalization, this chapter has focused on the negative aspects of state responses to diversity. Other chapters in this volume often point to more positive aspects of state policy. To give this negative view at the outset is to stress that there is at the very least a tension between the tendencies of states to centralize and to preserve themselves and the existence of a plurality of peoples and cultures. This tension resides particularly in the way in which states seek to perpetuate and aggrandize themselves through identification with a nation. Education has been one of the main structures whereby this myth has been implemented and reproduced.

Where this implementation has coincided with international or internal conflict, education systems have found themselves implicitly or explicitly engaged in the encouragement of warfare. If this alternative is to be avoided, other educational structures and curricular systems will need to be developed.

## References

Coulby, D (1996) 'European curricula, xenophobia and warfare', *Comparative Education*.
Coulby, D and Jones, C (1995) *Postmodernity and European Education Systems: Centralist Knowledge and Cultural Diversity*, Stoke-on-Trent: Trentham.
Ellin, N (1996) *Postmodern Urbanism*, Oxford: Blackwell.
Government of Romania Public Information Department (1995) *The New Education Law in Romania*. No further details.
Haarmann, H (1995) 'Multilingualism and ideology: The historical experiment of Soviet language politics', *European Journal of Intercultural Studies*, 5, 3, 6–17.
Hayward Gallery (1995) *Art and Power: Images of the 1930s*, London: Hayward Gallery.
Hobsbawm, E (1975) *The Age of Revolution 1789–1848*, London: Weidenfeld & Nicolson.
Hobsbawm, E (1962) *The Age of Capital 1848–1875*, London: Weidenfeld & Nicolson.
Hobsbawm, E (1987) *The Age of Empire 1875–1914*, London: Weidenfeld & Nicolson.
Hobsbawm, E (1994) *Age of Extremes: The Short Twentieth Century 1914–1991*, London: Michael Joseph.

Hoff, G (1995a) 'Multicultural education in Germany: Policies related to multicultural education', in Wulf, C (ed.) *Education in Europe: An Intercultural Task,* Munster: Waxmann.

Hoff, G (1995b) 'Multicultural education in Germany: Historical development and current status', in Banks, J and Banks, C A (eds) *Handbook of Research on Multicultural Education,* New York: Macmillan.

Labov, W (1969) 'The logic of non-standard English', *Georgetown Monographs on Language and Linguistics,* 22, 1–31.

Leavis, F R (1962) *The Great Tradition,* Harmondsworth: Penguin.

Letica, S (1996) 'The Genesis of the Current Balkan War', in Mestrovic, S G (ed.) *Genocide After Emotion: The Postemotional Balkan War,* London: Routledege.

Lieven, A (1993) *The Baltic Revolution: Estonia, Latvia, Lithuania and the Path to Independence,* New Haven: Yale University Press.

Massialas, B G and Flouris, G (1994) 'Education and the emerging concept of national identity in Greece', paper presented to Comparative and International Education Society Conference, San Diego, California.

Pesic, V (1994) 'Bellicose virtues in elementary school readers', in Rosandic, R and Pesic, V (eds) *Warfare, Patriotism, Patriarchy: The Analysis of Elementary School Textbooks,* Belgrade: Centre for Anti-War Action MOST.

Poulantzas, N (1973) *Political Power and Social Classes,* London, New Left Books.

Poulantzas, N (1978a) *Classes in Contemporary Capitalism,* London: Verso.

Poulantzas, N (1978b) *State, Power, Socialism,* London: Verso.

Royal Ministry of Church, Education and Research (1994) *Core Curriculum for Primary, Secondary and Adult Education in Norway,* Oslo: Royal Ministry of Church, Education and Research.

Said, E (1995) *Orientalism: Western Conceptions of the Orient. With a New Afterword,* Harmondsworth: Penguin.

Tomlinson, S (1981) *Educational Subnormality: A Study in Decision Making,* London: Routledge and Kegan Paul.

# 3.    Religion, Secularism and Values Education

Jagdish Gundara

## Introduction

Discussions about intercultural education cannot ignore the challenges posed not just by religious communities but by fundamentalists who challenge diverse secular polities. These fundamentalist systems are different and caused differentially in various contexts, which cannot be discussed here.

In India the Hindu fundamentalists have effectively used education and the electoral processes to undermine the secular system. In the United States by sharp contrast, these groups control their own broadcasting media, which extend as far as Central America. In Latin America, the failure of the Catholic Church to reform semi-feudalist elites has given access to American Protestant evangelists who are not only against the reform of social inequalities but are also opposed to the teaching of modern sciences.

In most instances, fundamentalism is a reactive phenomenon to rapid social change. In some other instances, it is a reaction to superior state power, as in Egypt, Syria, Iraq or Algeria. Where secularism has arisen because of foreign domination, the reaction to it is stronger. Hence, this chapter explores ways of indigenizing secularism and those local belief systems which counter-balance the patriarchal, reactive and anti-feminist tendencies of fundamentalists.

The general opposition to the modern condition in all civil societies needs to be examined in order to improve public policies and introduce educational innovations to strengthen the capacity of secular societies to protect all groups. Education systems have an important role in deconstructing the mythical pasts of societies, historical legacies and notions of identity(ies). The failure to establish critical engagement with such issues can lead to the capture of state power by theocratic groups, with grave consequences for diverse polities. Prophylactic educational policies are necessary in conjunction with other public policies to alleviate vast levels of inequality and injustice.

It is critical to acknowledge at the outset that such discussions cannot be undertaken without serious consideration of children's rights to accept, modulate or reject views and belief systems inherited from parents.

## Religion and secular issues

The notion of a theocratic city, where there are no divisions between the public and the private, with no civic culture, poses a new challenge and dilemma to modern cultures in both secular and theocratic societies. While secular societies confront competing claims from different belief systems and non-believers, those in theocratic states have to deal with sectarian, regional or linguistic cleavages. Although this chapter will confine the discussions to secular issues, some of the discussions may be relevant to education systems in theocratic states.

Given religious as well as sectarian diversity in many societies, it does seem necessary to have clear definitions about the secular nature of societies and the rights and obligations of various citizens and groups. Recent events in various countries have led not only to antagonism towards other religions, but, because this question is tied up with history, these issues have been dangerously conflated with xenophobia and narrow exclusive nationalisms.

This raises issues at two levels. One is how the different states ensure that within modern secular contexts others of different faith communities and non-believers will receive equal treatment and freedom of speech, accompanied by their duties and obligations as citizens. The second entails a much more serious issue for educators, namely, an accretion of feelings, ways of seeing and understanding by states of the rights of those citizens who are classified as 'other' and whose voices are ignored.

The notions of secularism therefore throw into much sharper focus our own understanding of the issues that teachers and teacher educators need to confront in intellectual terms, and their implications for schools in diverse societies.

The rise of theocracies in diverse societies in modern terms cannot be ignored. The rise, even in secular societies of electronic churches (as in the United States), is a pointer to the type of fundamentalism which may need to be faced because of its implications for the multi-faith nature of most societies. Since the symbol systems of religions strike a stronger chord than the diffuse systems of secularism in societies, educators (together with other social scientists) need to reappraise the nature of secular education and its role in strengthening the legitimacy of all citizens in currently narrowly defined nation states (see Batelaan and Gundara, 1993). The exclusion of groups on linguistic, religious, social class, gender or racial grounds, poses major challenges for all involved in teaching. Similarly, fundamentalist beliefs about the economy or the market can also have excluding effects, and can give rise to other fundamentalisms.

The critical question in this chapter, however, is the complex ways in which religion ought to be reflected within public institutions to bring about an inclusive value system, rather than strengthen exclusivities.

The rise of such strong belief systems in modern secular states may be a reflection of how secular states have failed to provide a safe and secure framework for diverse faith communities. It may also be partly attributable to strong assertions of human rights which are not accompanied by effective measures to ensure their implementation at both political and social levels. The divisions which occurred at the international conference in Vienna in 1993 between the western countries and Asian countries on individual and group rights is a case in point. Yet, we do need to question carefully the nature of this recognition of group rights, and its implications for a diverse polity. Given different social structures, the practice of individual and group rights is something that educators need to take on board to develop a more realistic practice of the rights of individuals and groups. This is an issue because of different social features and levels of autonomy in different societies.

Secularism is largely a legal system which provides the necessary frame-work to nurture equality for all citizens at the public level and to safeguard the sacred at the private level. The secular collectivity is not necessarily theistic, atheistic or agnostic (Verma, 1986). It therefore optimally provides a 'nest' for all groups and has a role to protect their citizenship rights. 'Positive secularism' or 'the nest' in this sense goes beyond merely the religious toleration of other groups (Gundara, 1994). It in fact moves towards the notion of 'belongingness' of all groups in society. The major issue is how the education system can legitimate the 'belongingness' of diverse groups, particularly if dominant groups assert otherwise.

The modern state has a major interest in education since it is considered as a way of providing the labour market with skilled personnel. Education, however, also has a role in providing equity and in transmitting humanistic, ethical and cultural values. For many groups and individuals these values have their roots in religion. Many secular societies are being challenged by the demand for religious education, or an education system based on one religion. These demands are in contradiction to the notions of positive secularism. Problems arise immediately with promotion or the dominance of one particular religion in public schools or when certain behaviour, based on religious conviction, is denied in schools (for instance the refusal in French schools to allow Muslim girls to wear headshawls). However, the issue is not whether religious education should be implemented in all secular schools for *different* religious groups, or whether pupils should be withdrawn for wearing a crucifix or a shawl. The issue is how to reconsider the consequences of secularism for education. Secular education as such is not neutral education.

Perhaps the role and the function of the school are misperceived, because the school ought to respect the individual autonomy of all students. The school, however, would be failing if it did not provide the students with a critical edge to their thinking, which can in turn provide them with a solid foundation to defend their belief system. An education which claims to be based on human rights, the democratic principles which claim to be opposed to domination, and which at least officially aims at mutual understanding, is not value free. But educators need to be aware of the pedagogical function of education and the basic values on which secular education is based. Therefore, it is important to define the basic ethical and cultural values which should be negotiated through secular education. These are not values to be imposed on students, but to be negotiated with them. This process of negotiation in itself ought to promote mutual understanding between students, parents and communities in which the schools are located.

It is being suggested here that notions of transmitting values are not sufficient in attempting to develop a shared value system. A more complex relationship between schools and communities exists and schools are not impenetrable.

Since education in most contexts is provided by the state, institutionalized education belongs to the public domain, while religion in a secular state belongs to the private domain. This division itself is problematic in a multicultural and multi-faith society and needs to be negotiated and mediated. Is it possible that good values, ethical and moral considerations can interpenetrate each domain in positive terms?

The division of the private and the public should be seen as an enhancing distinction. One of its functions should be to enhance the position of minorities or subordinated groups. This becomes a problem in those countries where different religious communities have a fundamental right to establish their own schools, but are not necessarily able to promote mutual understanding. Mutual understanding in diverse societies is more likely if there is a common and shared curriculum in a common school. Such a curriculum ought to be based on agreed and rational principles, rather than being imposed on the polity. A differentiated school system mitigates against development of common understandings, and yet may paradoxically be necessary to empower marginalized groups. This is particularly true of remote tribal groups and marginalized indigenous communities, as well as travellers and Gypsies whose ways of life are very different and under threat.

Since one religion cannot dictate to a heterogeneity of religions in a secular society, a distinction between private morality and law, as well as sin and crime, needs to be drawn. The nurturing of a secular morality and value system within the public institutions becomes incumbent on schools. The ensuing distinction between the metaphysical concerns of citizens and political ethics is important, to enable an encompassing confidence in the polity as a whole. The plurality of religious groups means that, since no dominant religion exists which becomes morally corrupt because of its strength, it becomes incumbent upon various groups to struggle to maintain faith. There cannot, however, be a prescriptive way in which schools can impose an across-the-board tenet since, given different features of commonality and weakness or strength of secular institutions, different action would have to be taken in different localities. Nevertheless, it is important for teachers to encourage in students the development of notions of a 'common good' or a broader 'public good'. In the final analysis this is a matter of public policy which needs to be considered by educational planners.

In principle, the negotiation of values through public education should be limited to the values of the secular state within the public domain. The school in a plural society should by definition not interfere in the private and in the autonomous individual's domain, because the essence of pluralism is the recognition of and respect for diverse life-styles and belief systems in the private domain of groups, families and individuals. However, the school as a social institution does have the right to foster and nurture the common good of all members of the school and the society of which it is a part. The school may not wish to ignore religious knowledge. As far as values belong to the private domain, teachers should teach *about* values in such a way that the good values of all children are validated.

Religious instruction may belong to the private domain, but religious, spiritual and philosophical knowledge and values form part of the public domain and can be taught to achieve the aim of religious knowledge, understanding and tolerance, which is a prerequisite for the maintenance of democracy. This is not a static context and requires a dynamic facility for being negotiated by teachers who bring to the school understandings of these complex issues. It is critical to understand that to maintain the autonomy of believers and non-believers alike, the school's role in religious instruction ought to be limited to providing facilities for prayers for those who need them.

The model presented here could also be used in the discussions between schools and communities. The pedagogic goals of education are aimed at the development of the attitudes and behaviour of individuals based on an awareness of values (Haydon *et al.*, 1987).


## Minorities and religion

Ethnic and religious communities require substantive protection from various forms of discrimination. In 1981 there was a UN Declaration on the Elimination of all forms of Discrimination and Intolerance, and all nations have agreed to participate in its educational dissemination and implementation. A dialogue amongst the socially diverse religious bodies is one hopeful sign for developing a new pedagogy, a pedagogy which can incorporate values or standards through the vehicle of higher norms in particular societies.

Simply stated, values as agreed upon by humanity are frequently not respected. And, as was mentioned earlier, exclusion of groups on religious, social class, linguistic, gender or racial grounds, poses major challenges for all involved in teaching and pedagogical planning.

When religions and other belief systems, including secular systems, speak of human rights, frequently they can only make utterances from behind the barriers of privileged positions, protected under domestic law. The religious factor can be met with an appreciation of agreed-upon standards of values such as those found in international and regional (eg, EU) legal documents.

These are also useful teaching tools. They may serve as a point of mutual intersection between the state and the distinct societies in which belief systems operate. In addition to the United Nations Charter and the UN Declaration of Human Rights, several other international, national and regional instruments also proscribe the principle of the freedom of religion and belief. Since values and belief systems (theistic and non-theistic) go hand in hand, human rights education can serve as the linchpin.

There can be no competing claim for social or religious rights unless they are subordinate to the right of humanity (and the environment) to live and survive. The application of human rights principles within the major world religions goes a long way towards the enhancing of human dignity – in concert with the multi-religious and multicultural nation states. The role of education can be to teach about the enhancing distinctions and overlaps between the sacred and the secular.

Common values based on a political culture assume an educational process which ensures that all groups and citizens are knowledgeable about the complexity of modern societies. Human rights principles, from ecology to economics, belong most of all to the value goals of young people. Because we are operating in a world culture newly informed by human rights standards and legislation, there is no way religions should avoid the responsibility of encouraging the teaching of human rights knowledge as a major educational component. The reverse is also true. Religious behaviour is also a subject of human rights education. When it comes to how a state treats its citizens under the law, the sacrosanct principle of state sovereignty has broadened during the last few decades. State sovereignty is now the interest of other nations under international human rights law. Likewise, how religions behave can no longer be their own 'private business'.

If it is intended to develop an ethical system which the young generation adheres to, this cannot be drawn from one cultural tradition without taking into account the different contexts in which teachers are interacting with students. How do educators engage the imaginations of young people on such major issues?

Many young people have little control of their own lives. The role of the school in teaching civic or political education can ensure that all children are able to participate within the civic culture. In addition to its pedagogic function, the school has other institutional functions. The school should also provide:

- a safe place for children, where they feel accepted and not threatened, humiliated, rejected or exploited;
- a place where real issues are addressed, where a connection exists with the reality of the lives of the children;
- a place where people are working according to the ethical principles which are taught; and

- a place where all children have equal opportunities to achieve academic success.

These all fit within the framework of the three underlying values necessary in diverse societies: non-discrimination, non-repression and democratic deliberation.

The need to include the religious factor in values education in socially diverse communities is becoming more obvious. Religious toleration is a universal value, among the most basic universal rights, and therefore does not extend to practices that conflict with other basic democratic rights.

The three underlying values necessary in diverse societies are required to give religious and other groups substantive protection. These same values are found in most international and regional legal documents. These standards of values may serve as teaching tools for educators and points of dialogue for religious believers. The coalescence of religious and educational leadership in the promotion of fundamental rights and freedoms for all would be revolutionary in terms of human dignity and strengthening the polity.

Education dictates that students have an opportunity to receive a solid base not only academically but in the appreciation of intercultural values such as respect, equality and toleration. Although the religious factor may be perceived as being in the private domain, certainly we can argue that religious knowledge and understanding can be taught in the school curriculum as a contribution towards the development of the common or public good. Where schools and teachers are prepared, this would even suggest that intrinsic (value-centred or growth) functions be measured with regard to religious and other group motivations.

As educationalists and others attempt to overcome potential conflict through sustaining a democratic union of many diversities, here it is suggested that the secular curriculum can offer an approach to values in which communities can engage in a dialogue about that which is sacred or special in human relations. World religions can contribute to enhancing values education within multicultural encounters by sharing a commitment to precepts and standards to which most states have committed themselves internationally.

Two countries which confront these problems differently can suffice to illustrate the issues: England and Wales and India. In England and Wales, the Christian faith is represented as the religion of the state and the school.

The mere provision for children of other faiths to worship (ie, withdraw) suggests that only Christianity has a recognized status. In children's minds other faiths remain second-class and exotic. This detracts from the understanding of other faiths and is in itself divisive. Such divisiveness may in turn lead to conflict, with faiths like Islam being equated with fundamentalism *per se.* Furthermore, all Asians may get constructed as 'Muslim fundamentalists' and notions of religious equality may be thrown to the winds.

At another level, this privileging of Christianity raises serious issues for the multi-faith nature of British society and has implications for the secular nation state. More importantly for schools, moral values derived from Christianity or Islam are but one dimension of the more complex value dilemmas confronting the younger generation. This is particularly the case since youth and peer group values themselves are an important feature of the culture of the school (Gundara, 1993).

In India a totally different issue is highlighted, by structuring a group as being non-indigenous and therefore not being able to belong. This is the case for Muslims in the state of India, even though the overwhelming proportion of them come, not from outside the country, but from indigenous families that converted to Islam. Thus, the construction of Muslims as non-indigenous fanatics by Hindus is not only a travesty of reality but a denial of the loyalty of the millions who have consciously chosen, or happen, to live in secular India rather than in Muslim Pakistan. Such narrow constructions by the Hindus not only twist historical and contemporary realities but are partially a result of the failures of the education system to address such questions. While Muslims, Parsees, Jews and Christians are as Indian as any Hindu, the evocation of a mythical Hindu past is an obscurantism which has been politically mobilized. The gullibility of its advocates is partly a result of low-level elementary education, which means educators, who have access to the long history of Indian tolerance of difference, are not propagating it. Rather, they are using literacy to misinform and create bias – both of which can be dangerous. For example, in 1992, Vidya Bharati prepared a new set of history textbooks which were to be used in schools in states controlled by the Bhartiya Janata Party. In their textbooks:

> The revivalists depict the Mughals as foreigners and oppressors, and inter-pret Indians' achievement of freedom from English rule as but the latest episode in a long ongoing struggle to free India from foreign influences. Muslims are, by this interpretation, the contemporary incarnation of the Mughal pattern of dominance (Kumar, 1993, p.121).

The challenge posed to secular schools and the Indian polity by Hindu revivalism is great, and their hegemonic views require a concerted effort, including educational initiatives, to re-legitimate the broad social diversities in India.

Unfortunately, the educational and political elites of the country are pro-foundly out of touch with the concerns of the masses. Any educational project which enables minorities in India to belong has to re-evaluate the role of religion in contemporary society. A re-examination of the public space in light of the re-emergence of the sacred can only take place if the educational and political concerns of the masses are met. Also, in India, secular and religious ideologies compete for the public space so a new balance of freedom and rights cannot be imposed from the top but needs to be made more locally relevant (Gundara, 1994).

## Conclusion

This chapter has examined the role of intercultural education at a time when secular societies have been destabilized, partly as a result of the strict divisions of the public and private domains. It has argued that a creative engagement and cross-fertilization of the good values from across public and private domains may enable secular and multicultural democracies to become more stable as well as dynamic.

The notion that secular societies only embody secular values and provide no space for good values from other domains of life has been discounted, particularly by pointing out the role of education in assuming greater responsibility in engaging with this critical issue.

Secular polities, however, have a fundamental obligation to preserve the rights of all individuals and groups, whether they are believers or not. The political and educational systems ought to use the various legal instruments to which governments are signatories as teaching tools to ensure that children understand their own rights and those of others in society. Religious belief systems, more often than not, flout their own principles in denying human rights to their own believers. Not only should they be doing the opposite, but the education and political systems can help in implementing the subtle enhancing distinctions and overlaps between the sacred and the secular. The function of education systems is therefore to ensure the development of a common and shared value system to enhance the public domain, which guarantees the rights and obligations of all groups in society. In this sense, faith communities cannot obviate their obligations to others in society who may or may not be believers: similarly, they must not only encourage ecumenicism but also subject their own religions to human rights tenets and legislation.

## References

Batelaan, P and Gundara, J (1993) 'Cultural diversity and the promotion of values through education', *European Journal of Intercultural Studies*, 3, 2/3.

Gundara, J (1993) 'Values, National Curriculum and diversity in British society', in O'Hear, P and White, J (eds) *Assessing the National Curriculum*, London: Paul Chapman.

Gundara, J (1994) 'Aspects of religion in secular education, in Gundara, J et al. (eds) *Education Rights and Minorities*, London: Minority Rights Group.

Haydon, G et al. (eds) (1987) *Education for a Plural Society*, Bedford Way Paper 30, London: Institute of Education, University of London.

Kumar, K (1993) 'Hindu revivalism in north-central India', in Marty, M E and Appleby, R S (eds) *Fundamentalism and Society*, Chicago, Ill: University of Chicago Press.

Verma, S L (1986) *Towards Theory of Positive Secularism*, Jaipur: Rawat Publications.

# 4.  Education and Linguistic Diversity

Euan Reid

## Introduction

The establishment of national compulsory education systems took place in what is now regarded as the 'First World' mostly in the 19th century. In terms of language and medium of instruction policy, the target was to be classes of pupils all more or less sharing a common language. Such classes were taught by teachers who would enforce and police that language as they guided pupils into initial literacy, even when they themselves knew and used other varieties or languages in their non-professional lives (Kroon and Sturm, forthcoming).

Benedict Anderson's work on 20th century nation-building (Anderson, 1991) suggests that similar patterns are being repeated in the developing world in the latter part of this century, as new 'imagined communities' are built, for example in Southeast Asia. Of course there have always been areas where 'national minorities' gradually establish linguistic and cultural rights, often after a long struggle. And there are border territories where special schooling arrangements are made, and sometimes recognized in international treaties and agreements (Stephens, 1976). But, on the whole, even in such areas use of a mixture of languages is not seen as acceptable in educational contexts. Within the minority areas, the same single-language 'territorial' ideology prevails within classrooms, and to an extent within playgrounds too: heterogeneity is still often seen as a threat to good order, and perhaps even to national or community cohesion.

It is striking that this 'monolingual ideology' is still so powerfully evident in education systems in almost every part of the world, even when confronted by the increasingly obvious reality that it is not only Bombay, Nairobi and Jakarta that are hugely multilingual places, together with 'immigrant' cities like Vancouver, Sydney and Sao Paulo, but now also London, Paris, Frankfurt and Moscow. New diversity has been created by the processes of economic and political migration in both old world and new world metropolises, and old diversities are being rediscovered in these same places. Yet school systems everywhere still seem to be designed to produce among their students a now dysfunctional monolingualism and monoculturalism. Teachers and curriculum planners everywhere need to move on to examine and change where necessary the mainstream curriculum, especially the language curriculum, since the job of schools everywhere now is to form the new citizens of a much more integrated global economy. Whatever the details of the political and institutional arrangements under which we shall all live in the 21st century, our children will be much more mobile, within and beyond their regions. They will have many more international contacts. Even in their home cities and communities, they will need to develop and use linguistic and other intercultural skills in their daily lives.

Many smaller countries have recognized this within their education systems, at least with respect to foreign language learning, but the larger countries, especially those with imperial or expansionist pasts, do not find it as easy to accept and to change their school systems and practices accordingly. However, if they are not to handicap their learners, they will have to do so, with reference not only to foreign language learning, but also to so-called 'mother tongue', more accurately considered as 'national standard language' learning.

Let us examine, first, some contrasting ideas about language and bilingualism, and about curriculum, which may be at the root of some of the conservatism evident in current mainstream educational approaches to linguistic and cultural diversity; and then in the last part of the chapter, consider some experience 'from the margins' which may point to some ways forward, before concluding with a 'cautionary tale'.

## Bilingualism and the curriculum: 'common sense' and some alternatives

There are some rather powerful 'common sense' ideas about bilingualism that condition the thinking of policy-makers in many parts of the world who are involved in making decisions about schools, and about linguistic diversity within schools. Here are five characteristics commonly attributed to bilingualism, all of which need critical examination, and in some cases replacement:

1. bilingualism is rare, exceptional and remarkable;
2. bilingualism is a characteristic only of the highly intelligent, belonging to intellectual elites;
3. being bilingual implies 'perfect', or 'native-like' command of two languages;
4. bilingualism implies the use of both languages in all domains of use;
5. 'proper' bilingualism means keeping the languages quite separate and apart.

In contrast, sociolinguistic and educational research (Romaine, 1989; Skutnabb-Kangas and Cummins, 1988) suggests that something like the following set of ideas about bilingualism are more likely to be productive in tackling the widespread linguistic diversity of modern school systems:

1. bilingualism is widespread and unremarkable in world terms;
2. bilingualism is common among whole societies in many parts of the world, and certainly not confined to social or intellectual elites;
3. the bilingual person's skills in one or both of the languages are often 'imperfect': just like monolinguals, individuals often have partial skills in particular domains of language use;
4. for bilinguals there is often a complementary distribution of functions across languages: people use one language for their family and domestic interactions, another for their educational or professional lives, for example;
5. for bilingual people, switching between and mixing languages is almost universal in situations of language contact, whatever the purists say about the negative consequences of such practice (Thomas, 1991).

We need, in the context of this Yearbook, to spend less time on the next set of ideas which interfere with productive thinking about linguistic diversity. These include notions of the school curriculum conceived largely in terms of 'subjects' – essentially academic disciplines deriving from ways in which universities working in the European tradition have divided up the world of learning. In this way of thinking, at the heart of the school curriculum lies command of the abstract systems of language and number, and there is an unproblematically 'transmissive' view of pedagogy. In the context of such ideas, wider social and cultural learning, as well as lessons learned from institutional structures and procedures, are often neglected and the school curriculum is seen as essentially isolated from and independent of the community, a matter for professional educators to deal with, not for community involvement.

An alternative perspective sees the curriculum and teaching methods as essentially based on social values and purposes and therefore on what are in the end different visions of what societies and countries are and should be. At the heart of the curriculum therefore, are not only cognitive but also affective, social, moral and aesthetic considerations, often highly contested and political. Learning is surely better understood as accomplished in interaction between teachers and learners, and between learners and learners, rather than being about the delivery of unproblematic 'facts' from unchallengeable and authoritative teachers to ignorant learners. In this view too, school structures and government are at least as important in, for example, moral and political learning, as anything said by teachers of civics or religious education, and the school's close interdependence with its local, regional and national communities is recognized.

The adoption of an approach to the curriculum closer to this last, as well as an understanding of bilingualism and multilingualism closer to that above, would make for a more fruitful exploitation of the almost universal potential located in the linguistic diversity of school populations.

Following on from this, in this next section, we look to experience on what are often considered the margins of school systems, to see what can be learned from ways of working educationally with 'minority' students, in the first place 'children of migrants' into north-west Europe, then of settlers in some of the OECD member countries.

## ECCE Intercultural: scope, findings and recommendations

The European Community Comparative Evaluation Project – 'ECCE Intercultural' – was an attempt to estimate the effect of various approaches to common situations of linguistic diversity in educational contexts, arising mostly from the labour migrations from Mediterranean countries and beyond into the more industrialized countries of north-west Europe. These approaches took the form of pilot projects in a range of countries, focusing on the linguistic needs of what are still commonly referred to as 'the children of migrant workers'. The function of the ECCE Intercultural Project was to document the scope of the different projects, estimate their effectiveness, distil the lessons to be learned and then to disseminate the findings (Reid and Reich, 1992).

The range of pilot projects was wide, with many of the early ones focusing on so-called 'mother tongue teaching' in the primary schools, for example of Arabic in Marseilles, Turkish in Limburg and Italian in Bedford – all to children of people who had moved from countries where these were the national languages. The fact that in many cases the migrants in question came from regions of their countries where other languages or varieties than the standard national language were in common use was rarely recognized, by either the education authorities of the receiving or of the sending countries.

The later projects broadened their scope to include second language and foreign language learning, the learning of certain subjects through the medium of the children's other languages, and indeed some which did not have a language focus at all – for example one in Leiden on 'Materials for Intercultural History Teaching'. The ECCE evaluation team, which was a multinational one, concluded that there had been a lot of useful, detailed work, for example on how to develop literacy in two languages in a coherent and systematic way. In spite of many teachers' doubts about this, biliteracy was shown to be both possible and valuable in an ordinary school context, with ordinary children. The Brussels Foyer Project (which was about the learning of Italian and Arabic in conjunction with the conventional medium of instruction, Dutch), and the London Mother Tongue Teaching Project (which took Modern Greek and Bengali as its main focus), both demonstrated this in the early 1980s (Houlton, 1984). The London Project, which had an explicitly intercultural basis, also showed how projects based around the teaching of one particular language need not be chauvinistic in any sense: in the Greek-learning and Bengali-learning materials which they produced for primary-age pupils they included not only Greek and Bengali folk stories, but also stories from the Caribbean, Africa, Ireland and England, but in the Greek and Bengali languages.

The pilot projects were also successful in that they showed how it was possible to give a more extensive role in secondary school to 'other mother tongues' – that is, to use languages other than the national language as media of instruction. For example in two further projects in the Limburg region of Belgian Flanders, Italian and Turkish were used for the teaching of some subjects, including geography and art. In Berlin some very successful approaches and materials were developed for teaching Turkish in the place of a first foreign language – although there were also problems with that project when it attempted to deal with some quite difficult intercultural themes in the language learning materials, such as racist jokes and stereotypes. This attempt was misunderstood by the Turkish national authorities and, as a consequence, they withdrew their full support for the project.

In spite of many positive experiences, however, there were severe limitations in this programme of pilot projects, in terms of their generalizability within the region. First, the projects were nearly all focused only on 'the migrant children', the incomers. These projects were what the ECCE evaluators came to call 'special programmes for special children'.

Second, even where they contributed to what might be called 'education for bilingualism', for example by encouraging effective and imaginative ways of maintaining and developing the original mother tongue, and at the same time learning the new language of the receiving countries, they did those two things in isolation. The projects failed to conceive of what they were doing as a form of 'bilingual education', and therefore to coordinate the learning of the two languages and make it more effective and explicitly intercultural.

Moreover, the project designs often left the teachers of the other mother tongues in marginal positions within the schools and education systems in general, working nearly all the time only with 'their' children, not with all the children in the class or school. Their success in terms of their 'intercultural' contribution, therefore, was in the end quite limited, and the positive strategies developed by the various project teams to meet linguistic diversity have only rarely been adopted since as ordinary practice.

In fact few countries have yet re-examined thoroughly the implications for their whole-school curriculum of adopting the goal of preparing at least bilingual people, preferably with a potential for learning additional languages, for an increasingly interdependent world. Some of the international schools have done so, but national school systems are lagging behind in this respect, caught up as they often seem to be in the increasingly nationalist rhetoric of resistance to allegedly, or actually, threatening 'superstates', or dominant nationalities within multinational polities.

## Education and Cultural and Linguistic Pluralism – basic messages and directions

There has been at least one other relatively recent multinational study which tried to document good practice with reference to linguistic diversity in intercultural contexts – the 'ECALP' (Education and Cultural and Linguistic Pluralism) Project. This was an attempt above all to find out what were the necessary conditions under which linguistic and cultural diversity could be a positive experience for children to succeed in school when they used languages at home other than the dominant national language of the school system (CERI, forthcoming).

The Project was set up by the Centre for Education Research and Innovation of the Organization for Economic Cooperation and Development (OECD) – the group of economically powerful nations of which most 'developed' economies are members. The conclusions of the cross-case study analyses by the team of international specialists commissioned to design and evaluate the various national studies undertaken are informative.

However, on the basis of some two dozen case studies of interesting and effective practice with reference to the schooling of linguistically diverse populations in OECD countries, ranging from Australia, through Canada and the US to Slovenia and Switzerland, the ECALP team concluded that at least the following key factors needed to be present for successful outcomes with particular reference to minority children.

- *Cultural and linguistic incorporation*: educational systems which exclude or even simply neglect to use the home languages and cultures of minority pupils will hinder educational progress in general.
- *Community participation*: failure to involve fully all the parents of children in school, and the wider minority communities to which some belong, and thereby to break down discontinuities between home and school language and culture, will work against wider curricular aims.
- *Open pedagogy and assessment*: the authoritarian transmission of unchallengeable and homogenized 'knowledge' and the testing of this by simple reproduction techniques will not produce the kind of critical and engaged people with the range of flexible perspectives necessary to succeed in a globalized and intercultural economic system.

## National Standard Language teaching: the key site for dealing with diversity

In relation to this topic, Bourne (1989) makes the important point that:

If we accept the argument that, however good the special projects and programmes, they will only ever impact on minorities within national school systems, then the focus for attention to linguistic diversity in an intercultural context has to be 'national standard language teaching' – Japanese in Japan, Italian in Italy, Urdu in Pakistan and so on. This is the major curricular space within which children, from majority and minority alike, are socialized into the major public language of the states in which they live. Whatever temporary arrangements are made, following major migrations, for special second language teaching materials and classes, in the end most so-called second language learners now learn alongside those for whom the same language is a first and often only language.

All the more important then that, even when we are primarily interested in education and linguistic diversity, we should begin to take more interest in what happens in National Standard Language curricula, just as the mainstream curriculum in general is where questions to do with cultural diversity as a whole will be most crucially dealt with (Delnoy *et al.*, 1992).

The link between studying the national language and learning how to behave as a national citizen of the country in question begins to seem close. Indeed, the space left for the development within school curricula of any kind of real diversity in terms of values and ways of behaving is probably vitally located in this curricular area (Herrlitz and Sturm, 1990). One of the themes of recent research on national standard language education is the way the teaching of so-called 'mother tongues' in various countries often has as at least part of its function the establishment of learners' national identities. It is as if by 'doing Japanese' you come to 'be Japanese', by 'doing French' you come to 'be French', etc. If this is so, then it obviously creates special problems for those many children in schools whose families have come relatively recently to the country in question – Brazilian Japanese returners to Japan, North African migrants to France, for example. They may not so easily be willing to adopt the national symbols, linguistic and cultural traditions of the new home, above all if it means giving up their existing languages.

Against this background, the final section of this chapter discusses, as a case study of the sometimes negative reaction to the promotion of linguistic and cultural diversity within a school system, some recent educational developments in the dominant nation within the UK.

## The school subject 'English' in England: an attempt to (re)create homogeneity in the face of diversity

It is probably necessary in a publication addressed to an international audience to sketch out some of the background to the present contention in England about the teaching of English in schools: it is currently a highly politicized question, touching as it does on disputed claims about what sort of country England is and should be.

Before the Education Reform Act of 1988, school English had evolved in some quite interesting and useful ways, in terms of its response to the increasing diversity of the school populations. For example:

(a) there had been a diversification, an internationalization of what was commonly read in schools;
(b) there was increasing attention to popular media such as film, television and teenage magazines;
(c) there was a recognition of the importance and value of varieties of English – including some from outside the UK – other than so-called 'standard English', which in practice amounts to southern British middle-class English;
(d) teachers were beginning to work on developing a systematic understanding of how language and languages can be analysed in their context of use, including attention to linguistic diversity and multilingualism.

Much of this was consolidated in the 1989 Cox Report on the teaching of English in schools (DES, 1989): this report, although prioritizing English in the curriculum, nevertheless recommended positive attitudes towards the other languages of bilingual learners.

However, after the 1992 general election in particular, there was a vigorous reaction against the Cox consolidation of the gains in understanding about language education from the previous 20 years. English teachers were instructed to 'clarify' and 'simplify' the curriculum, and the special role of the 'national language' was highlighted. Teachers of English were regularly portrayed from a right-wing perspective as being at the heart of national decline, subversive of traditional values and morals. Rules of grammar and punctuation were used as metaphors of social control, which was seen as having slipped away because of social reforms in the 1960s and 1970s (Marenbon, 1987).

Much of this can be seen as a reflection of a reactive English nationalism in the face of the UK's greater actual or potential integration into the European Union, and in the face of other important social and cultural changes in the composition of its population. Britain has always, of course, been ethnically mixed and linguistically diverse, but such diversity is now even more obvious than before, especially in inner city areas of large conurbations. A third or more of the children in inner London boroughs north of the River Thames speak languages at home other than or in addition to English. Furthermore, in many areas there are black children speaking in some cases local London varieties of English, in other cases also Caribbean varieties – or new syntheses (Linguistic Minorities Project, 1985; Rampton, 1995; Sebba, 1993,). There are comparable developments in most industrialized countries in Europe, in North America, Australia, and now in Japan too (Maher and Macdonald, 1995).

In the face of this, and in the guise of 'clarification' and 'simplification', the current UK government is offering the familiar slogan of 'back to basics'.

Teachers are to return, in the primary school, to teaching children to read using phonic methods and reading schemes – specially written school books devised on the basis of notions of controlled, graded, systematic progression through predicted and predictable stages. These approaches are to replace the combinations of whole-word and phonic approaches, reading schemes and real books which had evolved into more or less standard practice: such approaches are of course much more hospitable to the kind of cultural and linguistic diversity typical of urban school populations in most parts of the world.

As far as what books are to be read in future, the revised canon, while containing much of continuing interest and value, is a throwback to a previous generation of children's literature, much of it safe, conventional, nostalgic, unchallenging, and with only token representation of the kind of books which had come to be regular parts of the diet of reading offered to children at least in city schools. This more diverse diet included books written in English from the Caribbean, Africa and India, as well as from more traditional sources in the UK and the US. It also included books written about children from non-Anglo backgrounds living in England now, and books dealing with difficult topics like family breakdown, war and death – the particular and terrible experience of refugees everywhere. The UK government has also tried to insist that teachers drastically reduce, in some cases eliminate altogether, school study of popular fiction – teenage magazines; TV soaps; advertising; popular music. Even more incomprehensibly, less explicit attention is proposed for 'new media', the implications for writing, for example, of using word-processors and computing more generally.

In terms of pedagogy, all of this is to be accompanied by a return to more whole-class teaching (classes grouped by 'ability', determined by standardized national testing at ages 7, 11, 14 and 16) and by a drastically reduced role for course-work, based around individual and group-centred learning. Finally, an additional instruction supported by Ministers was that teachers were to be required to insist on spoken as well as written 'standard English', not only in class work, but also in the playground and the street.

The likely effect of all of this on learners in general, and on 'bilingual learners' in particular, is predictable. Remember that this is the only English curriculum there is in England: UK education authorities did not proceed down the road of a special 'English as a second language' curriculum – partly on the grounds that in the end there is only one target for everyone, whether they are 'first' or 'second' language speakers (Bourne, 1989). Many of the proposed changes, strongly resisted by many teachers of English but being steadily forced upon them by the current government, will have a profoundly negative effect on second language learners in particular, and on the promotion of linguistic diversity in general.

As far as reading methods are concerned, the transfer of reading skills built up in one language to another will be minimized if the focus is entirely on the particular (and peculiar) relation between the orthography and phonology of the single language English, rather than on meaning construction in general. Teaching methods which take as their starting point that children learn best most of the time in whole-class groups listening to the authoritative teacher, and being assessed formally with paper and pencil tests, are also unlikely to take us forward. (It has to be said, however, that some parents of bilingual children, since this is the kind of teaching style most familiar to many of them, thoroughly approve of this reform at least.)

Above all, of course, the requirement for a more or less exclusive use of 'standard spoken English' will hit hard (assuming it can be made to work at all) those insecure and under-confident about their English – whether they are users of other varieties of English, or of new contact varieties, or of learner varieties (Hudson and Holmes, 1995; Reid, 1996). The function of this message from the British government is clear: it says that to be English, you need to 'do English' as it is imagined English has always been done. It says there is no room for ambiguity, complexity, or diversity. It says that teachers all know what school English is, especially teachers of English as mother tongue. Their special role is to act as guardians of the purity of the language (perhaps also of the nation?): *doing* a certain kind of English will lead pupils to *becoming* a certain kind of English person – narrow, chauvinistic, inward-looking, monolingual, ignorant.

One of the many problems about that version of the school English curriculum is that it provides no space for the bilingual, bicultural learner – no position for him or her to take up except as silent observer, or even victim. A school system which is to have any hope of preparing a diverse population for the next century must offer alternative positions which do permit a place to speak for the bilingual learners in our schools, not from the margins and by special permission but from the centre, alongside classmates from wherever they come.

## Conclusions

This chapter has argued that the promotion of linguistic diversity in general, and in particular as part of 'national standard language education', is crucial to any serious attempt to realize intercultural education. Educators are potential contributors to this whether they are developing particular repertoires of mother tongues like 'English' or 'Japanese', or teaching 'minority' mother tongues like Turkish or Urdu in the European context. Teachers can help, whether they are fortunate enough to be able to teach the two sorts of mother tongues in a coordinated way, within a comprehensive and systematic framework of bilingual education, or if they have to teach them in separate parts of the school curriculum.

It is by holding in our minds the complicated inter-relationships between studying national standard languages and growing into certain kinds of citizens, of whatever national or supranational polities, that language educators of whatever sub-category can contribute effectively to the production of good citizens of particular countries who are also able to function as good citizens of the world.

# References

Anderson, B (1991) *Imagined Communities,* London: Verso.
Bourne, J (1989) *Moving into the Mainstream,* Windsor: NFER-Nelson.
Byram, M and Leman, J (eds) (1990) *Bicultural and Trilingual Education: The Foyer Model in Brussels,* Clevedon: Multilingual Matters.
CERI (forthcoming) *Dimensions of Cultural Pluralism,* Paris: OECD/CERI (Synthesis Report of the ECALP Project).
Delnoy, R *et al.* (eds) (1992) *Comparative Analyses of Case Studies in Mother Tongue Education,* Enschede: IMEN-VALO.
DES (1989) *English for Ages 5–16,* The Cox Report, London: HMSO.
Herrlitz, W and Sturm, J (1990) *Ethnographic Research in the Field of Mother Tongue Education: What can be Learnt from IMEN?,* Nijmegen: IMEN-IAIE.
Houlton, D (1984) *All Our Languages,* London: Edward Arnold.
Hudson, R A and Holmes, J (1995) *Children's Use of Spoken Standard English,* London: SCAA Discussions Papers No. 1.
Kroon, S and Sturm, J (eds) (forthcoming) *Multilingualism and Standard Language Teaching in Europe: Historical and Comparative Issues.*
Linguistic Minorities Project (1985) *The Other Languages of England,* London: RKP.
Maher, J and Macdonald, G (eds) (1995) *Diversity in Japanese Language and Culture,* London: Kegan Paul International.
Marenbon, J (1987) *English our English,* London: Centre for Policy Studies.
Rampton, B (1995) *Crossing: Language and Ethnicity Among Adolescents,* London: Longman.
Reid, E (1988) 'Linguistic minorities and language education: The English experience', *Journal of Multilingual and Multicultural Development,* 9, 1–2.
Reid E (1990) 'English as a Second Language in England', in Tingbjorn, G (ed.) *Svenska som Andrasprak,* Stockholm: Skriptor.
Reid, E (1996) 'Review of Hudson and Holmes', *BAAL Newsletter,* 53, Summer.
Reid E and Reich, H (eds) (1992) *Breaking the Boundaries: Migrant Workers' Children in the EC,* Clevedon: Multilingual Matters.
Romaine, S (1989) *Bilingualism,* Oxford: Blackwell.
Sebba, M (1993) *London Jamaican: Language Systems in Interaction,* London: Longman.
Skutnabb-Kangas, T and Cummins, J (eds) (1988) *Minority Education,* Clevedon: Multilingual Matters.
Stephens, M (1976) *Linguistic Minorities in Western Europe,* Llandysul: Gomer Press.
Thomas, G (1991) *Linguistic Purism,* London: Longman.

# 5. Educational Contradictions: The Education of Stateless and State-denied Groups

Crispin Jones

In Chapter 1, the concept of groups being stateless and/or state-denied was put forward and their especial educational provision indicated. Two broad groups of peoples fall into these categories, namely those nations or peoples denied validity and value by the states that encompass them and asylum-seekers and refugees. More precisely, the stateless are the asylum-seekers and refugees: although most have a formal state affiliation, it is one which they or their state have rejected. The state-denied are the groups who claim they have no state of their own and whose existence may be deemed problematic by their state of residence. With no state protection, internal or external, such people are particularly vulnerable. This would be true of many 'indigenous' peoples across the globe, such as the peoples of the rainforests in Africa and South America, the Aborigines of Australia, the Inuit and related peoples in Canada and the CIS and the Native Americans of Canada and the USA. (Again, language is revealing here, as the term 'indigenous', although perhaps easy to define, is difficult to apply, save in an operational sense.) It has also been true for peoples who have no state to protect them *in extremis*, such as the Roma and, until 1948 and the foundation of the state of Israel, the Jews. With no state protection, all such people are vulnerable and their children are likely to be the most vulnerable groups in state education systems, if indeed, they are present within them.

In many state education systems, provision for such groups has often been and frequently remains marginal and curriculum space for them is minimal or even denied altogether. Their history and presence is ignored. The example of the Roma in Germany and its precursor states is salutary in this respect. The Roma arrived in Hildesheim, in present day Germany, in 1407. The first discriminatory anti-Roma law was passed nine years later. Further major laws, expulsions and pogroms took place in 1500, 1531, 1580, 1659, 1710, 1726, 1830, 1899, 1905, 1907 and 1928. Hitler's policies towards the Roma were therefore not a new phenomenon, although their consequences were even more lethal. On 1 August 1944, '*Zigeunernacht*', four thousand Roma were executed and cremated in one day; by the end of the war, some one and a half million Roma had been killed, between half and three-quarters of all European Roma (details from Refugee Council, 1994). The lack of precision in relation to numbers is because few states had statistics on their Roma population, again indicative of their outsider status.

Other states have parallel histories in relation to Roma people, for example, Norway (Schluter, 1993). In his article, Schluter describes the forcible removal of Roma children from their parents, to 'save' them, a practice that continued into this century. It is, of course, a practice not restricted to Norway or indeed the Roma. For example, Australian Aboriginal children were, to all intents and purposes, kidnapped by the state in order to speed up their assimilation, a process which continued to relatively recently. The issue for schools operating in states with such histories is simple at one level, complex at another, namely, how much of this history could and should be told to all children.

That it seldom is, is probably a contributory factor to the rise of narrow nationalism, xenophobia and the continuation of vicious civil wars across the globe. That it should be taught is what this chapter hopes to demonstrate. Without such historical understandings, a state's demographic complexity can seem threatening and unclear to many students and pupils, a view that is often supported by various elements of the mass media, particularly when state controlled.

A similar range of educational issues relate to refugees and asylum-seekers. The educational needs of refugees, forced to flee their state, are potentially a massive extra demand on the education system of their receiving state, as the funds of the appropriate UN agency, the United Nations High Commission for Refugees (UNHCR) are rarely adequate and most receiving countries are already desperately short of resources, as many African instances demonstrate. To make matters worse, UN efforts in this area are divided. At least two other UN agencies also deal with refugees but in specific areas with specific groups of refugees, namely, UNWRA in relation to over two million Palestinian refugees and UNBRO in relation to Cambodian refugees.

Although refugees have been a permanent feature of all education systems, rarely does this seem to be remembered. Refugees are indeed as old as states and are a product of them. In English, the very word 'refugee' is both old and a reflection of this link with state practices of exclusion. The word 'refugee' derives from the description of themselves used by French-speaking Huguenots fleeing France to settle in England in the 17th century. Although concern had been expressed over refugees for many years, major international attention and systematic action had to wait until shortly after the Second World War. This was a period when the world experienced large movements of refugees, particularly in the Indian sub-continent, following partition, and in Europe, following the redrawing of state boundaries and the imposition of the Iron Curtain. At that time, the United Nations, in a 1951 Convention, defined a refugee as a person who has left his or her own country,

owing to a well-founded fear of being persecuted for reasons of race, religion, nationality, membership of a particular social group or political opinion.
(UN, 1951)

Such a person, having crossed an international border, is an asylum-seeker,
looking for refugee status in the receiving country. As all members of the UN
have subscribed to this Convention and the 1967 Protocol that followed,
refugee status should be readily given. However, being given refugee status
and having one's needs, including educational needs, met is another matter,
particularly in situations where large numbers of asylum-seekers arrive in a
country that is already poor, as is frequently the case. One major consequence
of this is a wide variety of practice between states and also within states over
time, the latter usually owing to the internal political views about particular
groups of refugees at any particular time. Classic cases of this latter point
would be the treatment of Palestinian refugees over the last 50 years and, in
Europe, the differential responses to Jewish refugees during the first half of
this century and to ex-colonial refugees during the second half. Indeed, as this
chapter was being written, the current Polish government apologized for the
massacre of Jews returning from the German concentration camps that took
place in Poland *after* the war.

However, refugees are a worldwide issue, with the overwhelming majority
of refugees never reaching the rich countries of the North. It is the poor
countries of the South which provide for the majority of refugees, as only some
5–10% of refugees are in the states of the North. The scale of this inequitable
distribution is made even clearer when the ratio of refugees to population is
examined. In Britain, for example, the ratio is one refugee to 318 of the
population: in Malawi it is one to nine and in Jordan, one to three (BRC, 1993).
However, accurate figures in this area are always hard to acquire owing to
significant numbers of asylum-seekers not being in official records for fairly
obvious reasons.

At this point it has to be reiterated that globally, refugees seeking asylum,
including education for their children, are nothing new. The Second World
War produced some 60 million refugees and even now, in a world supposedly
coming out of the cold war, the number of refugees worldwide has started to
grow again. It was estimated that some 15 million people were refugees in 1990
(Rutter, 1991, pp.26 and 35), a figure which had risen to 19 million by 1993
(Rutter, 1994, p.4) and is probably nearer 20 million in 1996. The devastation
of peoples is awesome. Taking into account both refugees and internally
displaced people, the numbers involved show a global catastrophe. Groups of
over two million internally displaced and refugee people include Angolans,
Afghans, Burmese, Burundis, Liberians, Mozambicans, Palestinians, Rwan-
dans, Somalis, Sri Lankans, Sudanese and former Yugoslavians (Rutter, 1994,
p.9). In other words, for every refugee, there is usually at least one internally
displaced person, also making demands on the state's resources, including

educational resources. Within Europe for example, the collapse of Yugoslavia has produced an estimated 2.5 million-plus refugees and displaced people, the majority of whom remain within the old borders of that state. By September 1992, when numbers officially began to peak, about 250,000 had arrived in Germany and some 30,000 in Britain (Rutter and Fischer, 1992).

A concern for numbers can frequently be a side track when considering refugees' educational needs. The numbers game is always a difficult one in relation to asylum-seekers, usually being played to deny, rather than to provide more adequately. Although innovative educational schemes have been evolved for former Yugoslavian refugees across the EU, for example in Italy (De Liva and Parmeggiani, 1995) and Germany (Morrell, 1996), an ongoing concern is with refugees in Bosnia, Croatia, Serbia and Slovenia.

Moreover, as Martenson's report for UNESCO on education for the refugees in former Yugoslavia indicates, despite huge efforts by the countries concerned, much remains to be done (Martenson *et al.*, 1992). Apart from offering specific advice, the report puts forward a conceptual framework that might be used in the assessment of refugee educational needs in a range of different contexts. Within the broad framework of human rights, the report advocates that the right to education provides a critical starting point. Analysing that right in terms of equity, quality and relevance provides the essential setting from which intervention strategy options (financial, advocationary and technical) may be derived and prioritized.

Martenson *et al.*'s report offers some useful pointers for policy-makers in countries with large numbers of refugees. For countries with few, like the countries of the EU, the issues would appear to be different but are in fact quite similar, centring on questions of relative equity within a specific state framework. Given this, what sorts of educational issues face refugee and asylum-seeking students if they can manage to get into a school? Six points, arising from work done in a number of EU states, seem worthy of brief discussion and may have a more general relevance.

## (i) Teaching about refugee issues to non-refugee children

Many refugee students face prejudice and discrimination when in mainstream schools, as no doubt they do in the wider society generally. Among many non-refugee pupils interviewed in the course of ongoing research work in the International Centre for Intercultural Education, there was general acceptance of refugee pupils on the surface but underneath there was quite a lot of hostility, some outright racism and a considerable amount of wearied acceptance on both sides. However, it was encouraging to find that, in most cases, if schools took a pro-refugee stance, this was accepted by the pupils. Pupils with strong anti-refugee feelings were generally disapproved of, although there is some evidence in London that inter-group relations among young people appear to be moving towards more complex alignments (ICIS, 1996).

However, even where refugee students are in separate schools, as they often are in the camps, similar issues of knowledge, understanding and tolerance arise, as the hostility that is often engendered by their presence is seldom actively opposed within the mainstream education system.

### (ii) Language issues, the languages of the home and the language(s) of the school

The amount of help given to refugee students in terms of language is seldom sufficient. Also, debates about language use are complex, a point explored in more detail in Chapter 4. Given the hope of return, continued home-language provision does seem important but resources are seldom provided for it, though there are exceptions (eg, Morrell, 1996).

### (iii) Giving appropriate emotional and other support

This is not just an issue in relation to post-traumatic stress disorder, a topic that quite correctly concerns many working in the area (eg, Jones and Rutter, 1996). Trauma covers other areas as well. For example, there are significant numbers of unaccompanied refugee young people in schools and they frequently require support to help cope with the often difficult positions that they find themselves in.

### (iv) The dangers of stereotyping refugee children

This issue links in with the previous one. Not all refugee students are traumatized, although many are in some way or another. Nor are they educational problems or failures as they are sometimes labelled. Many refugee pupils appear eager to use their schooling to the best of their abilities as a positive investment in a potentially better future life.

### (v) 'Yet another task...'. Resource issues

For many countries, the cost of helping their refugee communities is devastating. Providing anything but a minimum educational offering is difficult. This lack of responsibility towards the stateless is itself a revealing comment on the willingness of the modern state to provide for those that do not fit the state paradigm: it is also revealing in demonstrating the limitations and weaknesses of the relevant international agencies.

### (vi) Home/school/community links

This is another complex issue, with no two educational systems, or even schools within them, facing identical issues. For example, in schools in London which have many refugee students, they had strong links with some of the communities they served, weak links with others and in some cases, non-existent or even negative links with others. In this specific context, the negative links were often related to more general racial tensions in the area (CME, 1992; ICIS, 1996).

These issues raise further real issues for state educational systems. The vast movements of refugees, particularly the millions of people in the groups mentioned earlier in this chapter, quite clearly come near to collapsing any system of education set up for them. Being stateless, their main resource providers remain the international organizations, who themselves remain short of cash and in some cases are inefficient even with the relatively small sums of money available to them. As many remain in poor neighbouring countries, the richer countries of the North have generally adopted an 'out of sight, out of mind' approach, with spasmodic media coverage being the only chance for any significant change in the flow of resources to the refugee groups. It is therefor not surprising that recipient countries may seem harsh in their treatment of such people. With inadequately funded education systems of their own, why should precious and scarce educational resources be given to those who are not citizens? It is a clear sign of the inability of the modern state to deal with such a vast and widespread human phenomenon (Coulby and Jones, 1995).

States rightly prefer stability and peace in their societies. Refugees challenge this, as do the state-denied groups discussed earlier in this chapter. However, the dilemma for states between choosing stability and silence on the one hand, and fluidity and ambivalence on the other, is clear. Both tactics can lead to fission and fracture of the state. Such a dilemma ensures that the chapter ends on a note of indecision. However, the author would argue that this is indicative of a wider problem, namely the fact that the traditional state of the last two hundred years and its supportive education system is perhaps reaching the end of its useful life and that the preferred alternatives or variants are not clearly and currently visible. Indeed, the stateless and state-denied make this difficulty more apparent. Such views are at the heart of current debates about the future of the EU and the education systems that are found within it. As the German Chancellor, Helmut Kohl recently noted, when reflecting upon the late President Mitterand's commitment to the EU,

> We have no desire to return to the nation state of old. It cannot solve the great problems of the 21st century. Nationalism has brought great suffering to our continent. (Bremner, 1996, p.1)

Given that the nation state of old seems to refuse to lie down and die, and that the alternatives are unclear, this chapter is also a plea for idealistic pragmatism. In that sense, it is in accord with the view of the Irish Republican Army's (IRA) cease-fire taken by the Irish poet Seamus Heaney, when he said:

> I do believe that, whatever happens, a corner was turned historically in 1994. We've passed from the atrocious to the messy, but the messy is a perfectly okay place to live. (Lawson, 1996, p.2.3)

It is a view of recent events that many in South Africa, the CIS and other parts of the globe could well share. Change, even benevolent change, is painful, whether we call it symptomatic of postmodernity or not (Coulby and Jones, 1995). Its educational consequences are equally so.

## References

Bremner, C (1996) 'Nation state's day is over, Britain told [by Kohl]', *The Times*, 3 February.

British Refugee Council (BRC) (1993) *Who is a Refugee?* London: BRC.

Centre for Multicultural Education (CME) (1992) *Sagaland: Youth Culture, Racism and Education: A Report on Research Carried out in Thamesmead*, London: London Borough of Greenwich.

Coulby, D and Jones, C (1995) *Postmodernity and European Education Systems: Cultural Diversity and Centralist Knowledge*, Stoke-on-Trent: Trentham Books.

De Liva, W and Parmeggiani, A (1995) 'The reception of Bosnian refugee children into schools in Undine, Northern Italy', paper given at Intercultural Education Partnership Symposium 'The School in the Community', Edinburgh, November.

International Centre for Intercultural Studies (ICIS) (1996) *Routes of Racism: the Social Basis of Racist Action*, Stoke-on-Trent: Trentham Books.

Jones, C and Rutter, J (eds) (1996) *Mapping the Field: New Initiatives in Refugee Education*, Stoke-on-Trent: Trentham Books.

Lawson, M (1996) 'Turning time up and over', *The Guardian*, 30 April.

Martenson, J *et al*. (1992) *Report to the Director-General on a Mission to Slovenia and Croatia*, Paris: UNESCO

Morrell, C (1996) 'Refugee course to stay', *The Times Educational Supplement*, 23 February, p.15.

Refugee Council (1994) *Roma in Eastern Europe and the UK*, London: Refugee Council.

Rutter, J (1991) *Refugees: We Left Because We Had To*, London: The Refugee Council.

Rutter, J (1994) *Refugee Children in the Classroom*, Stoke-on-Trent: Trentham Books.

Rutter, J and Fischer, A (1992) *Refugees from Bosnia, Serbia and Croatia*, London: The Refugee Council.

Schluter, R (1993) 'Travellers: A forgotten Norwegian minority', *European Journal of Intercultural Studies*, 3, 2/3.

United Nations (1951) *Convention Relating to the Status of Refugees*, New York: UN.

United Nations (1967) *Protocol Relating to the Status of Refugees*, New York: UN.

# Section II:
# Regional Contexts

## 6. The Commonwealth of Independent States

Janusz Tomiak

### Introduction

The ethnic composition of the population in all the countries of the Common-wealth of Independent States (CIS) is highly diversified and for historical, political and economic reasons, interethnic relations are often marred by tension and discord. Developing respect and proper appreciation of the distinctive cultures of all nations, nationalities and ethnic groups through education can greatly help to eliminate the mutual suspicion and dislike which prevail among many different peoples living in the area. So far, intercultural education in the CIS states has, generally, not been accorded a high enough priority to ensure closer contacts and positive cooperation among the different nations, nationalities and ethnic groups. However, there is evidence that some educators have made real efforts to promote genuine interethnic under-standing and the dialogue of cultures. Concrete assistance from outside di-rected to this end can help to intensify this process and thus to ensure a lasting peace and stability in all CIS countries.

Geographically and politically the CIS represents a very different form of socio-political entity from the Union of Soviet Socialist Republics which ceased to exist in 1991. The CIS is an association of 12 independent states, with their own heads of state and their own governments. Each state is inhabited by a great variety of peoples, although in each case the numerically dominant nation decisively influences the political and cultural life of the country in question.

The ethnic composition of the population of each CIS state reflects a very complicated pattern of population movements over many centuries, west-ward, eastward, southward and northward, which involved many different races, nations, nationalities and ethnic groups. Superimposed upon this com-plex pattern of development have, over the last ten centuries, been various

political formations as well as religious and cultural influences which often
had their origins in much more distant lands. The result has been a very highly
diversified form of inter-group relationships which cannot be reduced to a
simple formula, valid for all countries constituting the CIS and each one must
be considered separately. Only then it is possible to grasp the true character
of the problems and difficulties which far too often have led to interethnic
tension, discord and confrontation.

## The socio-cultural background

The membership of the CIS includes the three important states with predominantly Slav population: the Russian Federation, Belarus and Ukraine. However, the first and by far the largest one is also home to some 120 different
nationalities and ethnic groups, speaking different languages and having
different spheres of cultural and religious influences which, despite all the
pressures of enforced urbanization and industrialization during the Soviet
period, are still very much able to orient their cultural and social life towards
the traditional values and norms deeply rooted in their past and their national
heritage. The other two Slav republics, despite the great importance that the
influences emanating from Russia have played in their history, significantly
declared themselves fully independent of the Russian Federation when the
decision concerning their political future had to be taken in the summer of
1991. But the presence of a large number of Russians, who have lived in both
Belarus and Ukraine for generations and still live there today, is of great
consequence. Apart from the Russians, there are also significant numbers of
Poles, Jews, Gypsies and many other groups who have lived in the two
Republics for a long time.

   One should also underline the cultural differences between Belarus and
Ukraine. The latter takes great pride in its distinctive cultural heritage, starting
with the Kiev Rus and stretching over many centuries, and embracing the
consciousness of a long struggle for free and unhampered cultural development. Smaller and historically less fortunate Belarus has had limited opportunities to develop its own language and literature, its own intelligentsia and its
truly independent cultural institutions. The declaration of political independence by Belarus could not in itself bring about a linguistic and cultural
revival in the absence of solid historical foundations, despite the efforts of a
small, but determined cultural elite (Tomiak, 1992, pp.33–44; Tomiak, 1993,
pp.393–409).

   Moldova, another member of the CIS, placed as it were at the periphery of
the old Tsarist empire as well as the former Soviet Union, possesses a population which includes a large proportion of Russians, mainly in the Transdni-
estrian region, Ukrainians, Jews and Gypsies as well as other nationalities who
have little in common with the Romanian-speaking Moldavians.

Armenia and Georgia, two ancient countries which have had to face continuous invasions from many directions over the last two millennia, take great pride in the fact that their written languages go back to the 4th century AD. Both countries embraced Christianity long before it spread across western and central Europe and both have produced over many centuries poets, writers and thinkers of distinction and high repute. Tsarist rule came there only at the beginning of the 19th century and both countries enjoyed a short period of independence between 1917 and 1920/1, when the Soviet forces overran them. Very much attached to their ancient cultural traditions and the heroic folktales which have been passed through countless generations, the two nations, surrounded by different ethnic groups and nationalities, have always resisted alien influences with all the means at their disposal. Bitter cultural conflicts, not cultural symbiosis, have inevitably been the central feature of human existence in that part of the world.

Again, the demographic and cultural differences between the two countries should not be overlooked. The Armenians constitute nearly 90% of the population of Armenia, while the Russians and the linguistically and culturally very different Azeris and Kurds largely make up the remainder. Territorially, Georgia includes two autonomous republics, Abkhasia and Adjaria, as well as the autonomous region of South Ossetia. Two-thirds of the inhabitants of Georgia are Georgians and one-third is made up of Russians, Ukrainians, Armenians, Azeris, Jews as well as several small ethnic groups. The capital, Tbilisi, despite the fact that the city recently was a battleground between the different factions fighting each other for political domination, still is a cosmopolitan centre with a mixed population of very different cultural backgrounds. Under stable and peaceful conditions cosmopolitan urban centres frequently are important focuses of trade and commerce which bring prosperity to their inhabitants. In times of instability, uncertainty and confusion they easily become the arenas for conflicting pressures where each interest group vies with all the others for the declining shares of wealth and diminishing opportunities. The sudden collapse of the USSR could not fail to affect Tbilisi adversely.

Azerbaidzhan, the third state in the Caucasus, occupying part of the region between the Black and the Caspian Sea, is almost as large as Georgia and Armenia put together. It is preponderantly populated by the Shiite Muslim Azeris with close historical ties to Iran. The Armenian-Azeri conflict over the Nagorno-Karabakh region in 1990–93 brought extensive devastation to this territory and death to many thousands of its inhabitants.

The ethnic composition of the newly independent states of Central Asia, that is Kazakhstan, Uzbekistan, Turkmenistan, Tadzhikistan and Kirghizstan is as diversified as that in the Caucasus. Kirghiz constitute less than half of the population of Kirghizstan. Tadzhik constitute only just over a half of the population of Tadzhikistan. Around two-thirds of the population of Turkmenistan are Turkmen and of Uzbekistan are Uzbeks. Large numbers of the latter live in the four newly independent states bordering Uzbekistan. Many Kazakhs live in Uzbekistan and Turkmenistan and many Kirghiz in Tadzhikistan. In all the newly independent states of Central Asia millions of Russians have lived for generations, though many of them chose to leave for the Russian Federation in the course of the last five years, fearing an explosion of nationalism in the different republics. Yet, many decided to stay on. In addition there are many smaller nationalities and ethnic groups residing all over the five republics in the areas which they consider to be their ancestral homelands. High birth-rates predominate almost everywhere, adding to the pressure of population on the means of subsistence and creating additional problems. Strong authoritarian governments have been able to prevent any outbreaks of direct confrontation so far, except in Tadzhikistan, where the civil war has already resulted in open armed conflict.

Most of the inhabitants of four out of the five independent republics which previously constituted the Soviet Central Asia, that is Turkmenistan, Uzbekistan, Kirghizstan and Kazakhstan, belong to the Turkic group. Yet, to this group belong also the Azeris, living on the western side of the Caspian Sea, the Tartars, the Bashkirs and the Chuvash, living in the very heart of the Russian Federation; the Yakuts, living in north-eastern Siberia; the Khakass and the Tuvinians who live close to the Mongolian frontier as well as the Karakalpaks, living in north Uzbekistan and the Gagauz, living in Moldova. Though so widely dispersed, they are all very conscious of their common roots. Over 90% of all Turkic people are historically of the Muslim faith, but the Chuvash, the Gagauz, the Yakuts and the Tuvinians have never been affected by Islam. Numerically much smaller Turkic peoples are the Karachays, the Balkars, the Nogays and the Muslim Kamyks living in the north Caucasus and the Altays of southern Siberia (Brown *et al.*, 1982, pp.65–70).

The many peoples belonging to the Turkic group often possess different physical features and the only common cultural feature is language. Yet, most of the Turkic languages have been developing independently of each other over the centuries and some in total isolation. This has resulted in a far-reaching cultural differentiation, further enhanced by direct contact and cultural intercourse with non-Turkic peoples inhabiting the same territory.

## Interethnic relations and the language factor

It is quite evident from the aforementioned data that there is a twofold dimension in the cultural diversity which dominates the scene in the territory of the former Soviet Union. On the one hand, each republic is a multicultural state. On the other, a particular language group is, as a rule, spread over numerous republics of the CIS. That means that it inhabits a number of independent – and sometimes antagonistically inclined – states where it often constitutes a significant and, frequently, a sizeable minority. Yet, such a minority has normally lived in a particular territory for generations. Each one considers that territory to be its homeland and it insists on being treated as a legitimate possessor of the territory and a distinctive category of citizens to whom full cultural rights should not in any way be denied (Zhiltsova *et al.*,1993, pp.65 and 75).

Under such circumstances, interethnic relations acquire a key significance and directly affect the political and economic stability of the area as a whole. Any tension or major dispute over whatever the different nations, nationalities or ethnic groups share within one particular political organism is likely to have far-reaching consequences outside it and, in certain circumstances, can easily lead to open conflict.

In trying to prevent such a danger, one should keep in mind that one of the particularly important factors influencing interethnic and national relations in a country is education. However, this is not always properly appreciated. One must never forget that in a multicultural state the language of instruction as well as the contents of the curriculum are of the greatest consequence. In particular, the teaching of history, literature, human geography, social studies and, clearly, religion – when it is incorporated into the course of studies – profoundly influences the formation of attitudes towards ethnic groups, nationalities and nations other than one's own (Council for Cultural Cooperation, 1987a, pp.4–8; 1987b, pp.7–20; 1993, pp.5–12).

In the old USSR there were many languages of instruction, although that did not mean that all children were in fact taught in their mother tongue. In many areas the population was a mixture of numerous ethnic groups, nationalities and nations. Under such conditions, the only sensible solution seemed to be to use the language of the largest group as the language of communication and instruction in schools. In addition, some groups were much too small or too dispersed to afford schools teaching in the mother tongue. Increasing geographical mobility of the population, which was imperative for economic reasons, produced also constant changes in the balance of local population in many areas. The official efforts to promote bilingualism which were understandable from the point of view of economic development, often produced covert resistance and, sometimes, open hostility. But the most significant development for the different ethnic groups and nationalities was the unintended growth of national consciousness and national loyalty which accompanied the teaching of national literature and national history, despite the Leninist formula of 'national in form and communist in content'. The spread of universal, free and compulsory education, first at the elementary, and then at the secondary, school level meant a growing familiarity with the national past and an increasing consciousness of the struggle of the different groups for cultural autonomy and political independence which had taken place in the ages gone by and resulted in the formation of negative attitudes towards 'the big brothers', dominating culturally and politically or even threatening the very existence of a particular ethnic group or nationality.

## The relevance of history and the geo-political dimension

Of direct relevance for all the CIS states is one particular aspect of historical development. This is the point of the original contact between the dominant and non-dominant groups. In general, whenever this takes the form of a military conquest, an enforced subjugation of the weaker by the stronger group, and it involves a subsequent exploitation – whatever form it may take and however subjective its perception may be – the consequence, almost inevitably, is a lasting antagonism and hostility. This may well remain hidden for a long time, but it is very likely to erupt and end in violence in the time of a crisis such as the dissolution of a large state, particularly if this process is resisted by the dominant group, determined to preserve the status quo (Buldakov et al., 1994, pp.11–26; Tomiak, 1991, pp.390–7).

If, on the other hand, the original contact occurs under different circumstances, in a peaceful way, without bloodshed and the groups involved see an advantage in the formation of a closer cultural or political link or economic cooperation, the intergroup relations progress along much more positive lines. That, unfortunately, does not happen very often. It, indeed, was not the case in the distant past when the Mongol invasions destroyed the Kiev Rus or, much later, when the Tsarist armies subdued the different parts of Central Asia and the Caucasus in the late 18th and early 19th centuries. On the other hand, the Russian eastward movement into western, central and eastern Siberia was, by and large, a peaceful process in which trade, settlement and development proceeded without bloodshed.

The interstate relations in the CIS today are, therefore, differently influenced by the memories of the past and have often more to do with present-day imperatives, among which economic considerations are of great importance, and the internal and external intergroup relations are not by any means fixed, but depend upon the policies pursued by the state authorities in each member country of the CIS. This precisely is the stage at which intercultural education can fulfil an important role in promoting better intergroup understanding by providing a generally acceptable basis for cultural development of all ethnic groups and nationalities inhabiting each state and thus laying down the foundations for a lasting peace and the reversal of negative economic trends (Tomiak, 1994, pp.415–27).

In the instances, however, in which open confrontation and armed conflict have recently been taking place, the propagation of positive attitudes has for both sides involved become very difficult indeed. The old animosities have been reawakened and the old wounds reopened – and what is much worse, deepened – by the human losses on both sides. Every effort, therefore, must be made to pursue intercultural education in all states and areas where there is an indication of a growing interethnic tension but where open confrontation has so far not taken place and can still be avoided if the roots of mutual suspicion and dislike are eradicated. This is, in fact, often the case in some of the CIS states and intercultural education must be considered there to be the top priority.

The challenge is a formidable one. Efforts to promote peaceful coexistence and, indeed, positive cooperation among all the nations, nationalities and ethnic groups inhabiting the vast territory of the CIS through intercultural education involve three different geopolitical dimensions. First, in each state the authorities responsible for the formulation of educational policy have to try to ensure mutual respect and positive attitudes towards each other among the nationalities and ethnic groups inhabiting that state, so that internal conflicts can be avoided. Paradoxically, this is often the most difficult thing to achieve.

Second, amicable relations have to be established between the neighbouring states within the CIS and all conflicts settled in a peaceful way to ensure political stability over the area as a whole. In one or two instances this also presents a real problem because of the traditional enmities that still persist between certain nations, nationalities and ethnic and religious groups, despite all the efforts made by some individuals who understand the likely catastrophic consequences of renewed confrontation.

Third, the relations between each CIS state and the neighbouring states which do not belong to the CIS have to be permanently put on a peaceful basis. Each CIS state borders at least one non-CIS state and the differences between the states that exist – political, economic and cultural – have to be respected. However, national chauvinism and imperialistic policies of the bigger states have resulted in numerous military conflicts in the past and the memory of the atrocities already committed dies hard. In some instances such memories can all too easily be reawakened, for example by ethnocentric policies pursued by the authorities representing the interests of the dominant groups, and ill-advised measures to promote national unity in the face of a supposed threat from outside.

## Educational priorities and intercultural education

It has to be conceded that, for a number of reasons, political and economic in character, intercultural education is not given a high enough priority in the CIS states. One can identify the principal causes of this unsatisfactory state of affairs. Determined efforts are made everywhere to use education to promote internal cohesion and political stability without a proper regard for the interests and sensitivities of the different minorities (Tomiak, 1994, pp.415–27). In addition, the main stress is nowadays frequently placed upon education which arises out of commercial and economic imperatives, that is the command of knowledge and skills important for direct application in production and efficient exploitation of natural resources (Kitaev, 1995, pp.1–22). Teaching respect for other cultures and ways of life is seldom regarded as vitally important and, at best, given secondary consideration. Human attitudes and

behaviour are then much more influenced by other agencies and social institutions, many of which are much more interested in the strengthening of the
inner ties within each group than in a dialogue of cultures and in promoting
respect for other beliefs and value systems.

When the CIS states constituted an integral part of the former Soviet Union,
social and ethnic relations were very much subordinated to the rigorous
demands arising from political imperatives and the pressures of modernization and industrialization. Any possible manifestations of interethnic hostility were avoided – apart from isolated instances – through a system of strict
controls from the centre, which were often ruthless but generally effective.
After gaining independence, the nations and nationalities inhabiting the
different CIS states made the development and strengthening of national
identity and cultural distinctiveness their primary concern (Schmidt, 1995a,
pp.10–20 and 28–42). In this way a direct clash of the different cultural
traditions, often reinforced by a renewed interest in the religious heritage of
each group, has become unavoidable. Intercultural education has, therefore,
become a matter of the greatest importance (Council for Cultural Cooperation,
1987a, pp.6–7). Yet, little evidence has been forthcoming from the CIS area in
the course of the last five years that the urgent need for intercultural education
has been explicitly acknowledged (Schmidt, 1995b, pp.30–36).

What efforts are then required of the governments and educational policy-
makers so that intercultural education could be introduced and pursued in
schools and other educational establishments, particularly in the regions of
intergroup conflicts in the Caucasus and Central Asia? Naturally, what one
does depends upon what one wants to achieve. Intercultural education aims
at the elimination of intergroup hostility, whatever its roots and wherever its
origins. And much more than that. It aims at a more genuine and lasting
understanding among nations, nationalities and ethnic groups which interact
with each other. It aims at a peaceful resolution of all problems, political, social,
economic and educational, through negotiation and open discussion. It paves
the way to a society in which rational thinking and genuine respect for other
individuals' and groups' rights are the rule without any exception. This
requires patience, perseverance and commitment, first of all among all those
who are responsible for the formulation of educational policy and the identification of the principal aims of education in each state. The latter must include
international understanding and intercultural cooperation, to make sure that
intercultural education is very much the focus of attention of all those who are
concerned with the education of the young.

It also means that the curricula which are in force and the teaching of all
subjects, but particularly history, national and foreign languages and literatures, social studies and geography, are oriented towards the creation of
proper respect for other cultures and never include the propagation of any
ideas which might lead to further deterioration of interethnic and international relations (Rust et al., 1994, pp.285–9).

In practice, everything depends upon the teachers. They have to be fully aware of the role they are to play in the intercultural dimension in education and act accordingly, so that the members of the younger generation can all fulfil their civic duties and obligations as the future citizens in each country.

Fortunately, good examples – albeit isolated examples, so far – of awareness of this responsibility of the educators of the young, can be found in the CIS. L N Bogoliubov and A Iu Lazebnikova, in their publication *Man and Society: The foundations of contemporary civilisation*, which has been recommended for use in schools by the Ministry of Education of the Russian Federation, state the following:

> the majority of nations live in multinational states. And this means that, however dear to us may be the historical memory of our own national roots, it is important that we also understand that we all live and will always live together with people of different nationalities. This demands from each one of us special sensitivity and responsibility in our dealings with the members of other nationalities. The more so that, among the various nations, there are more common features than there are differences and that this commonality steadily grows and with it grow the interdependence and the interconnections among nations and the unity of the world. Clearly, the drawing together of the different nations does not mean the repudiation of their national features. Just the opposite, it is the special features of their cultures which serve as a living testimony of the spiritual wealth of the whole of mankind and the infinite diversity of world culture (Bogoliubov and Lazebnikova, 1993, p.71).

The two writers go on to say:

> It is not only the cooperation between people as individuals [that matters]; there also is a dialogue of cultures, of civilisations. And today we understand that we must learn how to conduct such a dialogue; a dialogue that will help to make the achievements of the different cultures and civilisations the property of all mankind (Bogoliubov and Lazebnikova, 1993, p.7).

These words ought to be repeated and given the fullest consideration possible in every country of the CIS, without exception.

The source of another difficulty is the fact that the financial resources in all the CIS countries only too often preclude more fundamental research into effective programmes of intercultural education. The more important, therefore, is the help which can come from outside. Yet this is very limited, though fortunately not altogether non-existent. The Soros Foundation has recently been able to direct some of its resources towards intercultural education and intercultural studies. Kazakhstan, Kirghizstan, Tadzhikistan, Georgia, Moldova, Ukraine as well as Russia have now been involved in this kind of initiative. Thus, in the Caucasus, through the Arts and Culture Programme of the Open Society, Georgia, Foundation, support is given to a new generation of artists 'to build greater understanding among ethnic groups by promoting mutual respect for other people's cultural traditions' (Soros Foundation, 1994, p.46). In Moldova the aim of the Foundation is 'contributing to the normalisation of interethnic relations' (p.67). In Kazakhstan 'the Foundation is working to strengthen the local constituency for open society by undertaking and assisting efforts to promote the attitudes and values that such a society requires' (p.53) through the publication of new textbooks for schools and universities and the provision of seminars for authors, teachers and administrators. Such initiatives are important and should greatly assist in the promotion of intercultural education in the CIS countries. With their help should come the realization that this is the best way to ensure political stability and social harmony among all inhabitants, as well as economic improvement and peace in this part of the world.

# References

Bogoliubov, L N and Lazebnikova, A Iu (eds) (1993) *Ekonomicheskoe i sotsial'noe razvitie sovremennoqo obshchestva*. Materialy k kursu Chelovek i obshchestvo: Osnovy sovremennoi tsivilizatsii dlya uchashchikhsya 11 klassa srednei shkoly. (*Economic and Social Development of the Contemporary Society*. Materials for the course, 'Man and Society: Foundations of Contemporary Civilization', for Pupils of the 11th grade of Secondary Schools), Moscow: Prosveshchenie.

Brown, A *et al.* (1982) *The Cambridge Encyclopaedia of Russia and the Soviet Union*, Cambridge: Cambridge University Press.

Buldakov, V P, Bukharaev, V M and Litvin, A L (eds) (1994) *Fenomen Narodofobii. XX Vek. Materialy nauchnoi konferentsii* (*The Phenomenon of Dislike of Nations. XXth Century. Materials from a Scientific Conference*), Kazan: Kazan University.

Council for Cultural Cooperation (1987a) *Interculturalism and Education*, Strasbourg: Council of Europe.

Council for Cultural Cooperation (1987b) *Interculturalism: Theory and Practice*, Strasbourg: Council of Europe.

Council for Cultural Cooperation (1993) *Teaching about Society, Passing on Values: Civic Education*, Strasbourg: Council of Europe.

Heyneman, S (1994) *Obrazovanie v regione Evropy i Srednei Azii: Politika reform i sovershenstvovaniya* (*Education in Europe and Central Asia: Policies of Reform and Improvement*), Washington: The World Bank.

Kitaev, I (ed.) (1995) *Assessment of Training Needs in Educational Planning and Management (with Special Reference to Central Asia)*, Educational Forum Series No.5, Paris: International Institute for Educational Planning.

Rust, V D, Knost, P and Wichmann, J (eds) (1994) *Education and the Values Crisis in Central Eastern Europe*, New York: Peter Lang.

Schmidt, G (1995a) *Die Bildungsentwicklung in Kasachstan und Usbekistan: Umbruch und Neubeginn im Bildungswesen Mittel-asiens*, Frankfurt am Main: German Institute for International Educational Research.

Schmidt,G (ed.) (1995b) *Bildungsentwicklung nach dem Zerfall der Sowietunion: Kasachstan, Belarus, Litauen, Russische Foderation*, Frankfurt am Main: German Institute for International Educational Research.

Soros Foundation (1994) *Building Open Societies*, New York: Open Society Institute.

Tomiak, J (ed.) (1991) *Schooling, Educational Policy and Ethnic Identity, Comparative Studies on Governments and Non-Dominant Ethnic Groups in Europe, 1850–1940, Vol. I*, New York: European Science Foundation and University Press

Tomiak, J (1992) 'Education in the Baltic States, Ukraine, Belarus and Russia', *Comparative Education*, 28, 1, 33–44.

Tomiak, J (1993) 'Erziehung, kulturelle Identitat und nationals Loyalitat. Die Falle Ukraine und Belarus', *Bildung und Erziehung*, 46, 4, 393–409.

Tomiak, J (1994) 'Culture, National Identity and Schooling in Eastern Europe', in Thomas, E (ed.) (1994) *International Perspectives On Culture and Schooling. A Symposium Proceedings*, London: University of London Institute of Education.

Zhiltsova, E I *et al.* (1993) *Politicheskoe i dukhovnoe razvitie sovremennoqo obshchestva*, Materialy k kursu Chelovek i obshchestvo: Osnovy sovremennoi tsivilizatsii dlya uchashchikhsya 11 klassa srednei shkoly (*Political and Spiritual Development of the Contemporary Society*, Materials for the course, 'Man and Society: Foundations of Contemporary Civilization' for Pupils of the 11th grade of Secondary Schools), Moscow: Prosveshchenie.

# 7.  The Council of Europe and Intercultural Education

Verena Taylor

## Introduction

The Council of Europe, founded in 1949, currently unites 39 member states: Albania, Andorra, Austria, Belgium, Bulgaria, Cyprus, Czech Republic, Denmark, Estonia, Finland, France, Germany, Greece, Hungary, Iceland, Ireland, Italy, Latvia, Liechtenstein, Lithuania, Luxembourg, Malta, Moldova, Netherlands, Norway, Poland, Portugal, Romania, Russian Federation, San Marino, Slovak Republic, Slovenia, Spain, Sweden, Switzerland, the former Yugoslav Republic of Macedonia, Turkey, Ukraine and United Kingdom; five more cooperate under the Convention for Cultural Cooperation (CDCC): Belarus, Bosnia-Herzegovina, Croatia, Holy See and Monaco. Expressions such as 'intercultural education' or 'multicultural society' were not used by the founders of the Council of Europe. However, it was their clear wish that this institution would contribute to the creation of a Europe based not only on the rule of law and sound democratic constitutions, but also on respect for human rights and individual citizens, independent of their gender, religion or indeed cultural background.

Strasbourg was chosen as the seat of the new organization precisely because it is a place where, after centuries of fighting, different cultures had to learn to live together and to overcome prejudice and build their future together.

Achieving a 'true European union' is thus one of the principal aims of the Council of Europe. 'European union' means, in this context, to work together for the construction of a fair and democratic society, avoiding hegemonic tendencies; it means seeking international cooperation through learning from each other instead of by looking for a compromise which satisfies nobody entirely. Consequently the Council of Europe promotes cooperation between its Member states, on a voluntary basis, in a variety of fields linked to education and culture, health and legal affairs, including Human Rights. The European Cultural Convention, established in 1994, specifically fosters cooperation in the fields of education and culture and was designed to

> foster among the nationals of all Members, and of such other European States as may accede thereto, the study of the languages, history and civili-

sation of the others and of the civilisation which is common to them all. (CoE, 1994)

The Council of Europe's concept of European cooperation was never a closed one; cooperation with non-member states was envisaged from the beginning.

More recently, the Heads of State and Government of the Council of Europe member states, at their meeting in Vienna on 9 October 1993, made a strong political commitment against racism and xenophobia in the 'Vienna Declaration':

> Convinced that the diversity of traditions and cultures has for centuries been one of Europe's riches and that the principle of tolerance is the guarantee of the maintenance in Europe of an open society respecting the cultural diversity to which we are attached... Launch an urgent appeal to European peoples, groups and citizens, and young people in particular, that they resolutely engage in combating all forms of intolerance as they actively participate in the construction of European society based on common values, characterized by democracy, tolerance and solidarity. (CoE, 1993a)

The Vienna Declaration requests the implementation of a Plan of Action which gives a new impetus to the Council's activities in the field of intercultural education. Several aspects of this are specifically mentioned, in particular,

> promoting education in the field of Human Rights and respect for cultural diversity; strengthening programmes aimed at eliminating prejudice in the teaching of history by emphasising positive mutual influence between different countries, religions and ideas in the historical development of Europe. (ibid.)

Intergovernmental expert cooperation, as the Council's most important working method, is complemented by the Parliamentary Assembly, which offers a parliamentary base and assures coordination at both national and European levels. The organization works neither on military nor on macro-economic questions.

## Learning to live in a democratic society

As an organization working for European union, the Council of Europe carries out a wide variety of activities in the fields of legal cooperation, constitutional reform and human rights with a view to establishing the same standard in all member states. A legal framework is a *conditio sine qua non,* the very basis for the healthy development of democratic society.

A legal framework does not, however, teach citizens how to live in a democratic society, how to accept responsibility, how to solve conflicts peacefully, and how to respect each other. Even in those European countries whose democratic traditions go back many years, citizens, including young people, are often unable to live up to their responsibility to keep democracy alive. Political decisions seem to be taken far away from 'the people', and they feel that they cannot influence society anyway. Politicians tend to offer answers rather than ask questions, encouraging people to think for themselves and to take an interest in their physical and social environment.

Democracy is not an achievement which, once made, will remain forever. As a concept and as a reality it needs constant care and attention, readiness to change and to respond to new situations. It also requires a lot of effort to overcome one's prejudice and to combat notions of 'quickly settling conflicts' by violent or other non-democratic means.

All too often people's readiness to cooperate, to show solidarity, to seek peaceful solutions of conflict, or even only to only show patience, does not extend beyond the group they know best – those who are 'like us'. The media report nearly every day that intolerance, xenophobia and racism are rampant and are directed against all sorts of groups and minorities who have one thing only in common: they are different.

The Council of Europe believes that participation and the active development of a multicultural society through intercultural education and learning are key concepts for achieving a more just and tolerant, and therefore more democratic, society. Encouraging young people to take responsibility for themselves and their environment is one of the big challenges for schools today; intercultural education is the other.

This chapter focuses on intercultural education in the context of formal education in schools. Sectors of the Council are active in this field, but with slightly different emphases. In particular, seminars, research and training activities carried out in the European Youth Centres, and the grant system for international youth activities offered by the European Youth Foundation, are important. Both work with non-governmental youth organizations. (Further information on these activities and a free subscription to the Youth Directorate's newsletter are available from the Council of Europe Youth Directorate, 30 rue Pierre de Coubertin, F-67000 Strasbourg, France.)

## Education for a multicultural society

Traditionally, school is a place of national cohesion rather than for celebrating difference. If schools are to prepare children and young people for life in the 21st century, living with difference and the ability to cope with ambiguous, sometimes contradictory, codes and messages are arguably the most important skills of all to learn.

The Council's explicit interest in and activities on pluralism in school and education started in the early 1970s, in the wake of a phenomenon appearing in many European countries at that time: children and adolescents followed their migrant worker parents. Consequently, they had to go to school and it became apparent that not only was there a variety of approaches to how to integrate them into mainstream schooling, but also differences on whether this was at all desirable. From 1972 onwards the Council participated in this debate, starting with the launch of experimental school classes. The main focus of discussion has since developed. Now, in the context of formal education in the Council of Europe, intercultural education is referred to as a means of preparing young people for life in the highly segmented, multifaceted and multilingual society which seems to be developing in Europe. They are encouraged better to understand different concepts of culture and the fact that there are many layers of culture, that these layers overlap, and that culture is permanently changing. Three main areas of learning have thus been identified: awareness, skills and attitudes.

The aim is to raise awareness of belonging to a culture and the consequences of its characteristics on one's own feelings, thinking and behaviour; of the existence of other cultures with different characteristics; and of the differences between cultures and reasons for the differences. Skills which need to be learned include communication, both verbal and non-verbal, with people from different cultures and how to communicate about different backgrounds as well as living together with people from different cultures. The impact on attitudes is learning to respect and appreciate other cultures and cultural diversity.

Intercultural education is an important aspect of any educational activity. The following specific programmes run by the Directorate for Education, Culture and Sport of the Council of Europe, represent a 'vertical' approach to intercultural education as a subject as well as a method. They are concerned with teaching history and European cultural heritage, language tuition and linguistic skills, school links and exchanges, and with teacher training.

## Teaching history

Intercultural education is based on the premise that there is no hierarchy of cultures or nations; that being born in one or another town, region or country does not make one a more or less valuable person. It contributes to developing respect for people as they are for what they are, on the basis of a profound knowledge of oneself, one's values and cultural framework. Intellectually, it stimulates young people to learn about other people's points of view and to discover that there is more than one, their, truth. This is particularly important when attempting to overcome nationalist prejudice as often perpetuated in history lessons:

> The school version of the history of national states, old and new, was often presented as an accurate and unquestioned account of what happened in the past, with a selective tendency to highlight the contribution of the great and good (Gallagher, 1996).

However, history teaching can also be used as a means for developing better understanding of the complexity of the European past and present, and of the interdependence of European and other cultures. The Council for Cultural Cooperation, in recognition of this fact, has developed a substantial programme of history teaching over the years. History teaching is one of the main projects of the next medium-term plan, from 1997 to 2000. Pilot projects and seminars in this domain range from a 'History and identity' project run between countries formerly united in the Austro-Hungarian Empire, to a Baltic history textbook project developed by the countries situated around the Baltic Sea, and Europe-wide projects on the Normans, Vikings and Celts as peoples who were important for the development of many regions.

It is important to keep in mind that the aim of such projects is not, and cannot be, to create a uniform 'all-European history' from which all traces of dissent have been clinically removed. Moreover, the idea is for young people and pupils (as well as their teachers) to become aware of the legitimacy of different views, to develop respect for other people's opinions and truths as well as to encourage a critical thinking and open-mindedness. Dialogue must be facilitated, difference experienced, and attitudes shifted.

New technologies are successfully employed towards this goal in many cases – international communication is not restricted to physical mobility. This allows the establishing of international history projects between schools. The Internet, in particular, is a much used means of communication which appears to be accessible and desirable to young people. While no hard data are available on this phenomenon at the moment, it has become a regularly reported and discussed item at meetings of education experts in the Council of Europe. For example, electronic school links was the theme of the fourth annual meeting of the Network for School Links and Exchanges in Stockholm in 1993 (for further details see CoE, 1993b).

Since it is often difficult to find appropriate and up-to-date resources for history teaching, the Council of Europe encourages innovative approaches in this field and helps to identify criteria for good textbooks. Occasionally teaching material is developed and published by the Council of Europe; a recent example is *The New Faces of Europe* (Foucher, 1995), which looks at social, economic and political developments in Europe and which may be used by both multipliers – in teacher training, for example – and in the classroom itself.

## Teaching European cultural heritage

There are many different ways to explore cultural heritage. Whether one looks at music or crafts, architecture or agriculture, heritage laws, monarch's wedding presents or the population pyramid in the 14th century, one aspect remains the same: there was no one culture in one place. What we are today goes back to a mixing and mingling of peoples and cultures, to mutual enrichment and learning, to appropriating developments which were initiated elsewhere.

European cultural routes and European heritage classes take this into account:

> Centred on themes and movements which have helped to shape the face and mind of Europe, the routes mark an attempt to reconnect Europeans to the past they share, helping them to forget about frontiers and purely local interests, so that they can meet and forge new bonds (Ibram, 1994).

The cultural routes encourage citizens to explore the making of Europe from such different angles as pilgrimage, 'The Silk Road', the Viking trails and the activities of the 'Hanse', parks and gardens or Roma and Sinti life. The programme works with the help of a network of local and regional authorities, non-governmental organizations and other collaborators under the political and educational responsibility of the Council of Europe. In addition to helping people find out about their common past, the routes contribute to a less 'touristic' and more respectful and interactive approach to visiting new places, since they make their users aware of the complexity of relations in history. (The newsletter *Routes* supports the network and regularly reports on new developments. It may be obtained from the Directorate of Education, Culture and Sport, Council of Europe, F-67075 Strasbourg Cedex.)

European heritage classes translate this approach for use in formal education. They also add an extra dimension to school exchanges, since they provide an immediate topic, a joint project pupils can work on together.

> A European Heritage Class will... offer a much richer experience. Their teachers will have decided their joint learning and social aims long before, and will have planned 'hands-on' experiences. Experts and artisans from the world of culture and work will be involved with the children. The language barrier will be overcome through a multidisciplinary approach, practical and novel techniques and a multisensory experience (CoE, 1995, p.3).

Most countries which cooperate under the Cultural Convention are now active in this area. The Council of Europe offers legal, educational and practical advice on the running of such classes and publishes information material for teachers. In 1996 a pilot project, 'The City under the City', will take place simultaneously in more then ten European countries. It will further develop working methods which can be put at teachers' disposal. (The newsletter *eXchange*, published twice a year with up-to-date information on European heritage classes, may be obtained from the Directorate of Education, Culture and Sport at the CoE.)

## Modern languages

The role of languages in intercultural communication and in multicultural societies is unquestioned. While linguistic skills can improve communication possibilities, vehicular languages often also bring a certain cultural 'luggage' with them.

The promotion of language learning and teaching is necessarily a permanent aspect of the Council of Europe's work, because it contributes to all other
aspects of international cooperation – it depends on the ability of all sections
of the population to communicate directly and effectively with each other. The
aims of the Council's modern languages project are to make the means of
learning to communicate more effectively with other Europeans through each
other's languages more widely available to all sections of the populations of
member countries in order to facilitate free movement of individuals, to
further understanding between peoples through personal contact, to improve
the effectiveness of European cooperation, and to overcome prejudice and
discrimination.

Language learning is no longer about studying the grammar of some
far-away language, but it includes an increasingly important element of
sociocultural competence, of language learning for European citizenship. (For
further details see reports CC-LANG (93) workshop 13a and CC-LANG (94)
workshop 14 'Language Learning for European Citizenship', Council for
Cultural Cooperation, 1993 and 1994.) In this context, sociocultural competence is defined as the ability

> to bring different cultural systems into relation with one another, to interpret
> socially distinctive variations within a foreign cultural system, and to man-
> age the dysfunctions and resistances peculiar to intercultural communica-
> tion... [and] it is postulated that the construction of sociocultural knowledge
> involves a transformation of attitudes, of initial representations of things
> foreign (Byram and Zarate, 1994).

Teacher training is given a high priority by the Modern Languages Project,
which has organized over 60 workshops for teachers and other multipliers. At
the same time, new assessment methods are sought which take cultural
competence as well as linguistic achievements into consideration.

The Council of Europe's work on modern language has been complemented, since 1995, by the European Centre for Modern Languages in Graz,
Austria, established by now in more than 20 member states though a Partial
Agreement. It offers seminars for teacher trainers, emphasizing the close link
between intercultural education and language learning. Special attention is
also paid to the relationship between majority and minority languages, vehicular languages and lesser spoken ones, as well as bilingual education and
aspects of cultural mediation.

## School links and exchanges

The Council of Europe promotes school links and exchanges as a concrete and
practical contribution to the development of a Europe based on the principles
alluded to earlier. In 1991, the Council for Cultural Cooperation launched the
project, 'A Secondary Education for Europe', the aims of which are to give
young people the knowledge, skills and attitudes they will need to meet the

major challenges of European society; prepare young people for higher education and for mobility, work and daily life in a multilingual and multicultural society; and to make young people aware of their common cultural heritage and their shared responsibility as Europeans.

The project contains two parallel and complementary actions: for member states to reflect on and consult about their overall policies and strategies; and to develop the European dimension in the school curriculum.

It is in the framework of this second element that the Network for School Links and Exchanges was created in 1991, and its activities endorsed by the Standing Conference of European Ministers of Education, who, in their eighteenth meeting in Madrid in 1994, adopted a resolution on the promotion of school links and exchanges in Europe as an essential contribution to preparing young people for life in a democratic, multilingual and multicultural Europe.

Consequently, the Network for School Links and Exchanges has the task of promoting high-quality school partnerships and exchanges, including an element of structured and reflected intercultural learning. To this end a series of training courses for teacher trainers has been offered since 1991. They in turn inspired international teacher training seminars for school links and European awareness, and a code of good practice for school exchanges has been established. The Network members agree on some basic elements which are essential for a successful school exchange activity – it is certainly not enough to 'send children abroad'.

## Preparation

> The right experiences are those carried out in order 'to see'. New truths are not discovered by chance. Even if an unusual, unexpected event comes to our attention, our mind has to be sufficiently alert to notice it and to realise that it can make us change direction and our frames of reference. (Vanbergen, 1993, p.11)

Knowledge about a partner country's languages, history and traditions is useful and has to be included in the preparatory work. However, the most important element of the preparation is for pupils to get to know their own culture, their prejudices and indeed themselves. They will have to learn to cope with the unexpected, with not being able to understand, with difficulties in decoding messages. The Council of Europe has published a variety of documents and reports which deal with how to prepare an exchange activity. The workbook *Vis-à-vis*, for example, can be used by teachers and pupils to enhance the preparatory process.

## The exchange

Youth exchanges and school exchanges have arguably become 20th century Europe's initiation rites for young people. They can help them to become mature and responsible adults, as through the exchange experience they may be exposed to an unknown environment in which their hitherto safe and unquestioned concepts of life are turned upside down.

For this process to lead to positive results, it is useful to develop a common project together with the exchange partners. This is also helpful for practical and programming reasons, of course. When participants can concentrate on a joint project – building a statute, writing a play, cleaning a beach, etc – they find out about themselves and each other 'as a by-product' and can enjoy their achievements together. It is important to keep in mind that intercultural education is based primarily on the concept of social learning and whatever stimulates such a process is thus helpful.

*Teaching for Exchanges* (Vanbergen, 1993) stipulates that exchanges ought to adhere to the principles of 'parity and reciprocity' and of 'working together'. The concepts of parity and reciprocity include:

> recognising that participants, though of different origin, enjoy equal status; accepting interdependence; committing oneself to a collaboration contract and assuming co-responsibility for it; recognising that the other person has the right to criticise me and to participate in building another 'me', and vice-versa; looking at all factors, including building up identity, not from the centre but in terms of relations, contact, control. 'Working together' strengthens participants' interest to learn with, from, against each other; to activate people and release all their expertise; to increase autonomy; to develop one's ability to cooperate.

## Evaluation

Evaluating an exchange experience the process organizers and participants have gone through is an integral part of the activity itself. It is used as a means of 'confirming and explaining existing procedures' on the one hand, and in order 'to gain information to bring about innovation and change' on the other (Gabriella Gulyas, Budapest, input to a seminar for teacher trainers in Desenzano, Italy, October 1995).

Evaluation happens informally at all times, of course, but it is important to give the process a formal and appropriate structure which allows all aspects of an exchange to be examined, including the procedures as well as participants' personal growth. All partners in the event have a right to participate in the evaluation, since they all have a right to reflect on their experience in a structured manner and to draw conclusions from it.

## Pilot project, 'Visions of Europe'

The Network for School Links and Exchanges wished to develop a pilot project in order to put the various elements considered important for an international project into practice. 'Visions of Europe' involves teachers and students not only from all the corners of Europe, but also from Canada and Tunisia. After working on a collage expressing their 'visions' of Europe in mono-national groups, the young people spend a week together and work on the same subject in mixed nationality groups, confronting and challenging their own and each other's experience, attitudes and ideas, and creating, ultimately, their joint 'visions' of Europe. The project started with a teacher training seminar, since it was essential that the teachers involved should have gone through a process of cultural 'deconstruction', leading to greater tolerance of ambiguity in order better to accompany and support their pupils throughout the experience.

As a pilot project the activity does perhaps attract more attention than 'regular' exchanges. Still, the elements of which it is composed are of general interest and should be taken into consideration when an exchange is planned. Among them and in addition to aspects mentioned before, are clearly formulated educational aims. The participants should, of course, enjoy the project. But they are also subjected to an educational process which aims to leave them more knowledgeable about themselves and others, more open-minded and more tolerant.

One of the most interesting aspects of the pilot project is that it involves young people from non-European countries. The 'North-South-Interdependence' Campaign of 1987 highlighted worldwide international relations and interdependence and led to the establishment of the 'European Centre for Global Interdependence and Solidarity', which is situated in Lisbon. It develops educational programmes and exchanges, mainly in the non-governmental sector, for and with youth leaders, teachers, social workers, civil servants, journalists and other interested parties across the world, to increase general awareness of related issues. Most activities undertaken by the Education Department in Strasbourg are European in geography as well as content. They may, however, very well touch the lives and experiences of persons of non-European origins, since participation in activities and meetings depends on the country of residence, not the nationality of a person.

The issue of 'Euro-centredness' is a recurring one, especially in the context of history teaching and of the cultural routes. Awareness of global interdependence does not, however, change the Council of Europe's original vocation, which is to work towards European cooperation and, ultimately, unity.

## Teacher training

Teacher training is a key element in the Council of Europe's policy regarding intercultural education. After publication of several training manuals – the most important being the *Framework for teacher training for school links and exchanges* (CoE, 1996a) – the Network for School Links and Exchanges is keen to develop a strategy for teacher training in this field. The strategy will be valid from 1997 and will comprise a variety of complementary training offers. Initial teacher training is taken into consideration, as is in-service training. Both a basic training structure and the flexibility to respond to specific needs expressed by member states are required. Training may accompany ongoing exchange activities, but training activities can also provoke new ideas and initiatives from trainees. Due to its budgetary limitations, the Council of Europe has to be interested in developing pilot activities directed towards multipliers.

A pilot teacher training course took place in three stages in 1994/95. It brought together 35 teachers and teacher trainers from 16 European countries. After undergoing an initial intercultural learning process, the participants were encouraged to develop their own exchange and training projects. During the second and third phases of the course, the participants' own experience became the programme of the course: starting from the concrete, abstractions were made which led participants to understand general aspects of intercultural communication and cooperation. It is interesting that although all participants underwent the same initial training phase, their international cooperation projects are incredibly diverse. They range from 'straightforward' pupil exchanges to long-term multilateral teacher training courses, and, in one case, to the elaboration of a European Masters degree programme for intercultural education (CoE, 1996b).

The Network for School Links and Exchanges publishes the newsletter *Links*, which helps to liaise between interested partners, teachers, teacher trainers and civil servants in 44 European countries. Unfortunately, neither the newsletter nor the Secretariat can fulfil the role of matchmaker for schools wishing to enter into a quality exchange. Some, few, countries have central exchange bureaux, but all too often school exchanges are either commercial exercises concentrating on sightseeing, or else badly prepared trips which reinforce stereotypes rather than overcoming prejudice. The European School Exchange Data Base can, for a modest financial contribution, help with finding partners.

One problem lies in the fact that often school partnerships are seen exclusively from a linguistic point of view, not as a cultural exchange experience. This leads to a much higher demand for partnerships with 'language countries' than others. Training headteachers, teachers and education officials offers them the knowledge, skills and attitudes necessary to help choose a suitable partner school.

## The future

Schools, although by no means the only actors in the process, have an important role to play in equipping young people with the skills, knowledge and attitudes necessary to face the challenges of a European society which is becoming increasingly complex and mobile. Intercultural education will therefore not only remain on the Council of Europe's agenda, but will play an ever more important role. From 1997, two new projects on history teaching and citizenship education will start and a social-competence oriented approach to modern language learning will be continued.

New concepts can be put to the test in teacher training courses held in the framework of the Council of Europe In-Service Training Programme for Teachers, as well as the Centre for Modern Languages. The In-Service Teacher Training Programme allows member states to offer international teacher training seminars directly linked to the Council of Europe's main concerns. Often the seminars offer the possibility, in an experimental fashion, to try out new concepts, to share experiences from different cultural backgrounds, and to develop resource material for classroom use adapted to new developments and circumstances.

About one thousand teachers per year participate in these seminars, and several hundred more are involved in the modern languages training activities. They act as multipliers in the classroom, with their colleagues and even with parents. An important contribution to establishing intercultural education as a guiding principle of teaching and school life can thus be achieved.

## References

Byram, M and Zarate, G (1994) *Definitions, Objectives and Assessment of Socio-cultural Competence*, Strasbourg: Council for Cultural Cooperation.

CoE (Council of Europe) (1993a) 'Declaration and Plan of Action on combating racism, xenophobia, anti-Semitism and intolerance', adopted and signed in Vienna, 9 October 1993 by the Heads of State and Government of the member States of the Council of Europe (The Vienna Declaration), Strasbourg: CoE

CoE (1993b) *Report DECS/SE/Sec (93) 35*, Strasbourg: Council of Europe.

CoE (1994) *The European Cultural Convention*, Strasbourg: Council of Europe.

CoE (1995) *The European Heritage Class: A Way of Understanding Cultures* (Report on the 69th European Teachers' Seminar in Donaueschingen, 9–14 October, 1995), Strasbourg: Council of Europe.

CoE (1996a) *Framework for Teacher Training for School Links and Exchanges*, Strasbourg: Council of Europe.

CoE (1996b) *Training for School Links and Exchanges: Report of the Long-term Training Course*, Strasbourg: Council of Europe.

Foucher, M (1995) *The New Faces of Europe*, Strasbourg: Council of Europe.

Gallagher, C (1996) *History Teaching and the Promotion of Democratic Values and Tolerance – A Handbook for Teachers*, Strasbourg: Council of Europe

Ibram, C (1994) 'Paths of discovery – Europe's cultural routes', *Forum*, 3.

Vanbergen, P (1993) *Teaching for Exchanges*, Strasbourg: Council of Europe.

# 8. Intercultural Education and the Pacific Rim

Robert Cowen

## Introduction

It would be useful if there were a theory of intercultural education which covered the period of, say, 1450 to 1850, for the Atlantic Rim. In that period the Atlantic Rim became a major source of wealth and was an arena for economic and political struggle and the movement of peoples. Amid these processes, major programmes of education were devised and experienced by many peoples with varied consequences. Thus a theory of the Atlantic Rim would explain how political interest, economic power and cultural assumptions shaped forms of intercultural relations, understandings and education. The theory would no doubt also demonstrate why categories such as 'states' or, later, 'nations' were inadequate for handling the complexities of the analysis; and why the concept of 'Atlantic Rim' was better. Such a theory does not exist but asking about it acts as a catalyst to pull into focus several issues, most notably some of the cultural idiosyncrasies and assumptions built into aspirations for intercultural education which can be illustrated by a discussion of the Pacific Rim.

The Pacific Rim, like the Atlantic Rim, is a geographic and geological concept recently taken into the common sense discussion of world economic relations (Gibney, 1992; Naisbitt, 1996). Somewhat like calling the New World into being to balance the Old, the Pacific Rim needed to be invented, as a concept, because of the rapid economic development of its other half – its western edge. Thus the idea of the Pacific Rim contains strong ethnocentric and ideological elements: especially when viewed from its eastern boundaries, or from a position within the older economies of Europe, it is an economic threat and an economic opportunity, and it is, like the New World, a metaphor, though a less optimistic one, for the rebalancing of power relations – economic, political and cultural – with an older world.

The idea of a theory of intercultural education of the Atlantic Rim for the period 1450 to 1850 also gives another hint of unease and displacement. Manifestly such a theory, noting different forms of colonialism and different styles of diaspora, would simultaneously explain intercultural educational assumptions in the Brazil of the Jesuit period, in the America of Jefferson, and the peculiar mixtures of social stratification, domination, minority identity, schooling, religion and slavery in the Caribbean, in the southern states of the United States, in Mexico – and the other crucial other half of the rim, Europe, especially its maritime nations of early empire: France, Portugal, Spain and Britain.

However, we probably would not, in the 1990s, call what happened between many of those countries and the educational formations they constructed cross-nationally, 'intercultural education'. In general the educational messages were not a celebration of the possession of two cultures (say, Brazilian Indian and Portuguese; or the world views of the Mohican and the Puritan) but were primarily an intended European cancellation of one of the New World cultures. In a completely different way, to ask about intercultural education in the Pacific Rim highlights the point that the phrase 'intercultural education' carries forward, though subtly, strong ethnocentric and ideological elements. The contemporary intercultural project is not intentionally hegemonic, but it is culturally framed. We are asking about the progress of an idea and educational policies which have intellectual and political roots in European history, for example in the thinking of John Locke and other social contract theorists as they began redefining the principles on which contemporary democratic societies should be based. Intercultural education, as an extension of social contract theory, is itself a localized idea, one which it has taken a long time to invent and one which is now being exported.

The fictive notion of a theory of intercultural education of the Atlantic Rim raises another variant on this theme of exportation: what is the relationship, over time, between the national and the international? That is, what is the interplay of domestic educational histories and contemporary international educational relations – who is saying intercultural education is important, who is not listening and why? And what is the time dimension? The idea of the Pacific Rim takes its routine sense from the notion of space: geographic and cultural space. But cultural spaces contain the long-waves of history, memories of past wrongs – discords – as well as a variety of older philosophic traditions of hierarchy and harmony. It is important not to accept casually an invitation to compress social time.

This chapter will extract only three themes from this considerable puzzle, all directed to locating comparatively the implications of universalizing an honourable aspiration – intercultural education – within an international space only named about 30 years ago. First, the theme of getting to the start line: the complexity of the contemporary influences which construct both the need for and the difficulties of anticipating forms of intercultural education appropriate within the Pacific Rim. Second, the theme of the politics of time and international educational dissonance with which the creation and non-creation of intercultural education in national schooling systems is linked; and third the interplay of ideas about the global, the national and the local in the definition of intercultural education.

## Getting to the start line

As indicated, the 'Pacific Rim' is a shorthand statement of changed international power, especially economic power. For this reason perhaps, Ecuador or the Cook Islands or Papua New Guinea are not normally central in discussions of the Rim. So the concept does not stress a listing of all of the countries around the Pacific Rim and a sketch of their interrelations; it stresses events away from the Pacific Rim. The phrase acts as a succinct metaphor for the economic rebalancing of the hemispheres, even though the United States is still one of a very small number of major economic powers able at the moment to affect productive capacity in both Europe and Asia. But the Pacific Rim is not merely a contemporary economic metaphor. It is also an historical arena characterized by memories of British, Dutch, French, American and Japanese colonialism in the 18th, 19th and 20th centuries. The historical balancing of accounts continues with mutual embarrassment and occasional urgency, whether in Hong Kong, South Korea, Okinawa, Tahiti, Indonesia, New Zealand or the Philippines. Another characteristic of the Pacific Rim is its sociology of diaspora: not merely the magnificent voyages of ancient peoples across the Pacific but the emigration, frequently for reasons of misery and under miserable conditions, of large numbers of people to other parts of the Pacific Rim in the last couple of centuries. The Chinese diaspora, in particular, is an excellent example of the ways in which the international has intersected with the domestic, in Vietnam, in Indonesia, in Malaysia, in Canada and in the United States.

Thus the 'intercultural problem' – and by extension, intercultural education – poses questions: in what ways is the Pacific Rim an arena of conflict as well as opportunity in economic terms; how, in a given country, are the multiple identities of people – often the residues of colonial policies – to be addressed politically and educationally within a huge range of possible examples which include the impact of Spanish culture on the original 'minorities' on the western seaboard of Latin America and the position of the Ainu and the Koreans of Japan; and what are the terms on which major and economically powerful minorities (such as the overseas Chinese in Indonesia or Malaysia) are to be educated and understood (Lam *et al.*, 1993)?

The simplest answer is the most moral. Everywhere it is a matter of urgency to put into place programmes of intercultural education which (of course) distil the best from world practice and are adapted to local conditions by local people. Relevant local programmes must be devised, teachers educated, pedagogic strategies worked out, and so on. But the best answer is a long-term answer which, if embraced with too much immediate optimism, permits the complexity and varieties of the problem to be obscured. And these complexities and varieties of the problem may destroy the simple answer.

The Pacific Rim is an arena where competing and different economic systems meet: the socialist market principles of China, the corporate capitalism of the United States and Canada, the carefully protectionist capitalism of states undergoing rapid economic development with indigenous forms of corporate capitalism (eg, the *zaibatsu* of Japan or the *chaebol* of South Korea), the family-network capitalism of the overseas Chinese, and the dependent capitalism of the islands of the South Pacific (Crossley, 1993; Gibney, 1992). There is also considerable incomprehensibility emerging in the Rim area over human rights, an issue most visibly raised in recent GATT talks held in Asia or in the tensions between China and some of its trading partners, such as the United States or Germany. Human rights, like intercultural education, is an idea with a long history dating back at least to European debates in the 16th century with earlier roots in some of the questions of the Greeks. So many countries of the Pacific Rim, in their brilliant extensions of economic forms invented in Europe, are confronted with external voices declaiming the correctness of a European notion of the rights of man, subsequently taken up and magnified by several of the international governmental and non-governmental agencies. And these contradictions work themselves out in countries very much concerned with rapid nation-building (or re-building), in which social and political cohesion are central to a modernity project that is very urgent, as in Chile, China, Indonesia, Malaysia and the Philippines.

Philosophically then, there is a start line: the United Nations Declaration of the Rights of Man. Economically, there is a most uneven start line, with sections of the Pacific Rim already falling behind in an unequal race toward a post-industrial future. Sociologically, there is a pluralistic maze of mixed sub-national identities, clustered within the state formations around the Pacific Rim. Politically, there are the urgent anxieties of nation-building and national cohesion. And educationally, the long-waves of history offer a warning about misplaced confidence in the immediate efficacy of intercultural education as a 'solution' to a 'problem'. The Pacific Rim exists, by a convention internationally understood, in the same chronological time: say, on any couple of days in June 1996. However, the Pacific Rim also exists piecemeal in different sociological and educational 'times'.

## The politics of time and international educational dissonance

One of the clichés of comparative education is that schooling systems reflect the societies in which they are located. The cliché, soothing because it seems to offer an intellectual work agenda of some complexity, is useful because it hides several key questions: about time, about international influence, and about the filtering actions of state political decisions and the reactions of those who are marginalized in societies. Thus, for example, the cliché hides the considerable differences in the detailed process of the construction of ideas about intercultural education in the United States, in Canada, in New Zealand and in Australia. All four countries, for much of their educational history, have interpreted themselves as white, Christian and monolingual.

In New Zealand and in Australia these older assumptions, which were strongly linked with an immigration policy that favoured the British and the Europeans, have broken up relatively recently. From the 1970s in both countries the educational and social position of the original inhabitants and of the newer immigrants from Europe and from Asia has been brought under urgent and sympathetic review. In both countries the shift was filtered by new political parties in government and by a new sensitivity, especially in academic communities revitalized by younger scholars, to international issues of rights, the history of indigenous peoples and the cultural difficulties of the intersections of 'western' and 'traditional' knowledge. What is impressive in both countries is the relative speed of change in newly confident democracies now very open to international influence and conscious of a new position on the Rim – but the change is even more obvious against the hegemony of silence which existed for so long about minorities in both countries (Spoonley *et al.*, 1990; Teasdale and Teasdale, 1994).

In contrast, in both the United States and in Canada, the issue of minorities has a far from silent history, which has affected school formation and school contents, more or less since the advent of the political independence of both countries. In the United States the most visible markers of the renegotiation of these ideas are the law cases of Plessy versus Ferguson, and Brown versus Topeka – public definitions and public renegotiations of what it is to be a segregated minority and what are the educational rights of the full citizen. The law cases are very visible outcomes of an immense social struggle which has been brilliantly analysed (Condit and Lucaites, 1993). The process continues contemporaneously in the definition of what it is to be 'Hispanic' and what are the rights and duties and the correct forms of education which attach to that status.

However, making the claims and taking the identities would have been even more difficult without the international influences on the construction of the American Constitution, and the importation of ideas of political liberties, rights, and some duties, taken into the centre of American political life by the Founding Fathers, notably Thomas Jefferson. Furthermore, at the specific level of educational provision, contemporary notions of intercultural education in the USA have had to be worked out against long-held cultural assumptions and educational policies which stressed Americanization (Goodenow and Ravitch, 1983; Tyack, 1974). The creation of a common American identity through the schools of the United States is a leitmotif of the 19th century, carried through by the cultural invasion of the identities of immigrants from Germany, Sweden, Norway, Russia, Poland, Hungary, Italy, China and, later, Japan. Each of these groups had to make difficult decisions about its own community's creation of institutions such as 'Saturday schools', the retention of their own language, their constitutional rights and when to make appeal to them, and the imperative to accept public schooling in their new country out of economic necessity and for economic success (Reese, 1986).

The construction of the idea of intercultural education in the Canadian context is equally complex but is also different, intersecting with religion (Protestantism and Catholicism) more strongly than in the United States. Similarly, appeals could be and were made to law (The British North American Act of 1867) to define educational rights and provision. There was a parallel issue of the education of the original inhabitants of Canada and, as in the United States, this became a matter of federal concern. The language issue also has been complex, but the stress on English so long typical of the United States was severely modified by the significance of Quebec, to the point where French became constitutionally one of the official languages of Canada. The result is that in the contemporary period other languages such as Portuguese, German or Ukrainian are not constitutionally protected. Thus, in the Canadian case also, the time required for the construction of contemporary policies of intercultural education has been over 100 years. International influences are also reflected in intercultural provision, including the British compromise on religion in education in the 19th century and the *in absentia* but continuous political presence of French cultural influence from the other side of the Atlantic.

The Canadian State has filtered the variety of educational claims not only of the First Americans but of older immigrant groups such as the Germans and the Ukrainians – and is currently filtering the educational claims of the new immigrant groups from Hong Kong, the Philippines, China and India. And the taking of identity, as with minorities in the United States, has been central to the historical experience of the French-speaking minority of Canada, which has had a political impact on Canadian education, and contemporaneously on Canadian national politics and national cohesion, far greater than could be linearly deduced from its numerical size. The consequence, despite or perhaps because of the latent issue of the continuing political unity of Canada from the Pacific to the Atlantic, is that Canada has devised very complex and sensitive provisions for intercultural education of such quality that they might be taken as part of a world model of good intercultural educational practice for application in the Pacific Rim (Bolaria, 1991; Mallea, 1989; Mallea and Young, 1984).

Manifestly, that cannot and will not happen. As has been sketched, the processes of construction of intercultural educational policies in particular domestic contexts are complex and frequently confrontational. International influence may play a part, through the impact of international declarations or through exposure to the experience of other nations. But there are domestic circumstances which deeply affect the permeability of international examples. There is and has been major variation in the domestic negotiability of the speed, degree and directions of change, from assimilationist to pluralist educational policies in the countries of the Pacific Rim.

It has been suggested that Australia, the United States, New Zealand and Canada have moved from strenuous policies of assimilation, often incorporating elements of racism, toward more pluralistic definitions of good education during the 19th and 20th centuries, with considerable difficulty, at different speeds, with different political techniques including the use of law, and with different levels of anger and bitterness. Clearly political elites must be brought under domestic pressure, international trade relations may become significant, and minorities themselves must mobilize (increasingly through international as well as domestic political visibility) to produce shifts in legal and educational rights.

This is true even within societies that have not merely a formally democratic political structure but also have as part of their politico-cultural inheritance the thinking of Grotius, Thomas Paine, Rousseau, Hobbes and Locke. This is also true in societies which have had a couple of centuries to work out their collective cultural identity (their 'national' identity) to the point where the concept has become so sophisticated that it can incorporate the idea of 'minorities'. Even where some of these conditions are met, the incredible delicacy and instability of the process and the fact that its reaffirmation must be continuous is confirmed by the experiences of Northern Ireland, of the former Yugoslavia (which was politically framed by an alternative tradition in western political thought but one which had an explicit place for 'minorities') and by the current tensions over the minority status of the Quebecois in Canada.

In contrast, several of the states around the Pacific Rim are in the process of nation-building (eg, Indonesia and Malaysia) or in the process of recovery from a recent past which is being partially rejected (China and Chile). In these circumstances the emphasis must be on national cohesion. Clearly if the recovery is from dictatorship – as in Chile – an emphasis, as part of the recovery of democracy, may be placed on the importance of acknowledging the rights of minorities, including their rights to education (Avalos, 1996). As all of these states belong to the United Nations there will also be a formal acknowledgement, perhaps even one built into the constitution, of the rights of minorities.

In China, influenced by the socialist tradition on the rights of minorities following the thinking of Lenin, there will be a major emphasis in official declarations on the position of minorities (Price, 1977). However, there will also be counter-balancing pressures. China, for example, is faced with the continuing problem of reasserting its cultural influence in Tibet. It also has a large Muslim population, as did the former USSR, and a delicate balance to walk between secular political and economic messages and cultural and religious messages. China will soon to have assert – to what degree and in what fashion is not yet known – its cultural influence in Hong Kong and Macao, which are shortly to return to Chinese political sovereignty. Again, there is an awkward balance to be established here between the need for political unity and cultural recognition, not merely in the abstract but at the level of curriculum contents and pedagogic processes, language instruction and the teaching of history.

Thus while the Chinese position on minorities in its official form is as sensitive as that of the official form of the former Soviet position, and while in both countries the tradition of rescuing local oral languages and creating written languages and of permitting the use of the mother tongue for elementary or secondary education is remarkable, the official position also hides some of the practical difficulties of implementing actual policy at the level of the classroom. Chinese education policy, at the official level, recognizes and respects a range of cultures. It is, in its official stance, multiculturalist but in its political stance it captures in a different mode the idea of *e pluribus unum,* making one from the many. The multicultural educational stance is offered and structured within a frame of the necessity of political cohesion.

Similarly, in Indonesia and in Malaysia, the official stance stresses, first, political cohesion. Both countries experienced difficult national independence movements which included an awkward mix, as in Vietnam, of nationalist and communist movements. Both countries are characterized by major ethnic diversity. Both countries have experienced pressures for renegotiation of political boundaries. Thus the Indonesian Law on National Education passed in 1989 is bluntly assimilationist, stressing the nation and the responsibility of each citizen to become Indonesian. The Malaysian political project has been sharply clarified: through the insistence on the use of Bahasa Malaysia, through compensatory economic and social policies which favour the Malays, one nation – strongly informed by Islamic beliefs – will be formed. In education, compensatory policies will be pursued which rebalance the cultural power and the occupational options of the Malays, redressing some of the inequities in wealth and skill and occupational success which have emerged between them and, particularly, the Chinese (Cowen and McLean, 1984; Jayasuriya, 1983; Drake, 1989; Palmer, 1965).

In such social and political contexts there are no serious possibilities that policies of intercultural education can be developed in the short-term; any more than (for different reasons) they could have been developed in the South Africa of the apartheid period. The international encouragement to develop programmes of intercultural education is cancelled, politically, by the nature of domestic political projects. The potential political risks of intercultural education in any but the most stable of societies are too high. Intercultural education, if it is to develop in Malaysia or Indonesia or China, will need to be created from within.

This does not mean that Malaysia or Indonesia or China will replicate Canadian or Australian experience. But it does mean similar if not identical processes of struggle by minorities and the slow acceptance by majorities, in those places, of the political and social importance of redefining the cultural content of education. It does mean that political claims have to be made and accepted about what can not be treated hegemonically (eg, some aspects of personal identity). It does mean that some notion of rights which are secular, political, attaching to individuals by virtue of citizenship, and some notion of a social contract between the individual and the state from which the individual, *in extremis*, may withdraw, has to be negotiated. This is a deeply disturbing proposition because it insists on the globalization of the secular.

## The global and the local

The nationalist project, that is, the idea of creating nations, is an idea which draws on a long line of thinkers that certainly include Fichte and Mazzini, which takes form and substance in a variety of revolutions in the 18th and 19th centuries, and which takes repetition and later adaptation to local circumstances in the hands of charismatic leaders in various places: Cavour and Garibaldi, Bolivar and Sarmiento, Ho Chi Min, Ghandi and Nehru, Sukarno, Abdul Rahman, and so on. The nationalist project is messianic and defines principles of inclusion. It does not respect regions and it does not, in itself, respect diversity. The history of nation-building in France, Germany and Italy in the 19th century is a story of the subordination of regions, whether Alsace, Bavaria or Sicily, to incorporation in a national project (Breuilly, 1982).

The strand in political thought which respects diversity, indeed which insists on it because it starts with the notion of natural rights which attach to the individual, is social contract theorizing – a group of political theories which certainly includes the thinking of Locke and Jefferson (Held, 1983; 1987). These theories have informed the political formation of several countries, but they have also – and here more importantly – informed the assumptions of many of the world international agencies. Thus the United Nations, for example, contains the Security Council, one of whose functions (that has never worked particularly well) is to deal with the world when it goes Hobbesian: that is, to apply force in accordance with international law when world order breaks down.

But how, in normal times, you achieve peace and order is through negotiation, through formal and organized social conversation (such as diplomacy and structured 'cooling off' situations), and through education. Here the remarkable assumption is made that since war begins in the minds of men, it is in the minds of men that the defence of peace must be constructed. Thus major international agencies such as the League of Nations and the United Nations have tended to incorporate in their philosophies and in their structures not only assumptions about voluntarism but also assumptions about reason and rationality in the minds of men that can be found in Jefferson and Locke. And reason and rationality, both Locke and Jefferson argued, can be strengthened by education.

It is these assumptions about reason and rationality which are cancelled by much of the messianic assumptions of philosophies of nationalism. Nationalism celebrates unities and emotional bonding and messianic notions of the future. The rationalism of Jefferson and Locke stresses contractual obligation, individual rights, and personal duties. The rationalism of Jefferson and Locke emphasizes the right to difference and the duty to differ when certain rights are violated. Bonding, social bonding, is contractual and conditional. The future is pragmatic, a matter of mutual construction and negotiation; and certainly not to be deduced from messianic principles.

Thus intercultural education is in its political assumptions rationalist. It draws from only part of the world's tradition. It diverges sharply for example from the claim to exclusivity implicit in *civis Romanus sum*. It is not the same as accepting the difference of others in a multicultural empire, such as the Austro-Hungarian or the Arabic Empire of the Mediterranean. Intercultural education is an effort to diminish and make understandable the cultural differences – potentially messianic explosive differences – which prevent the beginnings of a Lockean discourse. Inserting intercultural education into schools, in any of its normal forms such as development education or social studies, is of course a technical project. It is also a choice within a range of political philosophies and world views.

It is thus hardly surprising or a matter of self-congratulation that there is a differential acceptance of the intercultural project in education around the Pacific Rim. In those countries such as Canada, Australia, New Zealand and the United States, where the issue is being tackled more or less frontally, there is a continuity not merely of a political project but of a political tradition. In other countries, multicultural in their mixtures of ethnicities, languages and religions, intercultural education is not at the moment tactically acceptable in political terms: they are still engaged in their acts of nation-building. But it is probably also the case that the intercultural project is a strategic divergence from indigenous political traditions, interrupted but not fundamentally altered by western and other colonialisms of the 19th and 20th centuries.

This is a political dissonance within the Pacific Rim and major differences in the long-waves of national histories which will reflect in education and in the construction of approximations of intercultural education in future years. However, small-scale success is possible (Freeland, 1996). There must be complex and careful understanding of, and adaptation to local contexts (Aikman, 1996). But the optimistic globalization of intercultural education, incorporated at the national level into national policy, is dangerous and likely to be unfruitful – which is not to say that the Atlantic Rim, in its past years, has done particularly well in the creation of intercultural education and an effective pedagogy of harmony.

## References

Aikman, S (1996) 'The globalisation of intercultural education and an indigenous Venezuelan response', *Compare*, 26, 2, 153-65.

Avalos, B (1996) 'Education for global/regional competitiveness: Chilean policies and reform in secondary education', *Compare*, 26, 2, 217-32.

Bolaria, B S (1991) *Social Issues and Contradictions in Canadian Society*, Toronto: Harcourt Brace Jovanovich.

Breuilly, J (1982) *Nationalism and the State*, Manchester: Manchester University Press.

Condit, C M and Lucaites, J L (1993) *Crafting Equality: America's Anglo-African World*, Chicago, Ill: The University of Chicago Press.

Cowen, R and McLean, M (eds) (1984) *International Handbook of Educational Systems: Vol. III, Asia, Australia and Latin America*, Chichester: John Wiley and Sons.

Crossley, M (ed.) (1993) 'Education in the South Pacific', special number, *Comparative Education*, 29, 3.

Drake, C (1989) *National Integration in Indonesia: Patterns and Policies*, Honolulu: University of Hawaii Press.

Freeland, J (1996) 'The global, the national and the local: forces in the development of education for indigenous peoples – the case of Peru', *Compare*, 26, 2, 167-95.

Gibney, F (1992) *The Pacific Century: America and Asia in a Changing World*, New York: Charles Scribner's Sons.

Goodenow, R and Ravitch, D (eds) (1983) *Schools in Cities: Consensus and Conflict in American Educational History*, New York: Holmes and Meir.

Held, D (1983) *States and Societies*, Oxford: Martin Robertson and the Open University.

Held, D (1987) *Models of Democracy*, Cambridge: Polity Press.

Jayasuriya, J E (1983) *Dynamics of Nation-building in Malaysia*, Colombo: Associated Educational Publishers.

Lam, C C, Wong, H W and Fung, Y W (eds) (1993) *Curriculum Changes for Chinese Communities in Southeast Asia: Challenges of the 21st Century*, Hong Kong: Department of Curriculum and Instruction, Faculty of Education, The Chinese University of Hong Kong.

Mallea, J (1989) *Schooling in a Plural Canada*, Clevedon: Multilingual Matters.

Mallea, J and Young J (1984) *Cultural Diversity and Canadian Education*, Ottawa: Carleton University Press.

Naisbitt, N (1996) *Megatrends Asia: The Eight Asian Trends that are Changing the World*, London: Nicholas Brealey.

Palmer, L (1965) *Indonesia*, London: Thames and Hudson.

Price, R (1977) *Marx and Education in Russia and China*, Beckenham: Croom Helm.

Reese, W J (1986) *Power and the Promise of School Reform: Grass-roots Movements During the Progressive Era*, London: Routledge & Kegan Paul.

Spoonley, P, Pearson, D and Shirley, I (eds) (1990) *New Zealand Society*, Palmerston North: Dunmore Press.

Teasdale, R and Teasdale, J (1994) 'Culture and schooling in Aboriginal Australia', in Thomas, E (ed.) *International Perspectives on Culture and Schooling: a Symposium Proceedings*, London: Department of International and Comparative Education, Institute of Education, University of London, pp.174-96.

Tyack, D (1974) *The One Best System: A History of American Urban Education*, Cambridge, Mass: Harvard University Press.

# 9.  Intercultural Education in Latin America

Sheila Aikman

## Introduction

Over the last ten years, the term 'intercultural education' has become increasingly associated with a new approach to education for the indigenous peoples who live throughout Latin America. This has taken place most notably in countries with relatively large indigenous populations, such as Peru, Bolivia, Ecuador, Colombia, Mexico, Guatemala and Venezuela. Prior to this the assimilation of indigenous peoples had been promoted through, among other processes, the spread of western-style schooling in the Spanish language with the aim of what was initially termed 'civilizing' and more recently 'modernizing' indigenous peoples so that they could play a role in the development and progress of the nation (Morin, 1988; Pike, 1973). However, over the last 20 years, with increasing force and increasingly recognized legitimacy, indigenous peoples have challenged policies advocated by the national society for their complete assimilation or their integration with the conservation of a few selected characteristics (see Marzal, 1986). These policies designed to eradicate indigenous peoples as culturally distinct groups and make them disappear into a homogeneous and unifying cultural and linguistic national identity, have been giving way to governmental statements about the pluricultural and plurilingual nature of their countries where indigenous peoples contribute to the rich cultural diversity. Moreover, directorates have been established within ministries of education with responsibility for intercultural and bilingual education policy and programmes for indigenous peoples.

This chapter will look at the different political forces which have shaped the changes in government policy for indigenous peoples' education over the last decade. It will then investigate the nature and significance of this change and consider what it means in practice in terms of education programmes and schooling.

## Indigenous peoples of Latin America

Intercultural bilingual education (IBE) in Latin America is generally recognized as a form of education for the indigenous peoples of their respective countries. Indigenous peoples are the descendants of those who inhabited the land prior to the establishment of the state and who refer to themselves as indigenous. They define themselves as distinct from other groups or minorities within the nation state through their intimate relationship with their land and culture. It is this spiritual link with their land and territory and their role as its protectors and custodians for future generations which distinguishes indigenous peoples from other minority groups. However, indigenous peoples are also disadvantaged and often receive less opportunity for schooling and training than the majority population and have less access to medical care and other social welfare services.

Since the early Spanish colonial period, the indigenous peoples have been referred to collectively as 'Indians' as if they were a uniform group. The indigenous peoples of Latin America are culturally and linguistically diverse. They live in geographically varied regions and have very different histories of relations with non-indigenous Latin American society. For example, the Quechua peoples of the Andean Cuscoarea, where the Inca capital was situated, came into sustained contact with the colonizing Spanish powers some 500 years ago, while the Arakmbut people of the south-eastern Amazon area (only 30 minutes by plane from the town of Cusco) first experienced sustained contact with non-indigenous people in the form of Dominican missionaries in the 1950s. The Quechua peoples today number several millions and their territory now forms part of Ecuador, Peru and Colombia. Conversely, the Arakmbut number some 1,000 persons, belong to a language family of 1,500 Harakmbut speakers and comprise one of some 67 different indigenous ethno-linguistic groups in the Peruvian Amazon region (Aikman, 1994). Indigenous peoples, therefore, have a diversity of indigenous education practices, a diversity of experience of formal education, and a wide range of educational needs today.

## The developing concept of intercultural, bilingual education

The development of intercultural, bilingual education in Latin America has followed a slow but relentless course through the 1970s and 1980s, spearheaded by indigenous peoples themselves. At the same time, developments within the non-indigenous society, both in individual countries and in Latin America as a whole, have raised awareness of the need for change in the assimilationist approach hitherto espoused by governments and much of civil society and its institutions. Furthermore, over the last decade the influence of global trends and international declarations on education and indigenous peoples' rights have had a profound impact on the development of IBE policy.

Indigenous peoples have denounced the monocultural and monolingual education provided by states as ethnocidal and have been increasingly campaigning for a fundamental reconceptualization of education for indigenous peoples as part of a process of cultural decolonization and recognition of rights to self-determination. Throughout the 1960s and 1970s the plundering of natural resources on indigenous lands intensified, accompanied by forcible relocation, land sequestration and destruction, and unequal access for indigenous peoples to health and education services on a worldwide scale.

In Latin America this gave rise to the formation of indigenous peoples' own representative organizations which lobby and pressure for rights to their territories and the right to freedom of cultural expression and way of life. Amazon peoples, for example, set up organizations to tackle problems of the exploitation of oil, timber and gold which has devastated, and still continues to devastate, the fragile rainforest environment and the flora and fauna on which their way of life depends. Local-level indigenous organizations have also come together to establish national federations, such as the Bolivian Indigenous Federation (CIDOB) and the Confederation of Indigenous Nationalities of the Ecuadorean Amazon (CONFENIAE). These national organizations are also linked on the international level with the Coordination of Indigenous Organizations of the Amazon Basin (COICA).

In 1982 the United Nations Working Group for Indigenous Populations was established to consider policies, laws and practices of both governments and indigenous peoples. In 1994 it produced a draft Declaration on the Rights of Indigenous Peoples which is now being debated at the UN Commission for Human Rights. The draft Declaration includes the right of indigenous peoples to 'establish and control their educational systems and institutions providing education in their own languages, in a manner appropriate to their cultural methods of teaching' (Part IV Article 15, E/CN. Sub. 2/1993/29). Other international indigenous statements and charters call for the right of indigenous peoples to a culturally appropriate education which is bilingual and bicultural/intercultural (see the Earth Charter in IWGIA, 1992).

Indigenous peoples consider that IBE has a twofold potential for them: to equip them to participate as citizens of the country in which they live, and to support them in their right to practise and strengthen their own cultural way of life. Indigenous peoples do not necessarily want to be outside of the state; they are part of it and have been since its inception. However, they want to be able to be part of it on their terms, not to be subject to whims of governments and changing policies, to exploitation by national and transnational corporations and open to the pernicious influence of racism and cultural oppression. Some indigenous peoples articulate their aspirations for intercultural bilingual education as providing them with useful knowledge with which to defend their interests vis-à-vis the wider encroaching society and also as a means of revitalizing and strengthening their indigenous culture (see Sampaio Grizzi and Lopes de Silva, 1981). Indigenous peoples consider their right to self-determination, to their decision-making and control over the design and implementation of IBE programmes, as fundamental.

Education has played and plays a multifaceted role for indigenous peoples.

Formal education has contributed to ethnocide and cultural genocide while at the same time being instrumental in developing an awareness of their indigenous identity. Intercultural education has a potential to reinforce indigenous forms of education and learning which are the cornerstone of indigenous identity. It can also prepare children for the intercultural lives which they lead today. Few indigenous peoples live isolated from the wider society and many live in complex, demanding and oppressive situations.

The Arakmbut and the other indigenous peoples of south-eastern Peru provide a vivid illustration of the multiple and conflicting demands on indigenous peoples' intercultural lives today. They live in close contact and interaction with Quechua migrants from the Andean region engaged in illegal gold panning and agriculture on their lands; Mestizo traders sell manufactured goods by canoe on their doorsteps; local government officials establish illegal schools for colonists on their lands and at their expense; environmentalists monitor national parks on indigenous traditional territory and try to relocate them; and representatives of the Mobil company try to reassure them that oil exploration will not harm their lands while huge stretches of the northern Peruvian and the Ecuadorean Amazon lie devastated and polluted by oil exploitation. The Arakmbut, together with their regional federation, the Federation of Natives of Madre de Dios (FENAMAD), are at present coordinating an international campaign against Mobil. They are also struggling for support to develop an intercultural education programme which can serve them in their demanding situation and will also reinforce their cultural identity, which sustains them in their struggle for the maintenance of their lands and their self-respect. The monocultural and monolingual missionary-controlled schooling they receive at present ignores the reality in which they live.

## The 'Indigenists' and education for indigenous peoples

While indigenous peoples have been campaigning for IBE, there have also been changes taking place at governmental level and in civil society. Official recognition of the worth of indigenous languages, albeit until very recently in their use as a springboard for teaching indigenous children Spanish, was an important first step towards IBE. 'Indigenists' can be defined as non-indigenous individuals concerned with the lot of indigenous peoples. There have been *indigenistas* since there was first colonization but the term took on a new meaning during the 1930s and 1940s arising out of concern for justice and defence of the rights of indigenous peoples. In 1940 *indigenismo* became a continent-wide movement arising at the First Indigenist Interamerican Congress in Patzcuaro, Mexico. At this meeting 17 countries ratified an international convention declaring respect for indigenous culture and the need to gather information about indigenous languages as a basis for developing bilingual education. This and subsequent congresses received support from member governments, UNESCO, the Ford Foundation and a wide range of non-governmental organizations and individual linguists, anthropologists and lawyers. Governments set up Indigenist Institutes in their own countries (for example, Mexico, Peru, Brazil, Bolivia, Guatemala and Ecuador) affiliated to the Interamerican Indigenist Institute (III) in Mexico to carry out recommendations which emphasized the importance of using indigenous languages in schooling, although as a transitional policy towards Spanish learning. The North American missionary organization, the Summer Institute of Linguistics, began to be very active in studying indigenous languages and setting up bilingual schools in several countries at this time (notably in Peru, Ecuador, Guatemala and Brazil).

The Catholic church had its own forms of *indigenismo*, one of which was expressed in terms of indigenous liberation and was linked with the subsequent development of Liberation Theology at the Latin American Episcopal Conference in Medellin in 1968. The Medellin Document on education denounced the marginalized situation of indigenous peoples, while a 1971 Document drawn up by bishops from five Andean countries in Iquitos, Peru, indicated the Church's responsibility for ensuring that 'native groups' became aware of their situation vis-à-vis the national society, organized themselves and directed their own development (Sainaghi, 1976).

Though the Mexican government responded to these changes of ideological stance by making bilingual education official in 1964, other countries were slower to move. Most bilingual education programmes were transitional and in several countries these were run by the Summer Institute of Linguistics.

These different strands of *indigenismo* came under criticism in the 1970s and 1980s as being paternalistic and concerned more with the protection of indigenous peoples and their assimilation through mother-tongue education rather than their 'participation' and dialogue as members of the state (Anuario Indigenista, 1988). The 'critical indigenists' argued against a linguistic pluralism which serves the interests of the national society and national identity and in favour of cultural pluralism which contributes positively towards the maintenance of indigenous identity (Nolasco, 1984).

From the 1970s indigenous organizations began to have some representation at the III and subsequent congresses stated that formal education should produce authentic indigenous leaders without violating indigenous self-determination. In 1979 UNESCO initiated its Major Project to address problems of low achievement, high wastage and unequal access to education in Latin America and the Caribbean. The UNESCO regional office actively supported governments in combating these problems and organized a series of seminars with the III on indigenous education, which advocated a linguistically, culturally and ethnically plural approach (see Quintanilla and Lozano, 1983). The seminar also agreed that new forms of education for indigenous peoples, such as bilingual and intercultural education, would not have meaning if they were not carried out as part of a process of cultural decolonization.

## From bilingual education to intercultural education

While there has been a general move towards recognition of IBE as educational policy for indigenous peoples in Latin American countries with large indigenous populations, this has happened at different rates and with different degrees and forms of collaboration between governments, educational professionals and indigenous peoples. The 1980s in Peru provides an illustrative example of developments in intercultural and bilingual education.

In Peru in the 1970s, a socialist military government initiated a radical education reform which signified a move away from a crude policy of economic and social assimilation of indigenous peoples to one of integration into a multicultural and plurilingual country. It embodied a conceptual shift in bilingual education from mother-tongue teaching as a bridge to Spanish (a transitional policy) to mother-tongue teaching for the strengthening of indigenous language and culture (a maintenance or enrichment policy). This involved a reorientation of the status of indigenous languages not only in the education system but with implications for their status in society in general. It also implied a new focus on indigenous languages themselves, what people use them for and how they are intimately embedded in distinct epistemologies and identities.

Landmark educational projects were carried out in Peru over this period in the Ayacucho region in the exhilarating climate of the Education Reform and the officialization of the Quechua language. A primary school project was established in Quechua- and Aymara-speaking areas of Puno which couched the concept of IBE in terms of 'putting the learner, his beliefs, values and customs, his socio-economic and cultural situation at the centre of the education process' (Lopez, cited in Citarella, 1990). This project has had lasting effects for IBE in Latin America because of its wide range of teaching materials in Quechua, publications on language policy, and innovatory materials sensitive to indigenous perspectives of history and the social and natural sciences (see Dietschy-Scheiterle, 1987; Lopez et al., 1987; Valiente, 1988).

With the arrival of a right-wing democratically elected government in Peru at the beginning of the 1980s, the atmosphere changed dramatically. Many of the landmarks of the Education Reform of 1972 were undermined and, while the PEEB/Puno project continued, Ministry support declined. However, in the Amazon area, which had never received any attention from the Ministry of Education and where responsibility for bilingual education was in the hands of the Summer Institute of Linguistics, new small-scale developments began to take shape, independent of government.

Rebelling against the transitional policy of Summer Institute schools, indigenous bilingual teachers and their organizations began to experiment to find forms of education which met their educational needs in their intercultural lives. Making links with various non-indigenous support organizations, and with funding from international agencies, projects of varying sizes were initiated.

These projects included new forms of indigenous/non-indigenous collaboration where educational aims and objectives were identified by the indigenous communities (see, for example, PEBIAN project, San Roman, 1984).

In 1988, the indigenous Inter-Ethnic Association for the Development of the Peruvian Amazon (AIDESEP) and the Instituto Superior Pedagogico de Loreto initiated a radically new training course for indigenous teachers in IBE, the Programade Formacion de Maestros Bilingues – PFMB (see Trapnell, 1991). This programme developed out of dissatisfaction expressed by indigenous bilingual teachers and organizations with the nature of schooling for indigenous children and was based on an in-depth analysis of the educational situation in the Amazon region. It expressed its understanding and conceptualization of intercultural education in the following way:

> Its objective is to train new generations of indigenous peoples with the conscious ability to manage that ethnological, social, linguistic and autochthonous spiritual inheritance of their native Amazon societies and of the knowledge and values propagated by the surrounding society. (Gasch *et al.*, 1987, p.4)

By 1995 this programme had produced a new curriculum system for indigenous primary schooling which structured learning around community activities.

In 1987 the Peruvian government bowed to developments in IBE by creating a Directorate for Bilingual Education within the Ministry of Education which had a mandate to produce IBE policy and strategies. Its 1989 policy document states the aim of IBE as:

> To produce individuals with an optimum communicative competence in their mother tongue and in Spanish and allow for identification with the individual's culture of origin and the knowledge of other minority and majority cultures. (DIGEBIL, 1989, p.11)

Within this conception of IBE, the languages and cultural practices of different indigenous groups are expected to constitute the basic structure and content of the formal education process but, 'gradually and in a non-conflictive and non-substitutive way, all the thematic areas from the majority culture which the indigenous child requires will be added' (ibid.).

The Directorate's five-year plan proposed IBE and interculturality as the basis not only for indigenous peoples' education but for all of society by:

> Strengthening indigenous cultural identity, self-esteem, respect and understanding of different cultures. The adoption of interculturality is essential for social, economic and cultural progress not only in the indigenous communities and regions but throughout the country. (DIGEBIL, 1991, p.3)

While indigenous peoples and support organizations welcomed this proposal because of its potential to revolutionize not only indigenous education but the entire national education system (Zuniga, 1995), the government subsequently closed down the Directorate.

## Institutionalization of IBE

Today many Latin American countries such as Mexico, Guatemala, Ecuador, Bolivia, Venezuela and Colombia have official policies, offices and/or programmes for IBE for indigenous peoples. These vary from country to country in terms of their definition of intercultural education, the structure of IBE programmes and the nature and degree of indigenous participation. Many of the programmes have been conceived in close collaboration with indigenous organizations (such as in Ecuador and Colombia); others have been developed independent of indigenous organizations (such as in Guatemala); or have been top-down approaches (such as in Venezuela). This is reflected in the aims of their IBE policies. For example, the Guatemalan Programme for Bilingual Bicultural Education aims to 'sustain the coexistence of two cultures and different languages... in order to contribute to a national Guatemalan consciousness' (Acuerdo Ministerial No. 997, cited in Chiodi, 1990, p.248). The Mexican General Department for Indigenous Education has a less assimilationist flavour and requires bilingual, bicultural education to 'maintain the identity of the communities and avoid their destruction and cultural substitution' (cited in Citarella, 1990, p.70).

There is growing recognition of the importance of IBE for indigenous peoples and the pluricultural nature of society in Latin America. Now discussion of IBE is focusing on the concept of interculturality. For indigenous peoples the intercultural relations they have with diverse sectors of national and international society continue to be asymmetrical, exploitative and oppressive. Interculturality requires that the relations between indigenous peoples and other members of society are more just, equal and democratic. For this to happen there has to be a transformation of the relations of dependency between the national (dominant) society and the indigenous society (see Bodnar, 1990; Cusco Seminar, 1995).

## Conclusion

Indigenous peoples in Latin America are looking for support for the development of IBE based in their own learning practices, their knowledge and with respect for their ways of life. They share this struggle with indigenous peoples in many parts of the world. Many of the experimental projects taking place in Latin America at present receive recognition from governments but continue to be dependent on financial support from international NGOs and, in a few cases, from bilateral aid agencies (for example the 'Proyecto EBI' in Ecuador).

However, where governments control decision-making in policy and programmes a paradox has emerged which can undermine IBE and its aims of strengthening indigenous culture. In countries such as Venezuela, government attempts to provide IBE for indigenous peoples have deprived indigenous peoples of control and decision-making over central concepts such as indigenous 'culture' and how indigenous knowledge should be articulated in the intercultural education process. Curricula based on generalized characteristics, processes and practices are by their very nature top-down approaches to IBE which gloss over difference and diversity and risk a return to a conception of indigenous peoples as a homogeneous cultural group with only a few superficial differences.

With generalized IBE programmes, teachers are expected to make local adaptations of the curriculum to suit local circumstances, while fundamental differences in world views, cosmologies and ways of life remain unrecognized. IBE as conceived of by indigenous peoples presents a challenge to currently existing educational structures, institutional frameworks and conditions. It is rooted in indigenous educational practices and indigenous ways of life and bodies of knowledge, not in the subject-based division of knowledge or the constriction of time around national timetables and space within classrooms characteristic of westernized schooling.

The challenge of IBE is frustrated by a shortage of indigenous professionals who can provide a sensitive and appropriate transformation of the aims and objectives of IBE into practical programmes in schools and communities (see Chiodi, 1990). Many indigenous schools are staffed by non-indigenous teachers sent by educational authorities to what they consider are the least prestigious schools. Many of these teachers have little teaching experience and scant interest in listening to indigenous peoples' priorities, the dilemmas of indigenous youth, or to the traditional wisdom of elders who are the repositories of indigenous knowledge. The challenge facing indigenous peoples today is to establish and maintain decision-making control of the design and implementation of IBE for their communities and children. This would help them achieve their aims of both strengthening indigenous identity and way of life and equipping future generations to tackle the oppressive intercultural relations which dominate their lives.

# References

Aikman, S (1994) 'Intercultural education and Harakmbut identity: A case study of the community of San Jose in South-eastern Peru', PhD thesis, University of London.

Amadio, M (1987) 'Caracterizacion de la Educacion Bilinge Intercultural' in *Educacion y Pueblos Indigenas en Centro America: un balance critico,* Santiago de Chile: UNESCO/ORE-ALC.

Anuario Indigenista (1988) 'Indigenismo y Participacion', in *Anuario Indigenista* Vol. XLVIII. Mexico.

Bodnar, Y (1990) 'Aproximacion a la Etnoeducacion como elaboracion teorica', in Ministry of Education, Colombia, *Etnoeducacion: conceptualizacion y ensayos,* Bogota: Programa de Etnoeducacion PRODIC.

Bonfil, G (1984) 'Del Indigenismo de la Revolucion a la Antropologia Critica', in Junqueira, C and Carvalho, E (eds) *Los Indios y la Antropologia en America Latina.* Ediciones Busquedas.

Chiodi, F (1990) 'Ecuador', in Chiodi, F (compiler) *La Educacion Indigena en America Latina: Mexico, Guatemala, Ecuador, Peru, Bolivia*, Vol. 1, Santiago: Abya-Yala.

Citarella, L (1990) 'Peru', in Chiodi, F (compiler) *La Educacion Indigena en America Latina: Mexico, Guatemala, Ecuador, Peru, Bolivia*, Vol. 2. Santiago, Abya-Yala.

Cusco Seminar (1995) 'Educacion e interculturalidad en America Latina', Seminar hosted by Bartolome de las Casas/Centre for Human Rights, August 22–25, 1995.

Deitschy-Scheiterle, A (1987) 'Ciencias Naturales y Saber Popular: Dominacion o Complementaridad?', in *Pueblos Indigenas y Educacion*, No. 1, Year 1, January–March, pp.113–26, Quito.

DIGEBIL (1989) *Politica de Educacion Bilinge Intercultural*, Lima: Ministry of Education, General Directorate for Bilingual Education (DIGEBIL).

DIGEBIL (1991) *Politica Nacional de Educacion Bilinge y Educacion Intercultural 1991–1995*, Lima: General Directorate for Bilingual Education (DIGEBIL).

Fernandez, M and Vera, R (1987) 'Educacion Bilingue – Intercultural: un reto ante la condicion multilingue y pluricultural', in *Extracta*, pp.66–71, Lima: Cultural Survival Quarterly/CIPA.

Gasch, J, Trapnell, L and Rengifo M (1987) 'El Curriculo alternativo para la Formacion de Maestros de Educacion Bilinge Intercultural y su Fundamentacion Antropologica y Pedagogica', Centro de Investigacion Antropologica de la Amazonia Peruana (CIAP) and the National University of the Peruvian Amazon (UNAP), manuscript.

Heise, M (1993) 'Educacion Bilingue Intercultural para los Ashaninka del Rio Tambo', *America Indigena*, 4, 125–40.

ISPL/AIDESEP (1987) 'Proyecto de Formacion de Maestros Bilinges de la Amazonia Peruana', Instituto Superior Pedagogico Loreto (ISPL), Iquitos and Asociacion Intertnica de Desarrollo de la Selva Peruana (AIDESEP): manuscript.

IWGIA (1992) 'Indigenous Peoples in Rio: The Kari Oka World Indigenous Conference', *IWGIA Newsletter* (International Work Group for Indigenous Affairs), 4, 53–6.

Lopez, L E, Yung, I and Palao, J (1987) 'Educacion Bilinge en Puno: Reflexiones en torno a una experiencia… Que Concluye?', in *Pueblos Indigenas y Educacion*, Year 1, No. 3, pp 63–106.

Marzal, M (1986) *Historia de la Antropologia Indigenista: Mexico y Peru*, Lima: Pontificia Universidad Catolica del Peru, Fondo Editorial.

Ministry of Education, Peru (1992) *Politica Nacional de Educacion Bilinge y Educacion Intercultural 1991–1995*, Lima: General Directorate for Bilingual Education (DIGEBIL).

Morin, F (1988) 'Indios, Indigenismo, Indianidad', in *Indianidad, Etnocidio e Indigenismo en America Latina*, pp.13–24, Mexico: Instituto Indigenista Interamericano & Centre D'Etudes Mexicaines et Centramercaines.

Nolasco, M (1984) 'La Antropologia aplicada en Mexico y su destino final: el indigenismo', in Junqueira, C and Carvalho, E (eds) *Los Indios y la Antropologia en America Latina*, Buenos Aires: Busqueda-Yuchan.

Pike, F B (1973) *Spanish America 1900–1970: Tradition and Social Innovation*, London: Thames & Hudson.

Quintanilla, O and Lozano, S (1983) 'Presentacion', in Rodriguez, N, Masferrer, R and Vargas, R (eds) *Educacion, Etnias y Descolonizacion en America Latina*, Vol 1, pp.viii–xvii, Mexico: UNESCO/III.

Sainaghi, P A (1976) 'La Evangelizacion del Pueblo Shuar', *Mundo Shuar*, No 6, Serie 'B', Sucua.

Sampaio Grizzi, D C and Lopes de Silva, A (1981) 'A Filosofiae a Pedagogia de Educaao Indigena: Un Resumo dos Debates', *Comissao Pro Indio A Questao da Educaao Indigena* pp.14–29, Editora Brasiliense.

San Roman, G (1984) 'Programa de Educacion Bilinge e Intercultural del Alto Napo', *Shupihui*, 30, 183–92, Iquitos.

Trapnell, L (1991) 'Una alternativa en marcha: la Propuesta de Formacion Magisterial de AIDESEP', in Zuniga, B, Pozzi-Escot, G and Lopez, F (eds) *Educacion Bilingue Intercultural: reflexiones y desafios,* pp. 219–39, Lima: FOMCIENCIAS.

Valiente, T (1988) *Las Ciencias Historicos Sociales en la Educacion Bilinge: El Case de Puno,* Lima: PEEB/GTZ.

Zuniga, M (1995) 'Pueblos Indigenas y Educacion en el Peru', paper prepared from Meeting on Indigenous Populations and Education in Peru, 21–22 April 1995, Lima: Foro Educativo.

# Section III:
# National Case Studies

## 10. Intercultural Education in Canada

John Mallea and Jonathan Young

### Introduction

The discourses of race, ethnicity, culture and education in Canada, as else-where, do not have a shared or uniformly accepted terminology. Multicultural education and anti-racist education are commonly used interchangeably, although some authors have argued that they have fundamental distinctions. In Quebec, intercultural education is used instead of multicultural education to explicitly signal that the province's commitment to inclusivity and equity is located within the structures of a Francophone society. (See Kehoe and Mansfield, 1993, and Moodley, 1995, for a fuller discussion of this debate in Canada.) Indeed, issues of race, ethnicity, culture and education have significantly shaped the Canadian state from its very beginnings. They were a major determinant of the particular form of federalism Canada adopted and the key reason why education was designated a provincial responsibility under The British North America Act, 1867. Notwithstanding such constitutional arrangements, conflict rather than consensus has characterized efforts to reflect the nation's diversity in provincially funded systems of public education.

### Demographic and cultural background

Prior to European settlement, an indigenous population estimated to number 200,000 consisted of some 50 distinct cultural groupings with at least a dozen different languages. Four centuries of immigration from around the world have added greatly to that diversity.

The early 17th century saw the start of a period of settlement and exploitation of New France/Canada by French traders and colonizers. This initial period of French settlement was followed by British immigration after Canada was ceded to Britain in the Treaty of Paris in 1763, so that by the time of confederation in 1867 the British population outnumbered the French. At this time, of a total population of some three and a half million people only 8% were of non-British or non-French ethnic origin (Miller, 1989).

The final years of the 19th century and the early years of the 20th up to the beginning of World War I saw a second phase of large-scale immigration that significantly altered the cultural make-up of Canada. Between 1896 and 1914 some three million immigrants came to Canada including large numbers of settlers from Northern and Eastern Europe recruited to settle the prairies of Western Canada. Within the period 1901 to 1911, Canada's population increased by some 43%, and by 1911 people of non-British and non-French origins formed over 33% of the population of the three prairie provinces of Manitoba, Saskatchewan and Alberta (Palmer, 1984). Settlement often resulted in initial concentrations of certain nationalities within a particular geographic area, and these block settlements served to facilitate the maintenance of traditional linguistic and cultural patterns (Anderson and Frideres, 1981). This period also saw the arrival of significant numbers of Asian immigrants, many of whom came as contract labourers to build the Canadian Pacific Railway and later settled on the west coast in British Columbia.

While some immigration continued during the inter-war years it was only in the period after World War II that there was a large-scale renewal of immigration that once again significantly reshaped the make-up of Canadian society. In addition to continued immigration from Britain, large numbers of immigrants came to Canada from Europe including Italian, German, Dutch, Polish and Portuguese. Unlike their predecessors, these immigrants settled predominantly in urban rather than rural destinations.

In the mid-1960s in a context of a booming economy and the need for skilled labour to meet the human resource needs of an industrialized and urbanized society, revised immigration legislation replaced existing racially and ethnically discriminatory practices with more universalistic admission criteria based on level of education, occupational skills and demands, and personal adaptability (Moodley, 1995). A consequence of these changes to Canadian immigration policies has been a substantial globalization of immigration into Canada away from the predominantly European patterns of earlier years, contributing significantly to the 'racial', cultural and ethnic diversity of the country generally and its major urban centres in particular. (Quotation marks are used here in relation to the term 'race' to signal our recognition of the socially constructed nature of the concept of 'race', and, as distinct from the term racism, its dubious scientific utility.)

In 1993, 58.4% of the 252,000 people immigrating to Canada came from Asia, with Hong Kong, the Philippines, India and China being the four leading source countries. A further 18% came from Europe, 6.8% from Africa, and 5.6% from North and South America (Statistics Canada, 1994).

**Table 10.1**   *Canada's population by selected ethnic origin, 1991*

| | | |
|---|---|---|
| **Total population** | | **26,994,045** |
| | | |
| **Single origins** | | **19,199,790** |
| Aboriginal | | 470,615 |
| British | | 5,611,050 |
| French | | 6,146,600 |
| European origins | | 4,146,065 |
| *Western European* | *1,355,485* | |
| *Northern European* | *213,600* | |
| *Eastern European* | *946,810* | |
| *Southern European* | *1,379,030* | |
| *Others* | *251,140* | |
| Asian and African origins | | 1,633,660 |
| *South Asian* | *420,295* | |
| *East/SE Asian* | *961,225* | |
| *African* | *26,430* | |
| *Others* | *225,710* | |
| Latin, Central and South American origins | | 85,535 |
| Caribbean origins | | 94,395 |
| Black origins | | 224,620 |
| | | |
| Others | | 787,250 |
| | | |
| **Multiple origins** | | **7,794,250** |

Source: *Ethnic Origin: The Nation* (1993a), Ottowa: Statistics Canada. Catalogue 93–315.

## Structural responses to Canadian diversity in public education: an organizing framework

In looking at the variety of different ways in which cultural differences have impacted upon, and been reflected within, the Canadian public education systems, this chapter is organized around two themes: first, the extent to which cultural differences have found expression in distinct structural and organizational forms; and second, the extent to which various cultural groups have been allowed to participate fully within the existing educational systems.

These two elements provide the basis for a model of intercultural relations developed from the work of Schermerhorn (1970) and applied to education by La Belle and White (1984), shown in Table 10.2.

**Table 10.2** *A model of intercultural relations*

*STRUCTURAL RELATIONS*

| | *Separate Institutions* | *Common Institutions* |
|---|---|---|
| *Equality* | Different cultural groups exist together in society with separate and parallel sets of institutions and share equally in the resources of the society | Different cultural groups participate in the same societal institutions without discrimination |
| *POWER* | *(Corporate pluralism)* | *(Liberal pluralism)* |
| *RELATIONS* *Inequality* | Different cultural groups with separate institutions and unequal power and access to society's resources | Different cultural groups share a common set of institutions but within them have unequal access to society's resources |
| | *(Apartheid)* | *(Anglo-conformity or 'The vertical mosaic')* |

The utility of this model in considering intercultural education in Canada lies in the fact that while it sets up four 'ideal types' of intergroup relations, both axes of the model represent in reality a broad continuum of possibilities in terms of degrees of equality/inequality and of common/separate institutions, allowing it to describe many different and shifting arrangements. Furthermore, as Schermerhorn (1970) notes, what becomes of key importance is less the specific location of any particular cultural groups within this typology, but rather the degree of agreement between groups as to the appropriateness of that location.

In the remainder of this chapter something of the range of these struggles and accommodations is described in a variety of different educational settings across the provinces of Canada.

## Religious and linguistic dualism

While reference to the English and French as Canada's 'two founding nations' is made problematic by its denial of the prior place of Canada's Aboriginal

People/First Nations as well as its failure to acknowledge the presence of non-English, non-French populations, it has been struggles between these two powerful cultural communities around the place of both the French and English languages and Catholicism and Protestantism in Canadian political and constitutional arrangements that have provided some of the most visible and enduring issues in Canadian diversity. Furthermore, it is only these two cultural groups that have seen at least some educational rights entrenched in the Canadian constitution – affording their educational aspirations a degree of legitimacy and security not available to other groups.

Palmer (1984) argues that of the several objectives of the architects of Canadian confederation none was of more importance than accommodating the needs of these two cultural communities. In the British North America Act (1867) it was religion that served as the vehicle for protecting English and French minority education rights with Section 93 of the Act, guaranteeing the right of Catholic and Protestant school systems, where they existed prior to confederation, to continue to exist and to be publicly funded.

In practice these religious rights have not always been respected and Catholic and Protestant schools currently exist in a variety of different forms across the country, reflecting in part their status in each province at the time of confederation and in part the outcome of legal and political challenges since that time (Bezeau, 1989). In Quebec public schooling has traditionally been organized into a denominational system with two confessional school systems (Catholic and Protestant) existing in the urban centres of Montreal and Quebec City, while in the rural districts public and separate/dissentient school systems exist, each confessionally identifiable. The three provinces of Ontario, Saskatchewan and Alberta have both public (non-denominational) and separate (Catholic and Protestant) systems operating side by side and protected under the law. Yet other provinces, including British Columbia and Manitoba, have a non-denominational public school system, and parents in these provinces seeking a Catholic or Protestant education for their children – like those from other religious backgrounds – have to look to private schools.

Unlike any other province, Newfoundland has multi-denominational school systems. These have included a Roman Catholic system, a Pentecostal system, a Seventh Day Adventist system, and an Integrated system that comprises four denominations – Anglican, Salvation Army, United Church and Presbyterian. However, in 1995 the province has moved to substantially reorganize this system.

The existence of publicly funded Catholic and Protestant school systems has led other religious groups to argue a case for public funding for other religious schools within the public school system (Shapiro, 1985). These arguments have not been successful in Canadian courts and, with the exception of Newfoundland, all religious schools other than Catholic and Protestant schools exist outside of the public school system. Private or independent schools account for only some 5% of the student population in Canada. In most provinces they are eligible for some public funds. In the last decade or so a number of court rulings under the Charter of Rights and Freedoms have made starting the public school day with a Christian prayer illegal – an infringement of the right to religious freedom. Public schools are having either to become increasingly secular or to find ways that recognize the multicultural/multi-faith nature of Canadian society. What the courts will deem acceptable in the latter case has yet to be fully articulated.

While it might have been argued in 1867 that religion served as an effective 'marker' of French and English culture in Canada, the constitutional guarantees for Catholic and Protestant schools in the absence of any language provisions have proven to have very limited power to protect minority cultures, specifically French culture in the face of English pressures for Anglo-conformity.

Up until the beginning of the 20th century, schools systems across the country were likely to operate in both English and French where both populations existed, as well as in other languages such as German and Ukrainian (see Bruno-Jofre, 1993). The early decades of the 20th century, however, saw provinces other than Quebec either abolish or place very stringent restrictions on the use of French as a language of instruction in the school. As a consequence, for more than half a century in most provinces in Canada English became the exclusive language of instruction (except where Francophone communities established an essentially 'underground' school system within their public schools).

In the second half of this century the struggle around English-French relations in Canada has been largely recast in terms of language rather than religion. Section 23 of the Canadian Charter of Rights and Freedoms, entitled 'Minority Language Educational Rights', provides parents who speak the minority official language in their province with specific rights to have their children receive primary and secondary education in that minority language if they so wish. This provision has seen considerable political and judicial activity across Canada to bring existing practice into line with these new constitutional requirements.

This has produced a variety of different institutional and governance forms. Some jurisdictions have responded by establishing distinct programmes for Francophone students in existing schools. Others have recognized the broader educational and cultural arguments that call for separate Francophone schools. In the critical area of governance, recent court decisions pursuant to the Charter of Rights and Freedoms have required several provinces to extend to minority language groups greater control over their own schools and a defined role in the governance of all schools. This has led Ontario, for example, to reserve seats on some school boards for Francophone trustees and to create distinct Francophone school boards in Ottawa and Toronto. Manitoba meanwhile has established a single Francophone school board to serve Francophone schools throughout the province. Quebec has made several attempts to move from a system of school boards based on religion to one based on language, but has only recently been able to do so in a way that respects the constitutional guarantees to both Anglophones and Protestants.

While English and French, the official languages of Canada, have secured constitutional, legal and institutional protections, other 'non-official' or 'heritage' languages have been afforded far less support. While bilingual programmes – English-Ukrainian, English-German, French-German etc – exist in schools in several provinces, and heritage language classes in an extensive range of world languages exist both as a part of the regular curriculum and as after-hours classes in elementary as well as secondary schools in many provinces (Cummins and Danesi, 1990), their status within the public school system remains much more marginal.

## Aboriginal education

The same concern for minority protection in education afforded to Protestant and Catholic school systems was not applied to the situation of Aboriginal people. It is worth pointing out that, as with other terms in this field, the terminology associated with Canadian indigenous and Aboriginal peoples is complex and shifting. In this chapter we use 'Aboriginal people' to refer to all peoples who are the descendants of the original peoples of the land, including Indian, Metis and Inuit people. 'First Nations' is a term used to refer to the various governments of Aboriginal people in Canada. The terms 'Indian' and 'Indian education' are used only as legal terms that refer to specific legal (and not cultural or sociological) designations and arrangements between the federal government and particular Aboriginal people.

While education is generally a responsibility of the provinces in Canada, the historic relationship of Aboriginal people in Canada is with the federal government. The Indian Act, first passed in 1876, has regulated the way in which status Indians have been treated by the government.

For most of Canada's history, Aboriginal education was controlled by the federal government, delegated to the churches, and shaped by policies and practices which sought to assimilate Aboriginal young people into the lower strata of the dominant society. A number of different institutional forms were experimented with over the years, ranging from local day schools to residential schools often specializing in preparation for industrial, agricultural and domestic pursuits (Barman *et al.*, 1987a). Neglect vied with coercion as primary strategies, and by almost any indicator of educational well-being one could wish to choose, the picture painted across the country was of a school system that served Canada's Aboriginal students dramatically less well than the rest of the Canadian population (Henley and Young, 1990).

It was not until the 1950s that the federal government began to take direct charge of Indian education when the federal government's new vision was one which saw Indian students schooled in the various provincial school systems, an approach that received support during the 1960s through the Hawthorn Report, a comprehensive study of Indian conditions in Canada.

Initially favourable reactions to the Hawthorn Report changed quickly in 1969 with the release of a federal White Paper on Indian Policy (Canada, 1969). A product of a period which was deeply committed to the liberal tenet of equal opportunity for all individuals in society, this document proposed that the Indian Act would be repealed; the special relationships that Indian people had with the Government of Canada based upon inherent aboriginal rights and treaty agreements would be eliminated; Indians would become full members of Canadian society, but as individuals without historic group recognition or rights.

The outrage of Aboriginal leaders to these proposals, which were withdrawn in 1971, has proved to be a 'marker event' in the relationships between Aboriginal societies and all levels of government in Canada. It was the immediate impetus behind a movement towards Indian control of Indian education and Aboriginal self-government generally (Assembly of First Nations, 1988). In 1972 the National Indian Brotherhood released a policy paper entitled *Indian Control of Indian Education*, which was very specific as to where power in Indian education should lie. Indian parents should oversee the education of their children directly and so emphasis was placed upon the assumption of control at the local or Band level as the basis for First Nations' jurisdiction over education.

This policy was accepted by the federal government in 1973 and the first Indian communities to assume control of their educational systems did so in the mid-1970s. In 1991, 326 of Canada's nearly 600 Bands/First Nations had assumed control of their schools (see Table 10.3) and by the end of the century it is likely that virtually all will have done so.

**Table 10.3**   *First Nations enrolments by school type, 1990–91*

| School system | Students | % |
|---|---|---|
| Federal schools | 8,055 | 8.7 |
| Public and separate schools | 43,545 | 47.3 |
| Band schools | 40,508 | 44.0 |
| Total | 92,108 | 100.0 |

Source: J MacPherson (1991) *MacPherson Report on Tradition and Education: Towards a Vision of Our Future*, Ottowa: Indian and Northern Affairs Canada, p.8.

To date these developments, important as they are, have taken place without the benefit of constitutional or legislative change: the Indian Act remains intact and Aboriginal rights and treaty entitlement issues (including land claims) have yet to be fully addressed.

Furthermore, at the heart of the issue of Indian jurisdiction over education is the struggle for control of the curriculum and for curriculum change. For Aboriginal people self-government in education has to provide the opportunity and necessary pre-conditions to develop curricula that are not only qualitatively better but also substantively different: a curriculum that could provide an appropriate balance between Aboriginal and non-Aboriginal language, content and experiences, and which could offer both 'cultural continuity and occupational freedom' (Barman *et al.*, 1987b, p.5). Efforts at making this new curriculum a reality have been reflected in the development of many new educational programmes across the country (Assembly of First Nations, 1988; Henley and Young, 1990; Kirkness, 1992) ranging from those which have made only minimal additions of Aboriginal content to school programmes that are fully bilingual.

An additional element in the development of Aboriginal education has been the training of Aboriginal teachers. Without a cadre of teachers committed to the goals of locally relevant curricula and with the cultural knowledge and professional capabilities to translate policy into practice, the ideal of local control would have little meaning. Attempts to address this need have seen the development of some 20 Native/Indian/ First Nations teacher education programmes in Canada, starting in 1961 at the University of Saskatchewan (Allison, 1983; Nyce, 1990). A major consequence of these programmes has been a dramatic increase in the number of registered Indians preparing to become teachers and a similar increase in practising Indian teachers, particularly at the early and middle grades.

In Canada's urban centres, Aboriginal control of education is evolving in a variety of different ways that have seen efforts to establish structurally distinct and culturally relevant schools and governance systems, as well as efforts to create, within a multicultural urban public school system, a much greater Aboriginal presence in all aspects of curriculum, staffing and governance.

## Multicultural and anti-racist education

Multicultural, intercultural and anti-racist education are terms that have been used quite differently by different people in Canada (Kehoe and Mansfield, 1993), and all of the above examples of struggle for structural recognition and control of schooling might be properly considered examples of multicultural, intercultural and anti-racist education. However, for reasons primarily of organizational convenience, we have chosen in this section to use the terms in the context of mainstream provincial public school systems.

Changing demographic, political and ideological pressures in Canadian society at large that gave rise to the policy discourse of multiculturalism and, in 1971 a federal policy of 'Multiculturalism within a Bilingual Framework' (Canada, 1971), produced similar pressures for change within the Canadian public school systems. These pressures were felt most acutely in the larger urban centres such as Montreal, Toronto, Winnipeg and Vancouver that were the destinations for the majority of Canada's increasingly racially and culturally diverse immigrant populations and which were becoming the home of increasing numbers of Canada's Aboriginal population.

From the beginning of the 1970s in a number of these urban school boards there was a growing awareness that these societal changes called for a far more fundamental rethinking of the nature of schooling for all students than the limited response of expanded English (or French) as a Second Language programming for recent immigrant children that had taken place in the 1950s and 1960s. School boards across the country in the 1970s began to establish work groups and task forces which resulted in the publication in the late 1970s and 1980s of a variety of policy documents on 'multicultural education' and 'race' relations. (For example, Toronto: Multiculturalism Policy 1976, Race Relations Policy, 1979; North York: Race and Ethnic Relations Policy and Procedures, 1982; Vancouver: Race Relations Policy 1982; Regina: Intercultural Education, Race and Ethnic Relations Policy 1985; Winnipeg: Multiculturalism and Education Policy, 1988.)

It has been these urban school divisions/boards (sometimes on their own initiative and more often in reaction to strong and persistent community pressure) that have provided much of the professional leadership in multicultural and anti-racist education policy development in Canada. At the provincial level, where the vast majority of authority for public education in Canada resides, only a few Ministries of Education have developed their own policies in support of multicultural education. A consequence of this is that there exist across the country very varied levels of commitment to policy development and policy implementation, and individual schools and teachers working to implement such changes are generally required to do so in the absence of a broad base of system supports (see, for example, Alladin, 1996, and Smith and Young, 1996).

Public schooling in Canada is primarily a provincial and not a federal responsibility. There is no federal Department or Ministry of Education. At the district level, elected school boards exist to oversee the management of the day-to-day operation of schools and parent advisory councils in different forms exist in most schools. While schools have traditionally had considerable scope for shaping their own programmes, in the last few years school reforms have seen a significant move towards the centralization and standardization of public education provincially (and regionally by way of inter-provincial agreements) through the regulation of curriculum and the re-introduction of province-wide benchmark tests at different points in a student's career.

## Curriculum and language

As Tator and Henry (1991, p.16) note, it has been issues of curriculum that have provided a focal point for multicultural policies and practices. Curriculum initiatives have included the development of guidelines for identifying bias in curriculum materials; the development of new curriculum units and courses; efforts to infuse a multicultural or anti-racist perspective across the curriculum; and, in a few instances, the development of 'culturally focused schools' such as Black focused schools in Toronto and Aboriginal focused schools in Winnipeg, Toronto, and Regina.

In an initial attempt to challenge Eurocentric, racist and assimilationist features of curriculum materials, a number of jurisdictions have prepared guidelines for identifying and challenging bias in textbooks and other learning materials. Some Ministries, such as Ontario and Alberta, have prepared these guides for authors and publishers of textbooks, others such as Manitoba have prepared detailed guidelines for librarians as well as for classroom teachers.

As with multicultural education initiatives in other countries, curriculum initiatives have been widely criticized as often being additive and trivializing rather than integrative and systematic. Sustained and systematic curriculum development initiatives that are accompanied by sufficient professional development opportunities for the teachers who are expected to implement the changes tend to be relatively rare.

## Teachers and teacher education

As mediators of the curriculum, it is individual teachers who to a significant degree define whether or not multicultural and anti-racist education will be a reality in specific schools and classrooms. In this regard two issues have been of central concern in the discourse of Canadian multicultural education: first, the need to recruit and promote minority group teachers; and second, the importance of developing through pre-service and in-service programmes the appropriate sensitivities, knowledge and skills in all teachers.

For many advocates of multicultural and anti-racist education, a racially and culturally diverse teaching force constitutes a cornerstone of their vision, and while few jurisdictions collect detailed data on the diversity of their workforces, what data are available clearly indicate the under-representation of Aboriginal and 'visible minority' teachers within the profession in Canada.

While many jurisdictions have articulated in their policies support for employment equity, only a few have taken proactive measures that have led to significant changes in this aspect of their workforce. Where they have occurred, such changes have included the establishment of an Employment Equity Office, the collection of sufficiently detailed and updated data that can generate a comprehensive profile of the system's workforce, and the development of strategies, training programmes, timelines and monitoring systems for broadening the pool of qualified applicants for all positions within the system. In addition, one or two school boards have entered into collaborative ventures with neighbouring faculties of education to initiate programmes designed to attract minority students into teaching, provide school sites and teacher-mentors to work with them during their pre-service programmes, and to hire at least some of them back into the school system on graduation (Solomon, 1996).

At the provincial level, where responsibility for the certification of teachers resides, attention has been drawn to the barriers that continue to exist for teachers whose initial training and experience occurred outside of Canada (Ontario, 1989). While some steps have been taken in recent years to establish the equivalency of international credentials and to assist such teachers in meeting provincial certification requirements, substantial obstacles still remain.

Within the pre-service curriculum of Canadian faculties of education, specific attention to issues of 'race'/racism, culture and ethnicity and their significance to teaching have received varying degrees of attention, both in terms of what material is included and in terms of how, when and to whom it is presented. Different curriculum approaches have included: the integration of material into foundation courses; the provision of elective (and occasionally required) courses such as 'Multicultural education', 'Cross-cultural education' or 'Intercultural education', or more focused courses addressing specific aspects of Canadian diversity or particular ethnic groups; the integration of material into methodology courses and field experience; the provision of minor and major areas of specialization in either the education of specific minority groups (generally First Nations students) or in various dimensions of minority education; and, as already noted, the establishment of specific native teacher education programmes (Orlikow and Young, 1993).

The variety of different approaches that can be documented within faculties of education should not, however, be mistaken for any widespread or comprehensive commitment to multicultural teacher education and, with a few exceptions, faculties of education have not played a leadership role in the development of Canadian multicultural education.

The importance of in-service teacher education is only highlighted by such an assessment of the limitations of existing pre-service programmes, and while, once again, it is possible to identify initiatives by faculties of education, school boards and individual schools that provide models for systematic and sustained approaches to multicultural professional development, in many jurisdictions in Canada this agenda has hardly begun.

## Community relations and school governance

In as much as multicultural education is fundamentally about redefining power relationships within schools and addressing the exclusion of minority voices in educational decision-making, it is inevitable that multicultural education in Canada has been concerned with matters of school governance.

School system responses to demands for minority group inclusion have been varied, including the hiring of community liaison workers, joint management committees for schools, the establishment of school board advisory committees, the reserving of a certain number of seats on school boards for Francophone or Aboriginal representatives, and the establishment of separate Francophone and Aboriginal school boards.

The public hearings and consultation processes that accompanied many of the task forces on multicultural education and race relations in the 1970s and 1980s clearly documented the pervasive sense of distrust, alienation and powerlessness felt towards the school system by many minority group parents, and the gulf that existed between the two.

An early response to these issues was the recruitment by several urban school boards of community liaison workers whose task, generally defined, was to begin to bridge the gulf between teachers and parents, communities and schools. While these positions have served a valuable function in facilitating communication, understanding and problem-solving between parents and schools, they have not been without their difficulties and limitations, particularly when these workers as employees of school boards have taken on advocacy roles for their communities.

A further development in terms of minority group representation has been the establishment in a number of jurisdictions of advisory boards such as the Urban Aboriginal Advisory Board within the Winnipeg school division, and the Black Consultative Advisory Committee within the North York and City of Toronto school boards. While these committees have only advisory powers within their respective boards, the influence that they have been able to exert serves to demonstrate that when backed by an active community constituency, they are able to play a powerful advocacy role not only in focusing attention on their issues, needs and barriers but also in contributing directly to changes within the school system (Tator and Henry, 1991).

While advisory committees have provided a vehicle for influencing Canadian school boards, several provinces have enacted legislation that has required minority group representation on the boards. These initiatives have to date been limited to instances of mandating Aboriginal and Francophone representation in jurisdictions that have substantial Aboriginal or Francophone populations, and giving to those representatives exclusive authority over matters of Aboriginal or Francophone education. Other provinces have moved directly to establishing one or more Francophone school boards to oversee Francophone education, providing a governance model that has been advocated for urban Aboriginal education as well.

At the present time there appears to be a cross-current of change in school governance in Canada in which the institutionalization of legally mandated parent advisory councils at the local school level is countered by an increasingly centralized control of the curriculum and student assessment by provincial governments. While the emphasis on parent advisory councils is usually justified in terms of democratizing the school system, and while centralized curriculum documents now include the language of inclusivity, there seems little as yet to suggest that public school governance in the 1990s is truly a public affair.

## Conclusions

It has been possible over the past 20 years or so to identify a wide range of positive initiatives taken under the rubric of multicultural/intercultural/anti-racist education. They range across all aspects of school life: political, legal, financial, theoretical and practical. There is much to applaud in these initiatives. Yet few provincial or local jurisdictions have articulated and implemented a comprehensive and flexible vision of public education that fully validates and celebrates the increasingly plural realities of Canadian society.

Many obstacles to doing so remain. Given the currently pervasive neo-liberal approach to educational reform, located critically within a broader political and corporate rhetoric of global competitiveness, a technological imperative, and a reduction in the role of governments, they are more likely to increase than decrease. As a result, Canada's international leadership role in this area – widely acknowledged and emulated around the world – has undoubtedly been placed in question.

## Acknowledgements

We would like to acknowledge the input of Dick Henley, Tony Riffel, Tony Tavares and Benjy Levin, in their comments on earlier drafts of this chapter.

## References

Alladin, M (1996) *Racism in Canadian Schools*, Toronto: Harcourt Brace.
Allison, D (1983) 'Fourth World Education in Canada and the Faltering Promise of Native Teacher Education Programs', *Journal of Canadian Studies*, 18, 3, 102–18.
Anderson, A and Frideres, J (1981) *Ethnicity in Canada: Theoretical Perspectives*, Toronto: Butterworth.
Assembly of First Nations (1988) *Tradition and Education: Towards a Vision of our Future*, Ottawa: Assembly of First Nations.
Barman, J, Hebert, Y and McCaskill, D (eds) (1987a) *Indian Education in Canada, Volume 1: The Legacy*, Vancouver: University of British Columbia Press.
Barman, J, Hebert, Y and McCaskill, D (eds) (1987b) *Indian Education in Canada, Volume 2: The Challenge*, Vancouver: University of British Columbia Press.
Battiste, M and Barman, J (1995) *Indian Education in Canada, Volume 3: The Circle Unfolds*, Vancouver: University of British Columbia Press.
Bezeau, L (1989) *Educational Administration for Canadian Teachers*, Toronto: Copp Clark Pitman.

Bruno-Jofre, R (1993) *Issues in the History of Education in Manitoba*, Lewiston, New York: E Mellen Press.

Canada, Department of Indian and Northern Affairs (1969) Statement of the Government of Canada on Indian Policy, Ottowa: Indian Affairs.

Canada, House of Commons, (1971) *Debates*, 28th Parliament, 3rd Session, Vol. 8, 8546.

Cummins, J and Danesi, M (1990) *Heritage Languages: The Development and Denial of Canada's Linguistic Resources*, Toronto: Garamond Press.

Hawkins, J and La Belle, T (1985). *Education and Intergroup Relations: An International Perspective*, New York: Praeger.

Hawthorn, H (1966-67) *A Survey of the Contemporary Indians of Canada*, Ottowa: Queen's Printer.

Henley, R and Young, J (1990) 'Indian Education in Canada: Contemporary Issues', in Lam, Y (ed.) *The Canadian Public Education System,: Issues and Prospects*, Calgary: Detselig.

Kehoe, J and Mansfield, E (1993) 'The Limitations of Multicultural Education and Anti-Racist Education', in McLeod, K (ed.) *Multicultural Education: The State of the Art National Study, Report #1*, Toronto, Faculty of Education, University of Toronto.

Kirkness, V (1992) *First Nations and Schools: Triumphs and Struggles*, Toronto: Canadian Education Association, Toronto.

La Belle, T and White, P (1984) 'Education and Multi-Ethnic Integration: An Intergroup Relations Typology', in Hawkins, J and La Belle, T (eds) *Education and Intergroup Relations: An International Perspective*, New York: Praeger.

McAndrew, M (1995) 'Ethnicity, Multiculturalism, and Multicultural Education in Canada', in Ghosh, R and Ray, D (eds) *Social Change and Education in Canada* (3rd edn), Toronto: Harcourt Brace.

MacPherson, J (1991) *MacPherson Report on Tradition and Education: Towards a Vision of Our Future*, Ottowa: Indian and Northern Affairs Canada.

Mallea, J (1989) *Schooling in a Plural Canada*, Clevedon: Multilingual Matters.

Mallea, J and Young, J (1984) *Cultural Diversity and Canadian Education*, Ottowa: Carleton University Press.

Miller, J (1989) *Skyscrapers Hide the Heavens: A History of Indian–White Relations in Canada*, Toronto, University of Toronto Press.

Moodley, K (1995) 'Multicultural Education in Canada: Historical Development and Current Status', in Banks, J and Banks, C (eds) *Handbook of Research on Multicultural Education*, Berkeley: Macmillan.

National Indian Brotherhood (1972) *Indian Control of Indian Education*, Ottowa: The Brotherhood.

Nyce, D (1990) *Teachers-Plus: First Nations Teacher Education Programs in Canada*, Vancouver: First Nations House of Learning, University of British Columbia.

Ontario (1989) *Access! Task Force on Access to Professions and Trades in Ontario*, Toronto: Queen's Printer.

Orlikow, L and Young, J (1993) 'The Struggle for Change: Teacher Education in Canada', in Verma, G (ed.) *Inequality and Teacher Education: An International Perspective*, London: Falmer Press.

Palmer, H (1984) 'Reluctant Hosts: Anglo-Canadian Views of Multiculturalism in the Twentieth Century', in Mallea, J and Young, J (eds) *Cultural Diversity and Canadian Education*, Ottowa: Carleton University Press.

Riffel, J, Levein, B and Young, J (1996) 'Diversity in Canadian Education', *Educational Policy*, 20, 10.

Schermerhorn, R (1970) *Comparative Ethnic Relations: A Framework for Theory and Research*, New York: Random House.

Shapiro, B (1985) *The Report of the Commission on Private Schools in Ontario*, Toronto: Commission on Public Schools in Ontario.

Smith, J and Young, J (1996) 'Building an Anti-Racist School; The Story of Victor Mager School', in McLeod, K (ed.) *Multicultural Education: The State of the Art National Study, Report #3*, Toronto: Faculty of Education, University of Toronto.

Solomon, P (1995). 'Beyond Prescriptive Pedagogy: Teacher Inservice Education for Cultural Diversity', *Journal of Teacher Education*, 46, 4, 251–8.

Solomon, P (1996) 'Creating an Opportunity Structure for Blacks and Other Teachers of Colour', in Brathwaite, K and James, C (eds) *Educating African Canadians*, Toronto: Lorimer.

Statistics Canada (1993a) *The Nation: Ethnic Origin*, Catalogue 93–315, Ottowa: Statistics Canada.

Statistics Canada (1993b) *The Nation: Immigration and Citizenship*, Catalogue 93–316, Ottowa: Statistics Canada.

Statistics Canada (1994) *Report on the Demographic Situation in Canada*, Catalogue 91–209E, Ottowa: Statistics Canada.

Tator, C and Henry, F (1991) *Multicultural Education: Translating Policy into Practice*, Ottowa: Multiculturalism and Citizenship Canada.

# 11. Intercultural Education in France

Olivier Hinton

In our attempt to comment upon intercultural education in France or, as it turns out, the lack of it, certain aspects of the national educational system and the society in which it appeared are important. First of all, it must be stated that until recently the French education system was considered an unqualified success. It has always been openly meritocratic and, as such, selective. At first this selection took place within two streams, primary education for the masses and secondary education for the elite, but in the 1960s the systems finally merged (for a detailed description of the change to a single system see Prost, 1968).

The education system or *Education Nationale* was set up ten years after the defeat by the Prussians in 1871. It was widely accepted that the Prussian school teacher had won the war and therefore education for the nation of France, *la patrie*, was of paramount importance. It was created by Jules Ferry and a few close colleagues. The body of legislation establishing education is many-faceted and aspects such as its relation to the church and its schools were fiercely discussed at the time in the National Assembly and are the subject of many studies to this day. As we are reminded by Pierre Ognier (1988), though it only came into being a hundred years later, 'it is during the Revolution that the idea was born... that school is an essential tool in forging the unity of the state through an education with the same moral and civic values given to all' (p.32). Today we might wonder what defines the state, *la patrie* and hence the 'all' concerned, but in the 1880s it was 'revealed as a historical fact and a natural feeling' and it was also a 'fellowship of the souls' (Lécaud and Glay, 1934). The latter allowed for those in parts of the *patrie* which were not at the time part of France, as was the case for Alsace and parts of Lorraine until 1918, to be included in the grand design. In securing the *patrie* as a single entity, local customs and in particular all languages other than French were banned from school. It was not until 1951 that languages such as Breton were allowed to be taught in state schools though, and this is true to this day, only as an additional option and not used for teaching. This logic of assimilation applied to linguistic minorities in France also applied to the colonies. It was considered France's duty to herself and to others to expand its colonial empire and therefore spread civilization. Schools were acknowledged to be the medium for civilizing people and foremost among their aims was to ensure linguistic assimilation. Any indigenous person who learned French received a one-off bonus payment.

This will to assimilate at the heart of colonial policy is also at the centre of the republican democratic ideal that drove the people who established the educational system. The belief was that the Revolution had swept everything clean and that human beings had come of age thanks to it. What was needed in their time was a careful construction of the new age, built on reason. Schooling for all was a very important part of this and although at one level 'all' did mean humanity, in practice what was considered was France. One of the reasons why schooling for all could be considered was that, ever since Descartes, it was presumed that all had reason. By the end of the 19th century, people were absolutely convinced that reason, with the catalyst of education, could not only help in the advancement of science and technology but that reason also underpinned morality. The consequences were immense. First, there was no need for religious education at school because a lay republican morality was available; it was considered that religions had kidnapped this morality but that it was now free. Second, this morality, as it was daughter to reason, was automatically shared by all and as such was universal. One could hardly expect people who reasoned like this to have any leaning toward intercultural education and the relativism in values that it implies.

My point is that in a more diluted form and possibly unconsciously, this belief is very much alive today in France, including and perhaps particularly in the ranks of those linked to education. The system was built up in order to make all children the same or, at the very least, make sure they all spoke the same language, learned to love France, and helped to turn children into French women and men. The edifice still stands and in the new contract for schools of September 1994, the minister pinpointed the command of French as the most fundamental task in the fight against inequality (Ministere de l'Éducation Nationale, 1994). In the same document, the paragraph about diversity does not mention ethnic or linguistic diversity but relates to the different streams in secondary education designed to account for the students' varying 'problems, demands, rhythms, wants, needs' (p.7). In fact, in the whole document, no mention is made of the different cultural traditions of the children attending school.

Published slightly earlier the same year is an official report on the schooling of immigrants' children (Bocquet, 1994) which openly states that today's school has to do for the one million foreign children in its midst what it did for the young Bretons, Alsaciens, Occitans and Savoyards previously. It must integrate them into 'the nation, the republic'; this integration is not only economic, social and cultural but also implies the 'sharing of common values', those presumably shared by all endowed with reason. In quoting this report, mention has been made of one million foreigners; this corresponds to the people who do not have French nationality. This group is much smaller than the numbers who belong to ethnic minorities, the vast majority of whom have

French nationality automatically by virtue of being born in France. There is no way of counting their numbers as they are not recognized as different.

When one looks at what special education is available in France for the needs of migrant children, one discovers that the first measures were taken in the 1970s; that was the first time it was considered that the large numbers of migrant children in schools called for specific action to be taken. One might be tempted to say that for the first time foreigners were considered to be a problem, and this just at the time when France came to the end of the economic boom that followed the Second World War. Not surprisingly, given the system, the first reaction was to promote the learning of French in special classes known as CLIN (initiation class) in primary schools and CLAD (adaptation class) in secondary schools. These classes still exist and their explicit aim is to bring children up to the required level of French as fast as is possible so that they can enter the mainstream classes. It is interesting to note that, since being in separate classes would go against one of the fundamentals of French education, ie, equality of treatment for all, children attending CLIN or CLAD are administratively speaking registered in the normal class for their age, and that they are only part of a CLIN or a CLAD pedagogically speaking. In the aforementioned report on the schooling of migrant children, these classes are condemned for having never lived up to their expectation and for not fulfilling the needs of the children they were created to help: 'a totally unadapted pedagogy... serious slips such as the inclusion of French children, keeping the children in these classes whereas they were meant to be transitory, the risk of creating ghettos' (p.3).

A further step was taken in the 1970s with the so-called intercultural approach. It might be worth pointing out that despite Michele Tournier's attempt (in Adams and Turner, 1992) at separating them, multicultural and intercultural have tended to be used interchangeably. The ELCO – teaching of the language and culture of origin – classes are the result of bilateral agreements between France and some of the major immigration countries. In order to qualify, children have to be nationals of one of the participating countries: Portugal since 1973, Italy and Tunisia 1974, Spain and Morocco 1975, Yugoslavia 1977, Turkey 1978, and Algeria 1981. The nationality clause limits the numbers concerned since children born in France are French nationals but do not necessarily inherit their parents' nationality. It is the consulates of the countries concerned that have to bear the cost of the teaching, but they have the freedom to choose the teachers, who can be French, and the curriculum. This applies to primary school children for three hours a week (a ninth of the teaching time) but these classes have only come into existence where sufficient numbers of one nationality are concentrated to make the classes feasible.

The same arrangement also exists outside school hours for both primary and secondary school children up to a maximum of three hours a week. As the aforementioned report noted (p.3), 'the extent of this set-up remains very limited' – 20 years after the signing of the first agreement. It also points out that the language in the ELCO, being the official national language of the country, is not always the one of the home, for example Arabic as opposed to Kabyl. Furthermore, it is also said that this measure was never really accepted or even, in its opinion, acceptable. This is not surprising: trying to graft onto a system that prides itself on the equality of treatment it gives to all children even the weakest form of interculturalism was doomed to failure because it smacks of heresy. Surprisingly, given how little good is said about all these measures, they are still in existence today in parallel with the ZEP, to which we shall come later. The most obvious explanation for this is that they ensure that France satisfies the requirements of Directive 77/486 of the Commission of European Communities on the education of children of migrant workers.

In the early 1980s the spread of the heresy was halted and the zones of educational priority, or ZEP, were brought into being. As zones they are geographical so the emphasis is now on an area that is underachieving in school results rather than on specific populations. The fact that within ZEPs there might be a high percentage of migrant children is due to their being from the less favoured socio-economic classes and that the language spoken at home might not be French; it is not linked to the fact they are migrants. In other words, the specific problem of immigration has disappeared, to be replaced with the age-old problem of integrating certain minorities. These zones, often in the suburbs of industrial towns, are the new Brittany, Alsace and Savoy. The benefits of being made into a ZEP are linked to slightly increased budgets which allow for smaller classes and more staff being employed for the security of both children and teachers.

One is tempted to say that after a few hesitations the system has adopted a policy which is coherent with its fundamental nature. The problem is that the certainty on which the system of assimilation stood, from which it derived its legitimacy and effectiveness, has disappeared. No French politician stands up to say that the best thing that can happen is to be made French and that the national education system is designed for that purpose. On the contrary, the European Directive on the education of children of migrant workers guarantees, among other things, 'promoting the teaching of migrants' mother tongues and culture' (Adams and Turner, 1992). This seems to be incompatible with the will to have all children share in the same values.

The same report (Adams and Turner, 1992) reckons that this Directive came to life because, 'European bodies began to see migrants not just as workers from the third world, but as members of communities taking up residence in one of the EC member states' (p.10). I would argue that in France, you are either French or foreign, and migrants and some of their children are the latter, whereas their younger offspring, born in France, are the former and are therefore not part of any minority. It is only recently that the expression *jeunes issus de l'immigration* has appeared in the press and it seems to be the closest you get to a concept of ethnic or cultural minority, but it has not found its way into official educational discourse, as in the eyes of the law and of the EU they are French children. How in such a system could you conceive of intercultural education? In fact, when certain organized groups ask for specific treatment they are accused of *particularisme* (wanting to be particular). Many readers will have heard of the storm created by the girls who wanted to wear the Islamic veil at school; it proved totally unacceptable and the few girls who refused to take it off after being told to do so by the courts remain banned from school and are taught at home.

The system is certainly at a cross-roads, some authors say a crisis. For the time being it is reaffirming its fundamental beliefs in identical education for all with selection according to ability. The old meritocratic ideal still stands, slightly diluted in that vain attempts are being made to add to the perceived value of the technical and vocational branches entered when there has been a failure in the mainstream system. As the *jeunes issus de l'immigration* swell the ranks of these low-status streams or drop out of education completely, will it always be possible to account for this in terms of social milieu rather than in terms of ethnic and cultural differences? In the 19th century it was clearly expressed that some cultures were inferior to others and had to go for the good of those in them and for the good of France. Because this cannot be said today, failure at school cannot be linked to culture, which would imply that culture's inferiority; rather it has to be linked to social class because it is still acceptable to say that working-class kids need more help than those of the middle classes.

The situation is different from the 1890s in another important aspect. The *jeunes issus de l'immigration* might consider themselves French but they see themselves as different from the other French and have various ways of making themselves heard, from specific slang to demonstrations and riots. Should one of the latter appear, they are *jeunes des banlieux*, so the problem is geographical and social and the ZEPs are the appropriate educational answer to the social problems leading to these disturbances. I am not claiming that riots are linked to ethnic minority status but am trying to point out that groups of people are not conceptualized as ethnic or cultural minorities, so the whole issue of intercultural education is buried within the social problems of certain areas.

France does not have intercultural education. It does however have what is considered an excellent school system: except in cases where the choice of a religious school is paramount, it is the lower achievers who are sent to private school. It is also believed that no small reason for its excellence is its refusal to see any difference between children save on the grounds of ability. The fact that the original system of the forebears rested on two splits, masses/elite and male/female, has been totally removed from the present day myth and can therefore not be used to justify any modern equivalent to these splits (for an analysis of the contrast between the myth and reality, see Nique and Lelievre, 1993). Seeing the migrants as no different apart from the fact that they might need bringing up to speed in French is therefore an odd reaction, possibly a racist one. France does however have social problems linked to a slowing economy and growing unemployment and it is addressing these problems with the ZEPs in education.

The debate currently occurring in France concerning civic education, sheds further light on the expected results of school education. When interviewed on the subject, Luc Ferry, president of the National Council for the Curriculum, states that 'certain values must be transmitted by the state and others not' (Ferry, 1996). He adds that France as a lay republic must stay out of religious and political quarrels and to a certain extent moral ones. But *only* to a certain extent, for there are some fundamental values linked to the very idea of the republic, and the lay State 'cannot [for example] remain indifferent to the question of racism or the equality of the sexes'. Needless to say, given the status of women in certain religious and cultural traditions, this throws the state into some of the very quarrels it claims it wants to stay out of. 'Universalism, the dignity of the human person, etc... [which] stem from the very essence of the republican ideal' must be taught in French state schools, and these principles are paramount. Private morality in general and religion in particular are acceptable only within the framework of these principles. Any intercultural education in France would be bound by what are considered acceptable values in the eye of the Republic. Cultural relativism is possible only within these boundaries; anything outside is wrong and would have to be presented in school as unacceptable in a civilized society.

## References

Adams, A and Turner, K (eds) (1992) *The Changing European Classroom: Multi-cultural Schooling and the New Europe*, Cambridge: Department of Education, University of Cambridge.

Bocquet, J (1994) 'La Scolarisation des Enfants d'Immigrés', *Journal Officiel de la République Francaise*, No. 17, Avis et rapports du conseil economic et social. Paris: Ministere de l'Éducation Nationale.

Circulaire No. 86–119 , 13 March 1986, *Bulletin Officiel*, No. 13, 3 April 1986. Paris: Ministere de l'Éducation Nationale.

Commission of the European Communities (1984) *Report from the Commission to the Council on the implementation of directive 77/486/EEC on the education of the children of migrant workers*, Brussels: EC.

Ferry, L (1996) Interview in *Le Monde de L'Education*, 235, March 1996, 36–7.

Lécaud, A and Glay, E (1934) *L'Ecole Primaire en France*, 2 vols. Paris: La cité Francaise.

Ministere de l'Éducation Nationale (1994) *Le nouveau contrat pour l'école, 158 décisions*, Paris: Ministere de l'Éducation Nationale.

Nique, A and Lelievre, C (1993) *La République n'éduquera plus. La fin du mythe Ferry*, Paris: Plon.

Ognier, P (1988) *L'école républicaine francaise et ses miroirs*, Geneva: Peter Lang.

Prost, A (1968) *L'enseignement en France 1800–1967*, Paris: Armand Colin.

# 12. Intercultural Education in India

Tapas Majumdar

## Introduction

India will remain arguably the world's largest cultural conglomeration as a nation state at the beginning of the 21st century. Not surprisingly, for that very reason, it will also have to face one of the world's biggest challenges: how to first devise, and then carry out, a wide-ranging national education policy for the whole country that could provide a valid and at the same time interculturally acceptable curricular agenda for all the sections of the population.

The basic problem that India will have to face in the sphere of intercultural education in the coming decade is that the venture must prove itself operationally manageable as it takes into its ambit a vast population that has gone on developing unevenly over time, not only educationally and culturally but also economically. That this large and varied population continues to show quite unmistakable signs of a strong and abiding attachment to the norms of a federal democratic political structure provides an additional dimension to the issue of intercultural education in India. By any standards, it seems India's organizational task in this field in the coming years, particularly if one considers the level of basic education, will possibly prove to be far more arduous than what almost any other country will have to face.

Among the larger countries with multilingual and multicultural populations, both Russia and China have already encountered situations broadly of the kind that India will have to face. In fact, until quite recently the extent of intercultural education covered by what was then the Soviet Union was possibly larger than what used to be covered by India, in terms of both variety and content. As for China, it always had larger numbers to deal with in the aggregate, having been the only country whose vast population had consistently outnumbered India's, at least up to the last decade of this century.

Two facts of contemporary history may be recalled here – one very visible and of truly global dimensions, and the other not yet widely noticed even within the more modest Asian context. Both facts, however, have altered significantly India's relative position in the intercultural league, placing it ahead of both the Russian Federation and China in terms at least of the size of the problem that these countries are expected to have to contend with in the coming decades.

The first fact is that the disintegration of the Soviet Union has apparently given Russia a more monolithic cultural profile, at least in the perception of many third world countries. Having shed much of its Islamic and Asiatic subcultures, the Russian Federation of today, though remaining demographically a multicultural nation state, is nevertheless quite discernibly white, Christian and almost altogether of the west. Not that this shift in the cultural balance needs to be seen as necessarily contrived. But the result of the great change surely has been that the intercultural problems in education seem to remain for Russia more as headaches to worry about than as challenges. In any case, it no longer looks likely that India would find many positive lessons to learn from the colossal Soviet experiments of the past in the intercultural education of that very diverse cluster of nations that history had somehow held together for so long.

Less spectacular, but for the future of Asia rather more consequential, has been the way the Indian population has been growing over the years, compared to the populations of other developing countries, particularly China. The total population of India at the last count (GIRGO, 1992) was nearly 844 million as of 1 March 1991. China's population, counted a little earlier, as of 1 July 1990, stood at 1.16 billion. So far as the total population is concerned, India is still behind China, though it continues to grow faster.

For assessing the educational needs of the people, the numbers that are really important are not those that refer to the aggregate population of any country. What really count are the numbers in the age group 5–14 years, for these are the children for whom school places have to be found and the educational inputs provided. And it is in terms of these numbers that India has already caught up with China. It is currently estimated that the number of children in the age group 5–14 years will be 232 million in the year 2000 in India, compared to China's estimated 230 million.

In other words, India's system of education must now prepare to cater for the world's largest population in the relevant age group. It is mind-boggling to think that this vast student population also belongs to nearly 20 different main language groups, almost each endowed with a script of its own, and drawn from almost all the major religions of the world.

## Religion and intercultural education

To give an example of the numerical magnitude of the diversity of the Indian population in terms of religion alone, one may recall that though Hinduism happens to be the creed of the majority of Indians, the Muslim minority actually constitutes the largest Muslim community in the world outside only Indonesia. Every linguistic group in the country has a sizeable Muslim community. Similarly, every linguistic group contains a much smaller but equally vibrant Christian community.

In many cases the cultural and educational needs of a religious minority within a linguistic group are subtly distinct and the fine distinctions are often cherished and sought to be protected, not only by that minority but also by the entire society. The basic educational and cultural rights of the religious and linguistic minorities in the states of India are recognized in the Indian Constitution itself, which lays down the broad parameters for the pursuit of intercultural education in the country. One must remember though that the gap between societal intention and the actual outcomes of high-sounding policy has often been allowed to remain unconscionably large in the social sector in India, the sphere of education being no exception.

## Constitutional provisions for the right to education

The Indian Constitution came into force in 1950, nearly three years after independence. It codified six fundamental rights for the Indian people, among which the right to freedom of religion (Articles 25–8) guaranteed that every citizen could practise and propagate the religion of his or her choice. The citizens could also form religious bodies or institutions and run them for their own religious and educational purposes.

The fundamental rights also include the cultural and educational rights of the religious or linguistic minority communities in each state (Articles 29–30). A minority community has the right to keep its own language, script, literature and culture.

The Supreme Court of India has held in several recent public interest litigation cases that from these fundamental rights also flows the right to education. By implication, the latter would also encompass the right to education in an intercultural milieu.

Apart from the fundamental rights, which are legally binding, the Constitution of India also lays down a set of directive principles of state policy. A violation of the directive principles by a state authority, however, is not held to be 'justiciable' in the sense that a public interest litigant cannot go to court over it. But the directive principles are nevertheless powerful guidelines in terms of which, as the Supreme Court has ruled in several instances, even the fundamental rights have to be interpreted.

One directive principle which is provided by the celebrated Article 45 of the Constitution says that 'the state shall strive to provide free and compulsory education for all children up to the age of fourteen years'. It had for long been generally understood that Article 45 actually provided an escape clause to the state by only enjoining that it shall 'strive'. To this extent, therefore, the right to a kind of education that would be in accord with one's culture, language (and script) seemed obviously circumscribed by Article 45. A heartening recent trend in the development of Indian democracy, however, seems to have given new hopes to social activists trying to secure in full the educational and cultural rights envisaged in the Constitution for all the children of India. This new trend is being hailed (and in certain quarters feared) as the advent of 'judicial activism'. For the first time the higher judiciary of India (consisting of the Supreme Court and the state High Courts) is calling into question acts of commission as well as omission by various state authorities including the ones (such as the Election Commission of India) that enjoy considerable protection under the Indian Constitution.

A landmark judgement delivered by the Supreme Court in 1992 on a writ petition against the State of Andhra Pradesh (one of the major states of India) for the enforcement of the right to education may be cited as one of the early instances of judicial activism in India. It is in this case that the Supreme Court decided that the right to education flowed from the fundamental rights. It also had decided that though this right appeared circumscribed by Article 45, it was open to the judiciary to accept or reject the contention that the state could be truthfully described as 'striving', but conspicuously failing, even after four decades of such striving had passed, to provide free and compulsory education to all the children up to 14 years of age.

One likely consequence of the Supreme Court's pronouncements on the right to education is that the greater emphasis of intercultural education policy will now be placed on the education of children in the age group 5–14 years as envisaged in the Constitution. Since such education has to be both free and compulsory, the cost implication of delivering it through the medium of at least the 18 major languages so far given recognition in the Eighth Schedule of the Constitution would clearly be enormous. The number, in fact, would rise to 19 if English, the associate official language at the centre and a medium of instruction in nearly all Indian states, is also counted. Apart from these 19, there would be perhaps two dozen more, as will be seen below, each of which would deserve to be recognized either on the Eighth Schedule or at any rate regionally as an official language and a medium of instruction by some of the states.

## Different languages and different religions

Because of the rise of judicial activism in India referred to above, the Indian children's right to education in a multicultural setting, indirectly conceded by the provisions of the Constitution itself, can now be expected to be enforced more and more through future court decisions. Such expectation will have an obvious implication for national education policy too. The emphasis in it from now on has to be very much more on what concerns the educational needs of the children than what may be needed to satisfy the cultural aspirations of the adults.

At the children's level, the first question to decide about the mode of delivery of the curriculum is invariably that of choosing the appropriate medium of instruction. The cultural divide that would be of greater import for educational policy in that case would be linguistic rather than religious, even though religion is such an obtrusively divisive factor in Indian society. This does not imply that religion does not play an important part in determining the issues of intercultural education in India. It is only that at the level of basic education – and that level is basic in many senses – the religious factor asserts itself in education mainly through raising the question of which language to use.

Thus the Muslims in many Indian states prefer to have Urdu (both the language and its Arabic-based script) as the medium of instruction for children. In the same way, in several north-eastern states where the dominant populations are both tribal and Christian, people will have English (usually in addition to the respective tribal languages) as an associate language and use the Roman alphabet for their languages rather than the script of any regional Indian language derived from Sanskrit, like Hindi or Assamese, conceivably because of classical Sanskrit's perceived Hindu association.

## The language question and federal polity

The medium of instruction should ideally be, but in India often is not, the mother tongue of the child. In many cases the problem of providing a package of interculturally valid education to the child simply reduces to mainly transmitting more or less the same (or academically equivalent) curricular content in as many languages (and scripts) as possible. This needs centralized effort and large resources.

Within each linguistic group, however, the special features of different religious sub-groups often require special treatment for which mainly a more localized approach at the level of the states or even the districts may be found more effective.

The Constitution of India provides for a federal structure. In the distribution of powers under the Constitution, education, particularly school education, had originally been made only a state subject and it remained that way for many years. Even though an amendment of the Constitution in the mid-1970s had put education on its concurrent list of subjects for both the centre and the states, the bulk of government expenditure on school education still comes out of the state budgets.

More recently, in 1993, the federal structure of the Indian polity has been extended further by the 73rd and the 74th Amendments of the Constitution that have placed school education as a subject on the list for the village and the municipal local governments too. The Constitutional Amendments of 1993 have placed the responsibility for providing school education on the governments at all the three levels – the centre, the state and the district. The district level of government is itself made up of a three-tier structure comprising the village at the base, a group of villages (or a 'block') in the middle, and the district at the top.

The three-tier structure of local self-government has been called the Panchayati Raj. The Panchayat, incidentally, was the old village government of India, an institution that Gandhi greatly admired and had wanted modern India to reinstate. It is undeniable that India's comprehensive failure to operationalize Article 45 and provide free and compulsory education to all children has been mainly due to its inability to activate effort at the village level, the level that Gandhi had always considered crucial for even the survival of the Indian polity.

## India's linguistic divides – the Eighth Schedule and beyond

We have already said that the linguistic barriers constitute a major obstacle to the presentation of a more or less academically equivalent curriculum to all the school children of India. In this section we present a few facts to indicate how astonishingly difficult the language question is to cope with, particularly at the school level.

Since education appears on the concurrent list, the constitutional provisions discussed above apply to governments at the central as well as the state, and now local governments at the Panchayat level too. But the operational impacts of these provisions are naturally not the same at each level. For the centre, for example, the macroeconomic implication of having to provide the free and compulsory education of children that was enjoined by Article 45 of the Constitution could be the most crucial consideration. Similarly, making provisions for the minority institutions and the use of local language in the delivery of the curriculum may be of far greater concern at the state or the district levels. For the same reason, even the linguistic divides that separate the school children of India do not appear the same when seen from the centre and locally.

The first problem that arises in listing the languages of India, in any case, is definitional: what is the difference between one's regional language and one's mother tongue? The difference, officially speaking, turns out to be simply enormous in the Indian context. The most respected list of Indian languages is, of course, the one that appears on the Eighth Schedule of the Constitution of India. To be on the Eighth Schedule is an important measure of success for an Indian language, for then its speakers can claim the protection of the centre as a separate cultural community and, wherever it happens to be a minority group, it can also claim all the benefits of the fundamental cultural and educational rights guaranteed by the Constitution that have been mentioned in the preceding section.

There is also a serious political aspect to the question as to whether a language should or should not be included in the Eighth Schedule. Ever since the boundaries of the states of India were allowed to be redrawn on a linguistic basis, many new states were created out of the old Provinces and the Native States of British times. Quite understandably, constitutional recognition given to a separate language almost invariably raises hopes for a separate state – the cases of Sindhi, the language of refugees from Sind in Pakistan, and of course classical Sanskrit, being obvious exceptions. By contrast the idea of a separate mother tongue, if unrecognized as an Eighth Schedule language, carries no political overtones at the all-India level, though that too may have an explosive connotation within a state.

The Census of India 1971 (GIRGO, 1975) recorded more than 3,000 mother tongues as declared by the informant households. This stupendous number is possibly somewhat misleading. There could have been a substantial exaggeration in the counting, since the households were left free to name their mother tongues just as they liked, and very often the same mother tongue might have been given a different name. Moreover, the majority of declared mother tongues were found to have only a handful of speakers each.

Even so, the number of mother tongues spoken by, say, not less than half a million people each would be quite enormous in India. The 1971 Census listed as many as 33 Indian languages that were mother tongues for more than one million people each. The names of all these languages are fairly well known to most educated Indians, and their rich and varied literatures are important components of the fabric of modern Indian culture. But almost half of these languages are not on the Eighth Schedule. Table 12.1 lists the 18 languages currently on the Schedule. Of these, Hindi is actually a collection of several affine languages of Northern India all using the Hindi script, several of which (like Magadhi and Maithili) have rich literatures of their own and are populous enough to have been included in the 1971 Census list of languages referred to above. Hindi, of course, is also the official language of India, along with English which enjoys the status of an associate official language and a medium of instruction in most states.

**Table 12.1**   *Languages listed on the Eighth Schedule of the Constitution of India and the number of speakers of the languages (in millions) as recorded in the Census of India 1981* *

| Language | Number of speakers |
| --- | --- |
| Hindi | 264.2 |
| Telegu | 54.2 |
| Bengali | 51.5 |
| Marathi | 49.6 |
| Tamil | 44.7 |
| Urdu | 0.3 |
| Gujarati | 33.2 |

| | |
|---|---|
| Kannada | 26.9 |
| Malayalam | 26.0 |
| Oriya | 22.9 |
| Punjabi | 18.6 |
| Kashmiri | 3.2 |
| Sindhi | 1.9 |
| Assamese | no census taken |
| Sanskrit | 0.003 |

* Recent additions to the Eighth Schedule (since the Seventy-first Amendment of the Constitution in 1992) have been the languages of Konkani, Manipuri and Nepali. Source: GIRGO (1985).

There are also a large number of Indian languages, many of which are tribal languages (not dialects) that may not be on the Eighth Schedule or even among the 33 most populous, but are recognized as official languages in many states on account of their local importance. In a tribal belt stretching over West Bengal and Bihar, for example, live the Santhals (population: 3.7 million in the 1971 Census and included in the list of 33) whose language Santhali has been officially recognized as medium of instruction in these two major states.

In fact, in some of the smaller states, all situated in Eastern India, not one of the Eighth Schedule languages originally listed by the Constitution used to be either spoken by the people or accorded acceptance as an official language of the state. These states were Arunachal Pradesh, Manipur, Mizoram, Nagaland and Sikkim where, in addition to English, the official languages are Nissi/Dafla, Adi, Nepali and Wancho (Arunachal Pradesh); Manipuri (Manipur); Mizo (Mizoram); Ao, Konyak, Angami and Sema (Nagaland); Bhutia, Lepcha, Limboo and Nepali (Sikkim). Basic education of children in these parts of the country was almost inconceivable unless it was imparted through these languages. The absurdity of the situation has only slightly been diminished recently by the Seventy-first Amendment of the Constitution in 1992 which put Nepali on the Eighth Schedule (after prolonged agitation by the ethnic Nepalis) and, less controversially, Manipuri. The other Indian language that also made it to the Eighth Schedule through the Seventy-first Amendment was Konkani in Western India.

Against the almost stunningly variegated linguistic background one may be surprised to find that the Constitution of India has up till now had only 18 Indian languages on the Eighth Schedule. Whatever might have been the political compulsions behind an obvious national consensus in the decision to keep the Eighth Schedule relatively small, there are at least two other considerations that should be mentioned before concluding this chapter.

The first consideration is that of the total numbers that were already covered by the languages of the Eighth Schedule as it stood. It will be obvious from Table 12.1 that the number was very large even in 1981. In fact, 1981 Census figures showed that the Eighth Schedule, which then had 15 instead of the present 18 languages on it, already accounted for nearly 96% of India's population.

There is, of course, always an ominous ring to the 'overwhelming numbers' argument in a democracy. But whatever may be the political connotations, even from the point of view of the sheer economics of managing programmes delivered through too many languages at the central level, there would be a case for restricting the size of the Eighth Schedule. Surely, if not just the 18 or 19, but actually perhaps twice that number of languages had to be taken care of by the centre, then every time a large enough central scheme with a wide enough spread (such as, for example, the highly promising National Open School programme now under way) had to be sponsored, the entire education system would tend to break down.

The second consideration is that of the greater relevance of the state-level – sometimes even the district-level – initiatives in fine-tuning a system of intercultural education. The true Gandhian advocate of the decentralized statecraft may want government to be both downsized and structured down to the village level – mainly for the sake of following an excellent idea! India's amazing cultural and linguistic diversity, however, may well make that particular mode of democracy soon appear not merely as an end in itself but also, pragmatically, the only plausible means of dispensing education to possibly the largest multicultural society of the 21st century.

# References

Brass, P R (1974) *Language, Religion and Politics in North India*, Cambridge: Cambridge University Press.

Brass, P R (1994) *The Politics of India since Independence* (2nd edn), Cambridge: Cambridge University Press.

Government of India (1992) *The Constitution (Seventy-first Amendment) Act, 1992*, Delhi.

Government of India (1993) *The Constitution (Seventy-third Amendment) Act, 1993*, Delhi.

Government of India (1993) *The Constitution (Seventy-fourth Amendment) Act, 1993*, Delhi.

Government of India Ministry of Education (1966) *Education and National Development: Report of the Education Commission*, Delhi.

Government of India Registrar General Office (GIRGO) (1975) *Census of India 1971*, Delhi.

GIRGO (1985) *Census of India 1981*, Delhi.

GIRGO (1992) *Census of India 1991*, Delhi.

Government of India Ministry of Human Resource Development (GIMHRD) (1986) *National Policy on Education, 1986*, Delhi.

GIMHRD (1992) *Programme of Action, 1992*, Delhi.

Sathe, S P (1991) 'Secularism, Law and the Constitution of India', in Gore, M S (ed.) *Secularism in India*, India: Indian Academy of Social Sciences.

# 13. Intercultural Education in Israel

Leslie Bash

## Introduction

This chapter provides a perspective on intercultural education in Israel based upon the interpretations of the outsider. While there might be a claim that this brings a semblance of objectivity to social analysis, this claim will not be pursued since I admit to a degree of partiality. This is to be found in a committed cultural identity: a Diaspora Jew, raised in a Zionistically-oriented synagogue community, who has travelled to Israel on a number of occasions and has long-standing kinship and other personal connections in that country. However, this chapter does not aim to offer the kind of in-depth examination of issues based upon a widespread knowledge of Israeli education gained from having worked in the system over a long period. It is, essentially, a view from abroad where thoughts on Israel are mediated by reflections on other situations of intercultural complexity, such as the diversity which characterizes the metropolitan landscapes of the UK and the seemingly insoluble case of Northern Ireland.

At the same time, such a perspective is informed by social theory and educational practice which has given rise to the articulation of a host of issues and questions relating to diversity, power, inequality, and international relations. One important focus may be the interrelations between Israel and the 'Arab world', including the West Bank, and between Jews and Arabs with Israeli citizenship. Or, attention may be drawn to religious diversity and ensuing tensions amongst the Jewish population as well as between Jews, Muslims, Christians, Druze and others. Further complexities may be perceived in relation to issues of ethnic identity and language – and in relation to permeating socio-economic and gender divisions. The educational questions which might follow cluster around conventional notions of assimilation, integration and segregation, and the policy implications might be viewed in relation to institutional organization and curriculum.

Israel is accordingly characterized by what appears to be a fundamental contradiction: officially defined as a Jewish state, supposedly identified by a singular culture but, in reality, challenged by variants within that culture – and by others who would either seek to add a culturally diverse dimension, or by those who would challenge its very legitimacy. As a specifically Jewish state, Israel might have been expected to have experienced significant difficulties from its foundation in being able to accommodate non-Jewish cultures. It is a fact that the Law of Return gives the right of Jews in the Diaspora to live in Israel and to be Israeli citizens while denying the rights of Arab families who had left the country, whether voluntarily or coercively, in the wake of the War of Independence. On the other hand, once the borders of the state achieved *de facto* and *de jure* recognition, those remaining within those borders gained Israeli citizenship. A tension has thus ensued between the pluralistic reality of Israel, albeit against a backcloth of a Jewish majority, and a monocultural ideal which itself is beset with difficulties. It is these difficulties which now merit some degree of analysis.

## Zionism, modernism and traditionalism

Any assessment of the relations between the different communities in Israel, as well as relations between neighbouring states, needs to be undertaken against the background of an analysis of Zionism and its inherent tensions. At the heart of Zionist ideology has been the view that:

> the course of Jewish history must be reversed and the familiar patterns of Jewish life in the Dispersion must be transformed. The exile must be ended, the Diaspora wholly or largely wound up. (Vital, 1979, p.309)

Stated as such, this has provided the *raison d'être* for the establishment of Israel as a Jewish state. Technically, the state of Israel is an international creation, not exactly as intended by the United Nations in 1947, since the recognized borders are the outcome of war and the subsequent armistice in 1948. Prior to independence, the land over which Israel has sovereignty had been a focus for immigration and occupation by large numbers of individuals, groups and imperialist nation-states. Many would wish to refer back to the Biblical era and certainly, at around the time of Christ, it was evident that Palestine, as it was then known, was inhabited by a diverse population whose geographical origins were widely dispersed. Already a Jewish diaspora had begun to form beyond Palestine and its immediate neighbours, while the indigenous Jewish people was composed of many different elements, having incorporated numerous tribes over centuries. This was reflected in the linguistic changes which took place, with Aramaic supplanting Hebrew as the *lingua franca* of the Jews, soon followed by Greek with the addition of Latin as a consequence of Roman occupation.

Following conflict with the Roman occupiers, the Jewish population dispersed to different regions of Europe and beyond. It is at this time that the idea of re-establishing the Jewish nation gained a firm hold within religious tradition. For the last two millennia, an eventual return to *Eretz Yisrael* has been embodied in the liturgy, with a particular focus during the Passover festival where, at the *Seder* service in the home, those present will intone the words, 'Next year in Jerusalem!' Yet, it should also be noted that notions of return are rooted in Jewish Biblical history which pre-date the Roman occupation and the fall of the Second Temple in AD 70, with, for example, the invoking of the exodus from Egypt, and the Babylonian and Persian exiles.

There is little doubt that this almost permanent emphasis upon return in Jewish religious tradition has played an important role in the Zionism of the 19th and 20th centuries but it was not, in reality, the basis of the ideology. As Jewish populations took root in the regions of the Diaspora, such proto-Zionism, in a religious sense, remained largely symbolic rather than a political aspiration. Contemporary Zionism was essentially the outcome of other factors.

The generally accepted argument is that it was not tradition but modernity which gave the spur to this essentially *European* Jewish political movement. At the same time, it was also perceived as revolutionary and romantic, both a product of the Enlightenment and the process of Jewish emancipation – and a reaction to some of the consequences of emancipation. With the destruction of the ghetto and wholly segregated existence in western Europe,

> Antisemitism replaced anti-Judaism when the rejection of Jewish culture confined to the *shtetls* of Eastern Europe gave way to fear of the emancipated Jew who was identified with the universalism of science, trade and art. (Touraine, 1995, p.138)

Accordingly, modern Zionism was largely the intellectual product of emancipated Jewry who, apparently, perceived this ideology as a response to a world which articulated their suspicions of a people not for their separateness but rather for the opposite – their ability to assimilate. Touraine's comment is persuasive because it focuses upon deep fears grounded in the very structure and basis of broad European Christian culture. This culture, in its variant forms, derives from the legitimation of Christianity as a distinct universal religion precisely because it had not only broken the tie with Judaism – it manifested itself in important respects as anti-Jewish (illustrated by the consequences of the conversion/apostasy of Paul of Tarsus).

Zionism positioned itself as a political ideology specifically to attract Jews who might otherwise turn to various brands of socialism and liberalism as answers to disadvantage, deprivation and unemployment. In this latter respect, Marxism rapidly became the dominant influence within central and eastern European social democratic parties, promising universal emancipation from the consequences of an inequitable economic system. However, for many Jews, the universalism of Marxist ideology was illusory, since the class perspective failed to take account of their unique historical position: emancipation was therefore to be viewed in particularistic terms. The General League of Jewish Workingmen in Lithuania, Poland and Russia (The Bund) established in 1897, sought to effect political change along socialist lines while preserving a sense of Jewish national (if not religious) identity, since 'Jewish workers suffer not only as workers but also as Jews' (Kochan, 1976, p.270). Ultimately, though, the Bund's main consequence was to cement collective identity among secularized Jews rather than significant political change; in this way, it was but a short step to Zionism – the recognition that separate territorial existence was the sole answer to persecution.

At issue has been the claim by many Jews to the status of a nation and, moreover, a nation which is geographically located in the area occupied by present-day Israel. Yet the relationship with the land is by no means uncontested within the broad spectrum of Zionism. (There were some, including Theodore Herzl, the generally acknowledged founder of modern Zionism, who considered the possibility of territory other than that of Palestine as a Jewish 'homeland', notably in east Africa, although this was eventually rejected.) Paradoxically, it was the left-leaning secularism of the early Zionists which placed value on a distinctive space for Jewish rebirth, as the antithesis of the ghetto. Kochan (1992, pp.36–7) cites those Marxist Zionists who considered that a nation needed a specific territorial base for the class struggle to be waged successfully. Both ghettoization and assimilation denied Jews the normality of modern life with its secular social, economic and political structures, whereas the realization of Zionism meant that Jews could participate in its totality – as workers, as professionals, as leaders, etc. It was this that became the core belief of modern Zionism.

In practical terms, the Zionist project became reflected in the establishment of autonomous Jewish collective organizations in Ottoman-ruled Palestine. Of significance were those concerned with education and, indeed, the Jewish school system of contemporary Israel arose in part from provision in the late 19th and early 20th centuries from community organizations such as the Alliance Israélite Universelle of Paris and the Hilfsverein der Deutschen Juden of Berlin, and in part from the collective efforts of Jewish teachers (Hebrew Teachers' Association) with the objective of creating 'a new Hebrew culture and terminology' (Kleinberger, 1969, p.31).

## Israel – intercultural mapping through time and space

Whichever political stance might be taken, the idea that this turbulent region of the world might experience permanent stability appeared, in 1996, a distinct possibility within a relatively short space of time. The notion that Muslim Arab nation-states could enter into a normal relationship with a country, historically viewed by them as an occidental interloper which had expropriated the land and property of the 'indigenous' population, might soon become a reality. Yet, peace may simply denote the absence of war and open conflict; perhaps, more positively, it may also herald increased economic cooperation and development. What may be more difficult to achieve is the breaking down of cultural barriers between peoples, since there are sufficient obstacles to its attainment even within the borders of Israel itself.

There is a temptation to descend into cliché, when dealing with Israel, and to characterize the country as a microcosm of the world. The three major monotheistic religions lay claim to the country as a spiritual home (as well as those less well-known, such as the Druze and Samaritan sects and the more recent, such as Bahaism); its population comprises first, second and third generations and beyond from all parts of Europe, north and south America, north Africa, Iraq, Syria, Lebanon, Iran, Yemen and even India and other Asian countries. Even if those Arabs, defined as first-language Arabic speakers not having Jewish identity (usually Christian and Muslim), with Israeli citizenship were to be discounted, there would still remain, by any stretch of the imagination, a cultural plurality which transcends the supposed unity of the Jewish people. The modernity of this still young, post-war nation-state, with its main roots in the secular modernist Zionism of the turn of the century, is heavily compromised by the traditionalism of diverse orthodox Jewish groups with clear national/ethnic origins. In this context, we may speak, for example, of the Hasidic communities of the Mea Shearim district of Jerusalem or Safed, with their origins in the *shtetl* of eastern Europe, or of those of Moroccan descent, the largest national group within the Jewish population. When the non-Jewish population is taken into account, the intercultural complexity of Israel provides an extremely rich source for social, political and educational analysis.

Interculturalism in Israel is a constantly changing scene, but in 1996 a number of assertions may tentatively be made. In the case of Jewish–Arab relations, there seems to be increasing evidence of some degree of 'normalization', with Arabs no longer perceived by the Jewish population in monolithic terms. The Arabic-speaking population of Israel is itself perceived as diverse in terms of religion, political outlook, region, class and so on, while as far as the West Bank, Jerusalem and Gaza are concerned, even greater diversity is perceived. With the acceptance by Israel of Palestinian autonomy there appears to have been some impact upon the Arab population of Israel: a self-identification as Palestinians, culturally, while politically holding to Israeli citizenship. (Interestingly, one Israeli Jewish respondent preferred a reference to Israeli Muslims rather than Arabs, with the implicit suggestion that the religious distinction is the most salient, rather than linguistic or other cultural factors. Where those who have been conventionally seen as Christian Arabs stand, such as a high proportion of the population of Nazareth, is not altogether clear.)

Within the Jewish population the position of two identifiable groups exemplifies the current situation in relation to interculturalism: the Russians and the Ethiopians. Recent post-Soviet immigration has resulted in the emergence of different kinds of issues. One commentary on the approximately 165,000 Russian immigrants who came during the period 1968–1984 suggested that the value system of the then Soviet Union could be regarded as a 'dominant' culture and that the 'dissocialization' of such immigrants has proceeded at a slower pace compared with other newcomers. Moreover, although Soviet immigrants have on the whole found little difficulty in adapting to techno-logical aspects of a westernized society such as Israel, it has been noted that it has been harder to accommodate to the cultural norms of pluralism, compe-tition and democracy and there is accordingly evidence of significant dissat-isfaction with the extent of integration (Horowitz, 1986, pp.16, 27). One response to the situation of Russian immigrants, expressed by Israelis of other origins, has been that there has generally been a set of high expectations on the part of the Russians in terms of what the Israeli state could offer them, perhaps reflecting a previous dependency upon state provision of employ-ment and social security. Others have voiced prejudices in relation to the importation of mafia practices into Israeli business, seeing the Russians as having a potentially destabilizing effect upon the Israeli economy and Israeli society at large.

On the whole, immigration from Russia has occurred as a consequence of antisemitism and the subsequent experience after arrival in Israel has not always been a betterment of financial circumstances. In addition, immigrants from Russia have often tended to deviate from the conventional image of East European Jews: a tenuous and barely discernible link with Judaism, frequently of solely Jewish patrilineal descent, thus making them in a strictly religious sense non-Jews. However, the Russians now constitute a significant segment of the Ashkenazic population and, in practice, are even accorded a separate linguistic status (with a significant increase in the use of Russian on signs and notices).

Immigrants from Ethiopia have in some respects been at an advantage compared with those from Russia. Even though at the beginning there was a general reluctance to accept them as Jews (including by the Israeli rabbinate, who required Ethiopian rabbis to undergo further training), there has argu-ably been an increased recognition of their place within Israeli society. In this context, it is important to note that young people of Ethiopian origin have experienced the process of acculturation as members of the Israel Defence Force. Compulsory military service functions to assimilate those of conscrip-tion age (which includes women as well) to a common set of norms and values, in addition to bringing together people of diverse ethnic origins (apart from Arabs and members of the strictly orthodox communities). On the other hand, increased acceptance of linguistic diversity in Israel has not yet meant that Amharic has gained similar status to that of Russian. At the same time, their broader identity as Africans has remained and has been the target for standard Eurocentric racism in the context of an initial refusal to accept the blood of Ethiopians by the transfusion authorities because of fears concerning HIV infection.

## Intercultural education and the Israeli school system

Although it should be noted that education is compulsory from age 6 to 16 and free to the age of 18 for all Israeli citizens, in quite crucial respects it is questionable as to whether it is appropriate to speak of *the* Israeli school system. Arab schooling and Jewish schooling have quite separate origins: the former was the responsibility of the Government of Palestine under the British Mandate, although Kleinberger (1969, p.30) points out that in the last days of the Mandate only about 30% of Muslim children between 5 and 15 received any schooling at all, and only 10% of those attended for more than five years. In addition, there was an urban–rural divide where, for example, only 7% of Arab girls of school age in the villages attended an elementary school (compared with 60% in the towns and cities). Christian Arab children tended to fare better as a result of additional denominational provision from churches and missionary societies. Thus, Arab schools could be viewed as products of colonialism and neo-colonialism while, as has been noted earlier in this chapter, Jewish schools were largely the products of self-determination.

Currently, schools are divided into four groups, each comprising a 'mini-system'. There are Jewish schools which are divided into state (non-religious), state religious schools (emphasizing Jewish studies, tradition and observance), and independent *(Torah)* schools affiliated to diverse strictly orthodox groups. The latter are further divided along gender lines, replicating such schooling elsewhere, and functioning to instil strict norms of behaviour in addition to maximizing religious education and providing the basis for *yeshivah* (rabbinical seminary) training for boys. Finally, there are Arab and Druze schools where the language of instruction is Arabic and there is a special focus on Arab and Druze history, religion and custom, respectively.

This diversity within Israeli schooling is a clear reflection of the history, experience and aspirations of the different identifiable groups which comprise Israeli society. Apart from the explicitly segregated provision described above, further divisions have arisen as a consequence of patterns of settlement occurring along a socio-economic divide which may also be shaped ethnically. On the other hand, this is not generally perceived as an unchanging situation; class divisions are fluid and there is a degree of optimism concerning the increased participation of those of middle-eastern and north African origin at all levels in the Israeli social structure. This is reflected in growing equalization in attainment in high schools, even though this has not yet filtered through to the universities (Heller, 1992, p.232).

On the other hand, there have also been innovatory practices which, at least as far as the Jewish school-age population is concerned, have attempted to run counter to the segregated religious nature of the system. Thus, a state school, Keshet, was established as both a religious and secular institution in 1995 and has the aim of going 'beyond tolerance to a true pluralism in which both secular and religious ways of life are considered legitimate and respected'

(Mason, 1996, p.8). While such a school is evidently not targeted at the strictly orthodox, who would not be able to countenance anything other than the traditional form of Jewish schooling, segregated along gender lines, there is evidence that it may be attractive to religious parents who would be seen as less insular. To achieve this, each class has two teachers, one religious and one secular.

However, it is the continuing tension and conflict between Israel and the neighbouring Arab states which casts a shadow over the prospects for more promising relations between the Jewish majority and the Arab minority. A major obstacle in this regard has been the continuing presence of stereotypes on all sides. Not least is this reflected in schools, especially in curricular materials in which images of 'the other' are portrayed. In the Israeli context, there has been an evaluation of geography textbooks used in Jewish schools which, among other things, considers the images of Arabs which are found in these publications. Not surprisingly, a wide range of characteristics attributed to Arabs are suggested, such as 'haughtiness' and 'romanticism'. Some of the suggested characteristics may also be seen as contradictory, eg, 'disregard' and 'ethnocentrism' on the one hand, 'humanitarianism' on the other (Bar-Gal, 1991, p.32). While it may be argued that school textbooks are marginal in relation to the creation of stereotyped images among the young, with the peer group and mass media constituting more formative influences in western societies, they may nonetheless function to reinforce what young people already 'know'.

At central government level, however, publicity is more upbeat with regard to breaking down cultural barriers, so that it is claimed that, 'Innovative programs, used in both Arab and Jewish schools, are designed to dispel stereotypes, to enhance appreciation of each other's history and culture, and to encourage openness and tolerance' (Israel Information Centre, 1995, p.5). On the whole, though, Arab–Jewish relations have generally not loomed large as a dimension of educational practice. Before 1987, when the Intifada began, there had been at least one initiative at attempting to create mutual under-standing between Jewish and Arab children at elementary school level. This was dependent upon support from parents, to enable children from both communities to be educated side by side in an atmosphere where stereotypes could be broken down. In addition, there have been tokenistic but symboli-cally interesting programmes such as the organization of mutual visits to Jewish and Arab kindergartens by the respective children and a project where a mixed Arab-Jewish group of teachers team-taught in both Jewish and Arab schools (Kalekin-Fishman, 1996). This latter programme had the interesting result that Jewish teachers, for the first time in Israel, had the experience of being a minority. At the same time, regional differences prevail: Haifa, for example, has traditionally been a mixed Jewish and Arab city, with the University of Haifa having mixed classes of Jews and Arabs to a far greater extent than, say, Tel Aviv. At the same time, the village of Neve Shalom, containing a mixed population, survives as a testament to the continuing optimism surrounding Arab–Jewish relations.

## Conclusion

As far as the Jewish population is concerned, Israel approximates more closely to the 'melting-pot' ideal than many other plural societies. While diversity remains for the time being in relation to customs and language rooted in national origins, these are fast disappearing. The religious divide (observant v. non-observant, religious v. secular) is more significant – and cuts across both the Ashkenazi and Sephardi broad groupings. Visible differences of skin colour may have less significance in Israel than in other countries, although prejudice and discrimination remain. Intermarriage between Ashkenazim and Sephardim is well-established and there is little evidence to suggest that the same will not occur between Ethiopians and these groups. Economic divisions remain, typified by north Tel Aviv and the surrounding suburbs being largely populated by the mainly Ashkenazi middle class and the south, much poorer and predominantly Sephardi.

Thus, class and religious observance remain divisive elements within the Jewish population and partly manifest themselves in party political allegiance. National origin plays some part in this process, but not a decisive one, and is generally mediated by other factors. It is clear that a homogeneous Jewish Israeli culture is yet to be firmly established, despite some superficial outward appearances. The strictly orthodox Jews, especially the Hasidim, might be seen as equally at home in New York, London, Antwerp or Paris. If the notion of Zionist culture is accepted, then the very least that can be said is that it has undergone significant change in the last 30 years or so. The image of the kibbutznik (always a minority phenomenon) and the socialistically-oriented pioneer is fast being replaced by a picture of Western consumerism, and by 'Americanization' which has helped to 'blur the gap between Europeanization and Orientalization [through] the shared popular culture of the young generation, in film, music and dress' (Heller, 1992, p.232). Together with the apparent appetite for new technologies – the mobile telephone and the Internet are ubiquitous – there seems now to be a common aspirational image having a good deal of resonance among the young.

At the moment that the content of this chapter was first being considered, news came through of the assassination of the Israeli prime minister, Yitzhak Rabin. While, at one level, many felt emotions which they could only recall in connection with the death of a near relative, or of other public figures such as President Kennedy, there was also the suspicion that the event occurred because a comprehensive Middle East peace settlement might be near to fruition. Yet, it is with some irony that just as the finishing touches were being put to the chapter a change of government ensued in Israel with the *Avodah*

(Labour) coalition replaced by Likud under prime minister Binyamin Neten-yahu. The fragile peace process looked as though it might fracture altogether as 'fundamentalist' ideologies were seen once again to be in the ascendant on all sides and the prospects for further Palestinian autonomy seemed bleak. While normal domestic issues are far from removed from the Israeli political process, these have frequently been overshadowed by questions concerned with relations with the Palestinians and neighbouring Arab states. Indeed, now that the socialist dimension of politics has all but been eliminated (as in much of the rest of the world) the main agenda is defined on the basis of intercultural relations, whether they be secular-religious or Jewish-Arab.

Meanwhile, education still remains high on the agenda for all sections of the population. Minimally, it is perceived as the principal means of economic advancement both for Jews and for non-Jews and, to that extent, might serve in the long run to lessen the gaps between communities. However, the experiences gained elsewhere suggest the perpetuation of disadvantage and deprivation unless there is a process of equalization of provision and access. In addition, the Israeli state notes the capacity of Palestinian educational establishments to raise social and political consciousness, especially as far as the universities are concerned (hence the periodic closure of such places as Bir Zeit when conflict has ensued on the West Bank).

The future of Israel as a multicultural, multinational and multi-faith state remains highly problematic. At the moment, the educational response is largely to reinforce the *status quo*, with a continuing emphasis upon the assimilation of immigrant Jews. As far as the socialization of the young is concerned, however, the schools now constitute but one agent as the mass media have mushroomed and computer games help induct children into the competitive culture of the west. Thirty years ago, there was no television in Israel (except what could be picked up from Jordan); today, there is video, satellite and cable, and the universalistic nature of media-based culture func-tions to lessen the ethnic divisions amongst young Jews. For the strictly orthodox, these may be reminders of the profane nature of a supposedly messianic dream, and they will continue to be insulated from such depravities through immersion in the *shtetls* of the late 20th century. For those Arabs who hold Israeli citizenship there remain significant inequalities, and most lead separate lives, both culturally and geographically distanced from the majority. For the stateless populations of Gaza and the West Bank, only a political settlement would seem to offer any real opportunity for the creation of a basis for citizenship, economic advancement, and mutual understanding. Given such a settlement, schools might serve to foster, or at least not hinder, the development of a non-threatening Palestinian identity which could encom-pass both those living on Gaza and the West Bank and those Arabs living in Israel itself. This would be an important contribution to an evolving education structure which, while retaining a diverse character to cater for a diverse population, could at least be conceptualized on a future where cooperation and the mutual satisfaction of collective needs were the norm and suspicion and open conflict were largely eliminated.

## References

Bar-Gal, Y (1991) *The Good and the Bad: A Hundred years of Zionist images in geography textbooks*, London: Queen Mary and Westfield College.
Englander, D (ed.) (1992) *The Jewish Enigma*, Milton Keynes/London: Open University/Peter Halban.
Heller, J (1992) 'Zionism and the Palestinian Question', in Englander, D, op. cit.
Horowitz, T (1986) *Between Two Worlds: Children from the Soviet Union in Israel*, Lanham, MD: University Press of America.
Israel Information Centre (1995) *Education*, Jerusalem.
Kalekin-Fishman, D (1996) from an interview with the author, April.
Kedourie, E (ed.) (1979) *The Jewish World*, London: Thames & Hudson.
Kleinberger, A (1969) *Society, Schools and Progress in Israel*, Oxford: Pergamon.
Kochan, L (1976) 'European Jewry in the 19th and 20th Centuries', in Kedourie, E, op. cit.
Kochan, L (1992) *The Jewish Renaissance and Some of its Discontents*, Manchester: Manchester University Press.
Mason, R (1996) 'School of Many Colors', *The Jerusalem Post Magazine*, 26 April.
Touraine, A (1995) *A Critique of Modernity*, Oxford: Blackwell.
Vital, D (1979) 'Zionism and Israel', in Kedourie, E, op. cit.

# 14. Intercultural Education in Japan

Yasumasa Hirasawa

## Multicultural Japan

Japan has usually been portrayed as a monoethnic/monocultural nation: one ethnicity, one language and one culture. Until recently, most Japanese people shared this view. The seeming monocultural aspect of Japan has often been referred to as a secret of its economic success.

Today the picture is changing. The proportion of foreigners to the total population in Japan now exceeds 1.3%. As of May 1995, the number of foreigners was 1.64 million: 0.72 million Koreans, 0.27 million Chinese, 0.16 million Brazilians, 0.13 million Filipinos and others. Some may say that the 1.3% figure is minuscule. Indeed, it is much smaller than comparable figures of foreigners in most other nations. However, as far as the perception of Japanese society is concerned, Japan is rapidly becoming more multiethnic and multicultural; this is because the population of foreigners almost doubled in the decade between 1984 (0.83 million) and 1994 (1.64 million). When the percentage exceeded 1% in 1993, it was reported widely in major newspapers. Furthermore there is an increasing awareness of the needs of two neglected minorities, the Buraku and the 150,000 indigenous Ainu people, now mainly living on the island of Hokkaido.

Until recently, the majority of foreigners were Koreans, who accounted for over 80% of the non-Japanese population. For instance, the proportion of Koreans was 82% in 1984 (0.68 million out of 0.83 million). They are the descendants of Koreans forcibly brought to Japan as the result of the Japanese occupation of Korea in the early 20th century. Under the military rule of Japan, they were compelled to speak Japanese, use Japanese names, and acquire Japanese manners and customs. After the Second World War, they were deprived of Japanese citizenship, but circumstances necessitated most of them remaining in Japan as second-class citizens. Second and third generation Koreans were born and grew up in Japan, speaking the Japanese language, going to Japanese schools, working and getting married in Japan and paying taxes. But unless they naturalized as Japanese, they were not entitled to most basic rights. Many Koreans in Japan have faced discrimination concerning marriage, employment, housing and other social aspects. They were treated as 'out-group' members, but they were not perceived as 'foreigners' because for the majority of Japanese people, foreigners meant westerners like Europeans and Americans. These 'looking-like-Japanese-but-different' people were marginalized.

During the 1980s, the faces of foreigners in Japan dramatically changed because so-called 'new-comers' from overseas began to arrive in Japan. The Japanese economy had a shortage of labour ('pull' factor), while there was an abundant labour supply in Asia and other regions ('push' factor). Asians such as Filipinos, Thais, Malays and Bangladeshis came to Japan as workers and entertainers. South Americans of Japanese descent such as Brazilians and Peruvians suddenly became visible in industrial areas all over Japan because the revised Japanese immigration law of 1990 gave them special permission to work. Between 1986 and 1992, the number of Japanese Brazilians and Japanese Peruvians increased 68-fold and 55-fold respectively, and the Filipino population more than tripled. As a result, Koreans in Japan constitute only 44% of non-Japanese populations today (0.72 million out of 1.64 million as of May 1995).

The changing demography is a result of Japan's rapid globalization. Japan is now compelled to become tolerant and respectful of diversity, otherwise it cannot survive in today's multicultural reality, found both within and outside Japan.

## Government policy to internationalize education

The Final Report of the Prime Minister's Council for Educational Reform (1987), which has had a massive impact in reformulating Japanese education policies in the past decade, outlined six major directions for internationalizing Japanese education:

- to meet the needs of Japanese returnee/overseas children effectively and to set up internationally open schools;
- to improve arrangements to receive exchange students from overseas;
- to reform foreign language education;
- to improve Japanese language education;
- to reform higher education from a global perspective; and
- to help develop among Japanese students self-directed thinking and attitudes and relative viewpoints.

Earlier the Council had outlined four themes underlying these six recommendations. They were as follows:

1. To make schools more internationally open in order to nurture interest in and tolerance of difference, eg, active receiving of returnees and non-Japanese children; effective utilization of teachers with overseas experience; recruitment of non-Japanese educators; setting up new

   international schools; recognizing credits taken in overseas high
   schools.
2. To educate exchange students from the perspective of developing
   transnational human resources, eg, diversifying the destinations for
   Japanese students to study abroad; providing information and
   comfortable residence for students from overseas.
3. To enhance communicative language skills, eg, improving teaching
   methods and materials for foreign language (especially English
   language) education and Japanese language education; teaching Asian
   languages; promoting Japanese language education in the world.
4. To nurture self-directed orientation and relative ways of thinking, eg,
   knowledge of Japanese culture; emphasis on cross-cultural
   perspectives; developing social skills.

These themes were presented mainly from the perspective of educating
people capable of 'thinking and acting globally'. These corresponded to the
need for Japan to adjust to the new global environments that expected Japan
to be not merely an economic giant but also a contributor to world peace and
prosperity as an active member of the international community.

## Education of returnees

Interest in intercultural education developed initially in Japan out of concern
for educating Japanese returnees from overseas. Those returnee children were
born in or went to other countries because their parents had to move outside
Japan, usually as a result of overseas work assignments. As of May 1995, the
number of Japanese elementary and junior-high students staying overseas
reached almost 50,000 and about 13,000 such returnee children come back to
Japanese elementary, junior-high and senior-high schools annually.

   In Japanese society where children of international marriage have custom-
arily been referred to as 'half' (meaning half-Japanese) rather than 'double',
those returnee children have often been treated as 'strange Japanese' and their
different ways of thinking, speaking and behaving have been subject to
rejection by others and even to bullying. Many returnees were compelled to
assimilate by abandoning their uniqueness. However, such a problematic
situation came to the attention of educators and those who were trying to
make Japan more open to the world. They maintained that the returnee
children had a number of qualities that majority Japanese children did not
have: proficiency in foreign languages, ability to communicate and express
themselves openly, being active, sociable, and global-minded. They thought
that these unique qualities of the returnees should be positively utilized as
important resources in schools and in society. Rather than marginalizing the
experiences of returnees, the Japanese educational system started to respond

to their needs by setting up research centres, providing counselling services and designating a number of schools nationwide to promote intercultural education for the majority of Japanese children as well as for the returnees.

## Receiving exchange students from overseas

As of May 1994, about 54,000 students from overseas were enrolled in Japanese post-secondary institutions: colleges and universities, junior-colleges, technical colleges and special vocational schools. In 1983, the then Prime Minister of Japan, Mr Nakasone, committed himself to the idea of increasing the number to 100,000 by the beginning of the 21st century. Now the government is implementing a series of measures to realize this pledge to the world.

Over 90% of these students are from Asian countries, in particular students from the People's Republic of China, Republic of Korea and Taiwan, who account for 78% of the total. They face problems such as a shortage of housing facilities, lack of Japanese language skills, prejudice against Asians, and difficulty in obtaining higher degrees in Japanese universities. Unfortunately, some of these students have become anti-Japan rather than pro-Japan due to their unhappy experiences during their stay in Japan.

Now the Ministry of Education is initiating a reform initiative by setting up International Students' Centres in major universities and by improving programmes and services for overseas students. In some communities, these overseas students are actively engaged in community-level cultural exchanges by visiting local schools, making home-stays and organizing events for Japanese people in the neighbourhood. These exchanges provide important opportunities to promote intercultural education at the grass-roots level.

## Intercultural education studies

The Intercultural Education Society of Japan, was founded in January 1981. The aim was to study various educational issues resulting from Japan's globalization from the perspective of intercultural studies. Its inquiry initially focused mainly on the education of returnees from overseas and the education of exchange students, as well as on language education and education for international understanding.

Intercultural education studies has grown as an interdisciplinary process stimulating collaboration among comparative education, sociology of education, social psychology, mental health, ethnology, cultural anthropology, linguistics, religion, political science, economics and international relations. However, intercultural education as a distinct academic discipline has yet to be established (Ebuchi, 1994).

Recently, new concerns have been addressed by intercultural educators in Japan. For instance, intercultural education has become a major focus of the Intercultural Education Society of Japan. Issue No. 7 of *Intercultural/Transcultural Education*, the bulletin of the Intercultural Education Society of Japan, featured intercultural education and the education of non-Japanese children. In previous issues, the bulletin featured such themes as internationalization of education, international understanding, communication, teaching Japanese as a foreign language, exchange students from overseas, cross-cultural contacts and educational friction. This indicates how the major concerns of Japanese intercultural education have evolved in response to the changing reality of intercultural contacts in Japan.

## Minority education and intercultural education

Intercultural education has also attracted the attention of educators in Japan who are concerned about the education of minority group children such as Korean and Buraku children. The education of Koreans in Japan has evolved mostly as assimilation-oriented education. Immediately after the Second World War, the Japanese government decided not to accredit Korean ethnic schools as 'schools' defined in the School Education Law. As a result, more than 90% of Korean children in Japan have been enrolled in Japanese public schools. Because Japan has maintained strongly assimilatory education policies, the ethnicity and the culture of Koreans have not been properly respected in Japanese schools.

On the other hand, there have been civil rights movement by Koreans and other foreigners in Japan demanding proper respect for their fundamental human rights. Securing foreigners' right to vote and right to work as public servants, and respecting their culture and identity in Japan, are among the major concerns.

Recently, Kochi Prefecture and Osaka City announced their new policy to eliminate the nationality clause concerning the recruitment of local public servants. This move is contrary to the central government policy, which has repeatedly issued administrative guidance to local governments not to hire non-Japanese as civil servants because, according to the central government, 'such employment could create a situation where foreigners will possibly be involved in a national decision-making process'. This new development is indicative of growing multicultural awareness in Japanese society and of how local governments are taking the initiative to formulate intercultural policies.

In some areas such as Osaka Prefecture, after-school programmes for Korean language and cultural activities have been expanding with institutional support from local governments. Curriculum development on historical relations between Korea and Japan and on Korean experiences in Japan is pursued in many ways. These are attempts to respect Korean identity and to raise general awareness about resident Koreans. Moreover, an increasing number of non-Japanese-speaking children have been enrolled in public schools. As of May 1993, their total number reached 10,450 nationwide. These children live with their parents who have settled in Japan either as migrant workers, refugees, or returnees from China (bereaved in China during the Second World War). All of a sudden, understanding different life circumstances, respecting different cultures and teaching Japanese language and customs became an important agenda for schools enrolling non-Japanese children. New approaches to motivating, teaching and interacting with children had to be figured out. The philosophy and practice of intercultural education matched these new concerns.

Education of Buraku children (called Dowa education) has employed an intercultural as well as an anti-discrimination perspective. Buraku is the largest Japanese minority group, with a population of about three million. They are descendants of outcast populations during the Edo era (1603–1867) when the status system (warriors, peasants, craftsmen and merchants and former outcasts) was enforced to divide and rule people. The prejudice and discrimination against the outcasts has been sustained on a quasi-racist ideology. They are not different racially, linguistically, or religiously. It is impossible to distinguish Buraku people from majority Japanese just by appearance. There are about 6,000 Buraku communities, and two-thirds of them are located in western Japan. Although the Emancipation Edict of 1871 issued by the modern Meiji government abolished the status system, Buraku people have continued to face discrimination in employment, marriage and other social situations.

The proportion of Buraku children advancing to universities and colleges is about half the national average of 45% today. The education of Buraku children has emphasized the need for educators to learn from the lived reality of the Buraku. In a way, perceptions of opportunities in life have been quite different for Buraku and non-Buraku people. As a result of the cumulative effects of past centuries of discrimination, Buraku acquired an ambivalent, and sometimes even oppositional attitude toward schooling. Educators often had to read the unexpressed messages from Buraku to make schools more responsive to their needs, freer of discouraging practices and richer in empowering elements (for more detail see Hirasawa and Nabeshima, 1995). Because of this, it may be said that Dowa education has employed an intercultural perspective. Dowa education has learned from intercultural education such concepts as maximizing the potential of learners, meeting the needs of different learning styles, and a systematic approach to educational reform. Today the Dowa education movement is leading Japan's coalition of human rights education initiatives.

It appears that the concerns of Koreans and Buraku have not been well reflected in the inquiries into intercultural education in Japan, although intercultural education as a theme is beginning to attract wide attention. Probably, the fundamental issue here is how perspectives of minority populations and the concept of empowerment can be appreciated in the circle of intercultural educators.

This analysis leads me to argue that the concept of 'inter-culture' is applicable not only between nations, but also between cultural groups. Culture refers to those elements in life that guide and give meaning to what and how people think, feel, appreciate and act. Intercultural education is important because it provides opportunities to reflect on and re-examine assumptions and values and to acquire multiple perspectives in order to appreciate cultural differences. Obviously, its ultimate objective is to build tolerance, mutual respect, cooperative endeavours, and synergistic coexistence between different groups and individuals. The framework of 'interculture' needs to be further developed so as to incorporate perspectives of ethnicity, class, gender, age, religion, interest and even multiple aspects that dynamically make up human identity.

## Intercultural education outside schools

Education takes place not just in schools, but also at home, in the community, in the workplace and in wider society. Intercultural education has mostly been discussed within the context of schooling, but this limitation is now being questioned in Japan. There are a growing number of books published in Japan with such titles as 'Manual for non-Japanese residents for a better life', 'Guide for local governments to provide effective services for non-Japanese residents', 'Communicating with our non-Japanese neighbours', and 'Non-Japanese people's rights to education'. This reflects the reality in Japan today, where there are numerous opportunities to meet and interact with non-Japanese people in local neighbourhoods. They are not 'aliens' but fellow residents in the community, co-workers in the workplace, and friends in the school.

Even today, some of these non-Japanese residents have difficulty in finding places to live because they cannot rent apartments as some landlords are prejudiced against them. According to a survey conducted in the city of Ashiya (Hyogo Prefecture) in 1992, the majority of non-Japanese residents obtain the necessary information for their everyday life (eg, date and place of disposing of household rubbish; emergency phone numbers; types of services available from the local government) through their personal network of friends and acquaintances rather than from local government and other public sources (Ashiya City Office, 1992). It indicates that the quality of government services for non-Japanese residents is rather poor and reflects a lack of concern on the part of public administrators to meet the needs of non-Japanese groups more seriously. Intercultural education is needed to change this situation by educating average Japanese people (including public servants) so that they regard non-Japanese as their 'in-group' members rather than 'out-group'.

Some local governments are now providing innovative programmes and services to meet the needs of non-Japanese residents and to promote intercultural awareness among Japanese people, as follows:

- Multilingual handbooks of medical services (Spanish, Persian, Portuguese, Chinese, English and Tagalog) are made available at all medical institutions in the prefecture (Gunma Prefecture, 1993).
- Newsletters for non-Japanese residents are issued in five languages (English, Chinese, Korean, Spanish, Portuguese), providing information on Japanese administrative services and volunteer groups (Kanagawa Prefecture, 1993).
- A set of information materials consisting of 'guidebook for sight-seeing', 'local area map', 'handbook on daily life' and six other kinds of booklets are supplied to foreigners when they register at the city office (Sabae City, Fukui Prefecture, 1993).
- A booklet on 'Koreans in Japan' is issued to raise awareness about this community among Japanese speakers (Kobe City, Hyogo Prefecture, 1992).
- Intercultural school lunch menu from sister cities (Chinese, Russian, United States, Brazil) is offered in elementary and junior high-schools (Toyama Prefecture, 1993).

Many other programmes and services have been increasingly implemented, and adult educators are now paying close attention to these new developments. The Japan Society of Social Education, a nationwide umbrella body of adult and out-of-school education scholars and practitioners in Japan, recently published a book entitled *Multicultural/Multiethnic Society and Lifelong Learning*. This society has been concerned with such issues as literacy, interculturalism, human rights, ethnic minorities, collaboration with developing countries, as well as with lifelong and adult education.

Although the Society does not deliberately use the term 'intercultural education', what it discusses actually encompasses it. For instance, the book carries articles such as 'Research on adult education in multiethnic society', 'Volunteer activities to teach Japanese language', and 'Formation of ethnic identity among elderly Koreans'. Also, the book introduces topics of intercultural education from other countries such as 'Intercultural education in museums', 'Immigrant education in Germany', and 'Bangladeshi families and education of women in the UK'.

## Future agenda

UNESCO recently decided to place a renewed focus on human rights in formulating policies of international education when it revised the 1974 Recommendation for International Education. Also, the UN General Assembly resolved to designate the years 1995 to 2004 as the UN Decade for Human Rights Education and called upon every nation to formulate concrete action programmes for the decade. These and other developments are addressing major human rights-related issues in the world today (eg, ethnic and religious tolerance; gender equity; anti-racism; interculturalism; cross-cultural cooperation; non-governmental organizations and movements). Intercultural education is now expected to deal with these issues in more detail.

The UN Decade for Human Rights Education aims at building a universal culture of human rights (Office of the United Nations High Commissioner for Human Rights, 1995). Although the UN document does not specifically define the 'culture of human rights', it could be defined in the following terms. The culture of human rights refers to the whole set of ideas, value systems and behaviour patterns respecting human rights that are shared in a society and among those who live in that society. The culture of human rights guards individuals and groups from being unfairly treated due to their membership of a certain group (eg, race, ethnicity, gender, class, social origin, religion, language, sexual orientation, age, physical condition), promotes positive interactions between different individuals, groups and cultures, and supports diverse forms of self-directed civic actions to promote human rights by developing collaborative endeavours. The future agenda for intercultural education should be set up within such a conceptual framework of 'culture of human rights'.

This implies that a wide range of interdisciplinary studies on intercultural education need to be developed. I have indicated that there has been a high level of interest in Japan in a variety of issues of intercultural education. The Intercultural Education Society of Japan has a powerful network of wide-ranging scholarly disciplines and leads interdisciplinary studies on the subject. Another scholarly society, the Japanese Society for Social Education, has been concerned with the education of more or less marginal and disadvantaged populations. By combining these two scholarly and other initiatives, a large body of educators and scholars in Japan can be expected to engage in the study of many aspects of intercultural education. Scholars and educators from more diverse disciplines, experiences and fields should join hands to develop a broader network of intercultural education movements that has as its primary objectives to empower marginal populations, to nurture a rich culture of human rights in Japan, and to build a solid academic discipline of intercultural education.

# References

Ashiya City Office (1992) *Survey of Ashiya Foreign Residents,* Ashiya City Office.
Ebuchi, K (1994) *Ibunkakan Kyoikugaku Josetsu (An Introduction to Intercultural Education),* Fukuoka: Kyushu University Press.

Ebuchi, K and Kobayashi, T (1985) *Tabunka Kyoiku no Kenkyu (Comparative Studies of Multicultural Education)*, Fukuoka: Kyushu University Press.
Hirasawa, Y and Nabeshima, Y (eds) (1995) *Dowa Education: Educational Challenge Toward A Discrimination-Free Japan*, Osaka: Buraku Liberation Research Institute.
Office of the United Nations High Commissioner for Human Rights (1995) *United Nations Decade for Human Rights Education* (GE 95–18031), New York: UN.

## 15. Geopolitics Language Education and Citizenship in the Baltic States: Estonia, Latvia and Lithuania

David Coulby

### Shedding part of their heritage

In a telling passage, Braudel (1992) considers the expulsion of the Moriscos and Jews from newly-united Catholic Spain. He suggests that his own sympathies and notions of justice might be somewhat irrelevant to these events. The passage warrants quotation at some length:

> To call sixteenth century Spain a 'totalitarian' or racist country strikes me as unreasonable. It has some harrowing scenes to offer, but then so do France, Germany, England or Venice… at the same period. When they expelled the Jews in 1492, Ferdinand and Isabella were not acting as individuals, in the aftermath of the fall of Granada, victory as always being a bad counsellor: their action was encouraged by the poor economic climate and the reluctance of certain wounds to heal. Civilisations, like economies, have their long term history: sliding down a hidden slope so gradual that their movement is unaided and unheeded by man. And it is the fate of civilisations to 'divide' themselves, to prune their excess growth, shedding part of their heritage as they move forward. Every civilisation is the heir to its own past and must choose between the possessions bequeathed by another generation....The massive cohesion of Spain in the fifteenth century was that of a people who had for centuries been in relation to another civilisation the underdog, the weaker, the less intelligent, the less brilliant and the less rich, and was now suddenly liberated (pp.582–3).

This passage is cited at the outset not to condone expulsions, any more than Braudel is trying to exonerate the Catholic monarchs, but rather to encourage a longer, historical view, rather than a too precipitate leap into international comparison and judgement. It may be that a similar attempt at remoteness should be aspired to in considering the 20th century history of the Baltic States and in particular their current education and citizenship policies. Without at least such an aspiration, the outside observer is likely to remark complacently that two wrong legacies do not make a right policy and walk away with only a superficial understanding. This would be regrettable since the issues which face education, in particular in relation to language and citizenship, are ones which have previously been overlooked or scarcely understood by commentators on intercultural education, and furthermore are ones which can be replicated in many other areas of the former Soviet Union, for example, Moldova (Haarmann, 1995; Menter and Clough, 1995).

Distinctions between peoples in the Baltic States are not principally made on the basis of skin colour; rather they are made on the basis of either religion or language. It is the latter distinction – in particular between Russian on the one hand and Latvian and Estonian on the other – which forms the main focus of current politics and of this chapter. Language is conflated with ethnicity. The emergent independent states have attempted to portray themselves as linguistic or ethnic nations (this is a general historical trend described in Hobsbawm, 1962; 1987). It is possible that nowhere is the fallacy of the nation state (Coulby and Jones, 1995) more dangerous than in Latvia, Lithuania and Estonia.

To understand the first of these two legacies, it is necessary to have some knowledge of the history of the Baltic States during this century. The difficulty is that the interpretation and even the facts of this history remain deeply contested. Following the peace treaties which ended the First World War, Lithuania, Latvia and Estonia became independent states. At this point their demographic profile was substantially different from what it was in 1989. In all three countries there was a significant Jewish population, with some cities being historically and demographically important components of the diaspora, such as Vilnius in Lithuania and Daugavpils in eastern Latvia. In all three countries, but especially in Latvia and Estonia, there were also significant Russian minorities.

During the Second World War, the Baltic States were successively invaded by the Soviet Union, Hitler's Germany and the Soviets again. Baltic forces fought for both sides as well as independence movements. This was a period of atrocities. Responsibilities for these remain contested. By the end of the war, the Jewish population had been almost eliminated in local as well as distant death camps. In 1945, Lithuania, Latvia and Estonia became Soviet Republics. This was not the choice of their populations but reflected the military power of the Soviet Union across eastern and central Europe at that date.

The period of Russification between 1945 and 1989, which constitutes my first 'wrong legacy', involved demographic, economic, political and educational processes. Through waves of wholesale purges, Lithuanian, Latvian and Estonian people were transported en masse to Siberia. Others fled as refugees to the west. A parallel and opposite demographic movement of Russians into the Baltic States was implemented. This rested on the Soviet development of industrial facilities in the area and more particularly with military installations rapidly established in the warm-water Baltic ports. The demographic profile, especially of Latvia and Estonia, was radically transformed. In 1934 Estonians represented 88.2% of the population, in 1989 they were 61.5% (Estonia Institute, 1995). By 1993 Latvians represented only 54.2% of the population of the state (United Nations Development Programme, 1995), having been 75.5% at the high point of 1939 (Lieven, 1993). This demographic profile was most visible in the cities. In Daugavpils, to take an extreme example, out of a total population of over 120,000 in 1994, 56% are Russian, and Polish and Latvian speakers both represent about 15% (Multinacional Culture's Centre, 1995): this probably underestimates the Russian population (Lieven, 1993, gives 87% Russian speakers). Riga has 60% Russian speakers as against 37% Latvian; Tallin has just over 50% Russian speakers (Lieven, 1993).

The economic processes were such that the Russians in the Baltic States during this period were all too often seen to have the best-paid jobs, frequently in the military or security services. Political processes supported this: the newcomers were provided with new housing, while Latvians, for instance, subsisted in poor conditions. The politics of Soviet triumphalism were actually, in the south and west as well as the north of the state, those of the continuation of 18th and 19th century Russian expansionism. The Baltic States were being Russified.

Education played a major part in this process. Schools and universities were adapted to the production of the ideal Soviet citizen. The history of the 20th century was accordingly rewritten – not for the first or the last time. In particular the status of the Russian language became ever more important in the schools and universities. Russian became the first language of many schools and of higher education. It became the second 'international' language of all other schools. Lithuanian, Latvian and Estonian, or for that matter Livonian, did not have this status in the Russian-speaking schools where English or German were more likely to be the foreign languages. Russian rapidly became the language of the military, of commerce and of education. Russian was the language of daily transaction in the cities – as indeed in many it still is. Educational institutions encouraged the development of linguistic segregation and asymmetric bilingualism.

In order to understand the profundity with which this first legacy was perceived, it is necessary to see it from a conventionally defined Latvian or Estonian perspective. Dispersed, degraded and neglected, their language, their culture and their very 'people' seemed to be being systematically wiped out. Their history as languages, cultures, independent states and major European trading cities goes back centuries. It was as if it were all about to disappear under the onslaught of Russification, disguised as Soviet internationalism. Given the current status of Russians and the actual history of the Jews in the Baltic States during the Second World War, the people who magically appear outside international conferences in the Baltics carrying banners such as 'Stop the Genocide of the Latvians' appear incongruous. This is where it is essential to have some sense of history and to attempt, at least in part, to follow Braudel's consideration of the Catholic monarchs. When the three states achieved independence, heralding the total dissolution of the Soviet Union, they had succeeded in wresting political independence from the seeming brink of cultural ('ethnic') extinction. The education and citizenship laws which were rapidly put in place reflect this. It is these, of course, which constitute the second legacy.

## Education and citizenship

The core of this legacy is political, but educational issues are closely involved. The political legacy can be briefly stated. In Latvia, Latvian is the one official language. In Estonia, Estonian is the official language. In both states only people who are literate in the official language are regarded as citizens by the law. People not regarded as citizens have no vote and cannot engage in political activity. (In Estonia non-citizens can vote in local elections only.) They carry a different passport from citizens and there are thus restrictions on their ability to travel. A large percentage of the populations of these countries thus suffers discrimination in terms of civic rights on the basis of their language. Furthermore, 'there have been changes in the Latvian labour law code permitting employers to lay off employees who cannot fulfil their professional duties due to lack of Latvian language knowledge' (United Nations Development Programme, 1995).

The ability of people to learn a foreign language can thus determine their civil status. In this sense in Latvia and Estonia education and citizenship are vitally interconnected. To put it at its starkest: an old lady whose family have been living in Riga for many generations, who might herself have actively participated in the independence movement, now has to take a language examination before she is eligible to vote. Not official policy in either state, though part of the political discourse in both, is the notion that Russians should go 'back' to Russia. Although Russia has said that it will accept any who proclaim themselves to be Russian, the current political and economic climate in that state is not exactly one to encourage inward migration.

Educational policy is now a key characteristic of newly emergent or re-emergent states (see Coulby, 1995a; 1995b). The change in language policy is the most obvious. One asymmetric bilingualism has replaced another. Lithuanian, Latvian or Estonian have become the predominant language of schooling in Lithuania, Latvia and Estonia respectively (for a full description of language policy in Latvia, see Kamenska, 1995). Attempts are also being made rapidly to shift the language of higher education away from Russian. 'The Baltic universities increasingly operate only in the Baltic languages, and quietly discriminate against Russian applicants' (Lieven, 1993, p.314). Russian-speaking schools continue, though their numbers are being reduced, and in these either Latvian or Estonian is the first and compulsory foreign language. The foreign language of Estonian- or Latvian-speaking schools is no longer Russian but German or predominantly English. Thus all young Latvians and

Estonians will soon speak the official language but only some of them will speak Russian, the language of many cities and of their neighbour, trading partner and major regional power. A Russian teacher is quoted in *The Baltic Observer* as saying:

> I feel sorry if they don't choose to learn Russian. You can't escape Russia. It will always be our neighbour. The students will miss out on Russia's unique culture and miss out on contacts with people from the other Baltics (McDaniels, 1993).

All three Baltic states rapidly shifted their curricula away from the objective of creating ideal Soviet citizens. A more complex but equally urgent task was the invention or re-invention of a national culture. Great poets and artists, important scientific and technological developments, sacred landscapes and cityscapes are being discovered, rediscovered or, if necessary, invented. The history of the state, of its relations to the rest of the Europe and the wider world and of the various groups within the state, is being rewritten. In this way a version of the state's importance, its culture, its identity and its history are being encapsulated within the school and university curriculum and thereby legitimated and reproduced to succeeding generations.

It is crucial that this process of curricular redefinition should take into account not only the cultural diversity of the state but also the history of cultural diversity within the state. One example must suffice. Vilnius was for many centuries a major city of Jewish civilization. The city hosted a rich outpouring of Jewish culture which in turn gave it status and wealth. Can the curriculum of Lithuania afford to ignore this multicultural legacy and the brutal way in which it was brought to a close? Were this legacy to be over-looked or marginalized within the school and university curriculum, three things would follow. First, the citizens of Lithuania would be left in ignorance of a proportion of their cultural legacy. Second, the lessons concerning the dangers of cultural and religious intolerance which come from any study of the Holocaust would be left untaught and unlearned. Third, part of the long, rich history of cultural diversity in the Baltic region would be allowed to disappear as if it had never been, preserved only in university-level courses in Israel and the United States. There are positive signs that this will not be allowed to happen (Zujiene, 1995).

Religious education has been reintroduced as an optional subject in Estonia and Lithuania. The importance of Latvian and Estonian culture, in terms of folk music and dance, as well as in the discovery of a literary canon, is being stressed. Current and historic links with the West are emphasized in many activities: scientific, commercial, artistic, political. An official statement on education in Lithuania, for instance, stresses that 'The educational system is based on European cultural values; ...educational reform is based on the educational experience of democratic Lithuania and Europe' (Lithuanian Ministry of Education, undated).

What may be being insufficiently resisted is *the encouragement of xenophobia as a mode of state-building* and the involvement of educational institutions in this process. This possibility is obviously attractive in newly re-emergent states. A sense of statehood may be encouraged by emphasizing difference from other states, perhaps even distrust of the inhabitants of other states or a stress on their historical role in subordinating the 'true' citizens. The curricula of schools and universities implicitly or explicitly shift towards the encouragement of warfare (Coulby, 1996). Such a temptation may be particularly attractive with regard to the state and inhabitants of previously colonizing powers.

## Geopolitics in the eastern Baltic

Beyond saying that two wrong legacies do not make a right policy, it is necessary to do two things. The first is to recognize the extent of both legacies and the second is to consider some of the geopolitical implications of the current policy. It is necessary to recognize the extent of both legacies because otherwise, either the origins of the current policies or their geopolitical implications become lost to sight. It seems almost as if there were an element of revenge in the policies pursued by politicians, otherwise enlightened, with regard to the Russian speakers in Latvia and Estonia. Combined with other policies on housing and on the payment of pensions to previous Soviet military and security personnel still resident in the two states, this may well be the perception of the people involved. And it may also be the perception of the much larger Russian population across the land borders within Russia itself. On the other hand, from the point of view of Latvian or Estonian speakers, these are essential steps to preserve the languages and cultures which Russification almost succeeded in eliminating and to redress the economic and civil wrongs of the Soviet era.

The politics of this region are important in European and indeed global terms. All three Baltic states are actively pursuing political and economic links with the west. As capitalist democracies with a long history of western links, these are not hard to develop further. The Estonian currency has been successfully tied to the Deutschmark. All three states wish to become members of the European Union; they would furthermore welcome membership of NATO. In the medium term such developments would be not unwelcome to either of these international organizations. The Scandinavian countries in particular are keen to further their historical, geographical and commercial links with the Baltic States. They are also anxious to support all political developments which can assist in the establishment of stability in the region.

At this point it is worth mentioning the dimensions of each of the three states in demographic terms. The population of Estonia in 1990 was little over one and a half million (Estonia Institute, 1995); that of Latvia in 1993 was 2.6 million (United Nations Development Programme, 1995); that of Lithuania in

1989, 3.7 million (Lieven, 1993). Not one of them has as many people as, say, adjacent St Petersburg. No matter what their success in transforming their economies, these states can never become world powers. They could not even sustain the armed forces necessary to defend themselves against a militarily powerful neighbour.

Just such a neighbour exists. Russia has now almost completed its military withdrawal from the Baltic states though it maintains its naval base at Kaliningrad (Koenigsberg) on the Polish Baltic coast. Russia is not the only post-Soviet nuclear power but it is unquestionably the main one. Events internally in Inguchetia and Chechinia as well as externally in Georgia and Moldova make it clear that Russia is still prepared to use conventional military power. These military interventions have been made by a moderate ostensibly pro-western government. It is by no means clear that such an administration will continue in Moscow. The language and citizenship laws of the Baltic states, even without the actual or threatened expulsion of Russian speakers, are probably provocative to the people of Russia. They could certainly be made to seem to be so by any government with an expansionist eye on the Baltic ports and natural resources. These language and citizenship laws are a source of regional and European instability.

Legislators in Latvia and Estonia are faced with two sets of policy options. The first option (see Vetik, 1995) is to abuse the civil rights of Russian speakers and to erode the importance and status of Russian as a language. This option depends on the continuation of Russian weakness in the area or on the calculation that the existing and ever-strengthening links with the west would be sufficient to deter any Russian military intervention or the threat of such, or that, were there to be any such intervention, the western powers in the shape of the EU or NATO would actively intervene. The second option is to recognize that the economic collapse of Russia will not continue indefinitely; that Russia will remain a major trading power; that Russian speakers in the three states are an economic and cultural asset and should have equal civil rights; that educational policies and particularly language policies should recognize these issues of social justice and economic and political fact.

It is the first of these options that Latvia and Estonia are currently following. Only time will tell whether two wrongs do in the event make a right. Certainly the preservation of Lithuanian, Latvian and Estonian language and culture is to be celebrated, just as the abuse of the civil rights of Russian speakers is to be condemned. On the other hand, the final part of the calculation which underpins the first option – that the west would actually intervene to counter any move from Russia – seems rash in the extreme. By contrast the second option offers civic justice, educational progress and enhanced regional stability.

# References

Braudel, F (1992) *The Mediterranean and the Mediterranean World in the Age of Philip II*, London: HarperCollins.

Coulby, D (1995a) 'School and University Curricula in Multicultural States', invited paper presented at the International Conference on Multinational Society: Reality and Perspectives in Daugavpils. Daugavpils, Latvia. April, 1995. Published in *Kultura un Vards* (Culture and Word), Daugavpils, Latvia, March/April 1995, pp.5–7.

Coulby, D (1995b) 'Educational Provision in Multilingual States', paper presented at the 'Multilingual Workshop – The Baltic Republics Today', University of Joensuu, Finland, November 1995.

Coulby, D (1996) 'European Curricula, Xenophobia and Warfare', *Comparative Education*.

Coulby, D and Jones, C (1995) *Postmodernity and European Education Systems: Centralist Knowledge and Cultural Diversity*, Stoke on Trent: Trentham.

Estonia Institute (1995) *Facts About Estonia*, Tallin: Estonia Institute.

Haarmann, H (1995) 'Multilingualism and Ideology: The Historical Experiment of Soviet Language Politics', *European Journal of Intercultural Studies*, 5, 3, 6–17.

Hobsbawm, E (1962) *The Age of Capital 1848–1875*, London: Weidenfeld and Nicolson.

Hobsbawm, E (1987) *The Age of Empire 1875–1914*, London: Weidenfeld and Nicolson.

Kamenska, A (1995) *The State Language in Latvia: Achievements, Problems and Prospects*, Riga: Latvian Centre for Human Rights and Ethnic Studies.

Lieven, A (1993) *The Baltic Revolution: Estonia, Latvia, Lithuania and the Path to Independence*, New Haven: Yale University Press.

Lithuanian Ministry of Education (undated) *General Concept of Education in Lithuania*, Vilnius: Ministry of Education.

McDaniels, A (1993) 'Latvian School System Goes Back to the Drawing Board', *The Baltic Observer*, 24 September, p.16.

Menter, I and Clough, N (1995) 'Teacher education in "the New Europe": Some Lessons from Latvia', *European Journal of Intercultural Studies*, 6, 2, 3–11.

Multinacional Culture's Centre (1995) *Multinacionala Multinacional Daugavpils*, Daugavpils: Multinacional Culture's Centre.

United Nations Development Programme (1995) *Latvia Human Development Report 1995*, Riga: UNDP.

Vetik, R (1995) 'On Relationship Between Ethnic and Security Issues in the Baltic States', paper presented to the Fifth World Congress of ICCEES, Warsaw, 1995.

Zujiene, I (1995) 'Education in Lithuania – An Object of Reform', in Wulf, C (ed.) *Education in Europe: An Intercultural Task*, Munster: Waxmann.

# 16.  Intercultural Education in New Zealand

Lisl Prendergast

The New Zealand education system has at all levels become more sensitive to the needs of the indigenous minority of *Aotearoa* (the Maori name for the country) since the 1970s and more attuned to the demands of a multi-ethnic new settler population since the 1980s when ESOL (English for Speakers of Other Languages) programmes first began. Prior to the 1970s, New Zealand education was homogeneous and singularly assimilatory in its policies. Maori people were expected to conform to the linguistic and educational demands of strongly monocultural classrooms. The tradition of the early mission schools (1815–50) where Maori was used as a medium of instruction was lost, and Maori children were discouraged from speaking Maori at school and even punished for doing so. Migrant communities of new settlers fared little better and New Zealand literature records the struggles which early Dalmatian (Croat), Assyrian (Lebanese), Chinese, Indian and Samoan communities had in their new environment. Difference was not tolerated in the patriotic fervour of the Edwardian period, and New Zealand as a minor colonial power in the Pacific waged campaigns against independence movements like that of Samoa. It was a society suspicious of outsiders. White Anglo-Saxon Protestant xenophobia reigned supreme with newspapers exhorting caution against 'the yellow peril' and even new migrants from the 'Mother country' took a while to be embraced as full citizens of the colony and later the Dominion. Within this chilly wider climate, however, individual teachers can be acclaimed for their efforts to educate their students in more enlightened ways but it was not until the 1980s that genuine moves were made to acknowledge the special needs of a pluralistic society.

The colonial monocultural nature of New Zealand's primary school system was established by 1877 when the legislative assembly passed its first Education Act and was well entrenched by the 1900s when patriotism for Mother England gripped the small colony. Maori people had been decimated by disease and a loss of *mana* (pride, status, prestige) as a result of losing tribal lands after the Land Wars of the 1860s. Despite the many difficulties or perhaps because of them, there arose a proud tradition of Maori resistance, including movements with syncretist religious cults which included Christian and pre-Christian elements and which were great preservers of the Maori linguistic and cultural heritage. However, the four Maori Members of Parliament responsible for founding the Young Maori Party in the 1900s were all in favour of an education in English while trying to retain their own cultural heritage.

These men – Sir Apirana Ngata, Sir James Carroll, Sir Peter Buck and Sir Maui Pomare –were products of an Anglican Boys' College, Te Aute, which to this day maintains a tradition of bicultural education but with a linguistic accent on English. This is precisely the tradition that has come to be questioned by Maori educationalists today. The so-called Maori Renaissance began in the 1970s with groups like Nga Tamatoa (a university-based Maori rights movement) which combined aspirations for Maori sovereignty and a new political consciousness with a demand for bilingual and total immersion education. Maori sovereignty is a complex issue which aspires to *tino rangatiratanga*, in the words of the Treaty of Waitangi, or Maori control over all aspects of Maori life, including lands, welfare, health and education.

The Treaty of Waitangi is the cornerstone of New Zealand's foundation as a bicultural and, more latterly, multicultural society. It is a document unique in the intercultural affairs of the UK's history as a colonial power. It was signed in 1840 by the *rangatira* or chiefs of Northern New Zealand and then taken by a naval vessel around New Zealand to collect the other signatures and marks of the *ariki nui* (chiefs) of all tribal groups. It guarantees the rights of Maori people in terms of estates and cultural treasures. To Maori people the treaty is a sacred covenant, whereas many *pakeha* New Zealanders are more ambivalent about it, feeling very threatened by the climate of the 1990s which has seen the return of vast tracts of Maori land and a percentage of all fish resources from New Zealand's coast line. (*Pakeha* New Zealanders are those of European descent; the term *tauiwi* is now more generally used to describe people of non-Maori descent.) It is within this climate of a growing political awareness that a resistance to linguistic imperialism (linguicism) has emerged assisted by the research of the government-backed NZCER (New Zealand Council for Educational Research) and the work of Dr Richard Benton.

The development of bilingual schools was advocated in the 1980s, with some trial schools being set up. In the 1990s many Maori educators favour total immersion schools, and several *kura kaupapa* (Maori total immersion schools which also encourage traditional learning styles) are now in existence where the medium of instruction is solely Maori for all curriculum subjects. There are also Intermediate schools (Form I and II for 11- and 12-year-olds) and Secondary schools which have total immersion or bilingual units, but even the old Maori-operated Church Secondary schools have yet to adopt total immersion for all subject areas. The total immersion movement is thus largely confined to the *Kohanga Reo* or language nests for pre-school children and primary schools (5–10-year-olds). The language nests were the first move towards a non-assimilatory education policy and were argued for by Dr Richard Benton and NZCER researchers at a time when a change in policy seemed essential as only a small percentage (1– 5%) of Maori speakers were under the age of 5.

The language was and still is seriously threatened. There was also an aspect of what Jacques (1991) called 'the therapeutic approach' about this. This derived from the deficiency theories of the 1960s and 1970s using bilingual education as a pacification tool. This approach leads to ethnic groups being kept happy while a small elite carries on the business of running the country. In fairness though, whatever the suspect motivations, many *pakeha* educators also adopted a move to teach Maori language in primary and secondary schools with enthusiasm. The training colleges taught Freire's 1970s ideas that saw self-image and cultural identity as essential parts of academic success. Freire also predicted that this would lead to 'the development of a keen awareness of the sociological economic and political processes that condition their subordinate role' (Freire, 1970).

Maori people have developed a strong political consciousness which could have interesting consequences when the country moves to proportional representation in 1996. The country has always had four Maori seats in its House of Representatives as a legacy from its colonial past, but there are Maori political parties with well-developed policies on language maintenance and economic issues and these parties contest the general seats as well. The tribes all subscribe to language maintenance and the importance of the *Kohanga Reo* movement and, although there is only one language, there are dialect variations, especially between the North Island tribes and the *Kai Tahu* (Maori tribe) of the South Island. This was an issue when setting up regional Maori language radio programmes.

An important aspect of the *Kohanga Reo* is the level of parental and intergenerational involvement, with grandparents playing a leading role because of their competence in the language. This is a trend that has been noted by writers on the *Naionrai* or nursery schools in Ireland. Jacques (1991) noted that Maori parental involvement in bilingual school units and *kura kaupapa* Maori increased by 46%, and that many parents visited the school at least once a week and 84% visited at least once a term. Cummins and Swain (1986) noted that minority group parents are more likely to show an interest in education if the community has a degree of control over it.

Studies in New Zealand have emphasized the importance of self-esteem to Maori education (Spoonley, 1990) and a study of Maori students in the Maori environment of bilingual units showed that:

- students had a good knowledge of Maori and were confident in the performing arts;
- the teachers reported better attitudes to learning and achievement;
- the parents were pleased that their children were enjoying education and staying on at school;
- the students surveyed had a positive approach to learning.

There has been a lack of funding and research in all aspects of bilingual and total immersion education and for secondary schools wishing to implement such programmes. There is a lack of Maori language teachers who have competency in supporting curriculum subjects. In 1996 this is currently an issue between the New Zealand Post Primary Teachers union and the government and part of a dispute involving industrial action. Jacques (1991) pointed out that if the resources given to our early reading recovery programme had also been given to the emerging language programmes, New Zealand might well have as good an international reputation in this field as we have in the reading recovery field. Maori people are 12% of New Zealand's population and government funding agencies need to look carefully at the level of funding given to language maintenance initiatives, as currently poor training and lack of funds could lead to what Benton (1981) calls 'semi-lingualism' which results from poorly devised bilingual and total immersion education. A major study needs to be conducted which examines the quality of the education offered by *Kohanga Reo* and Maori language units. New Zealand's remodelled school inspectorate, the ERO (Education Review Office) can barely cope with bringing primary and secondary schools to account, let alone inspecting all the *Kohanga Reo*. There should be a special section of the ERO where Maori researchers look specifically at Maori education initiatives. This is an urgent need as some schools have the best of intentions but offer poor academic standards and poor quality teaching by untrained teachers. In some of the *Kohanga Reo* this education is also taking place in a substandard educational environment.

Most Maori people live in the North Island of New Zealand. Sixty per cent of the adult Maori population speak some Maori. However only 6% were very fluent in the language. This compares with a 1970s survey which showed 18% of Maori people as being fluent in the language. In addition 44% of fluent speakers are 60 years of age; only 3% are between 16 and 24 years old. The language is most used in the *marae* (ritual meeting places), churches and schools. In 1995 there were 35 *kura kaupapa* Maori schools offering instruction in Maori. Apart from these, Maori is offered as a subject in most high schools and all New Zealand schools have Taha Maori programmes which teach simple greetings, songs and some vocabulary.

Of all students enrolled at July 1995, 3.7% (25,284 students) were involved in Maori Medium Education, where students are taught curriculum subjects other than *Te Reo Maori* in both Maori and English (bilingual) or in Maori only (immersion). An additional 77,904 students (11.4%) were learning *Te Reo Maori* as a separate subject.

New Zealand also has a large Pacific Island population comprised of Samoans, Tokelauans, Nuieans, Tongans, Cook Island Maoris and other smaller groups. There are already Samoan language schools and some groups encourage Saturday morning language maintenance programmes for the children. The largest Pacific Island population is in Auckland and Auckland schools have offered cultural clubs, language programmes and strategies for better community liaison since the 1980s.

New Zealand education has been slow to respond to other aspects of intercultural education too. The standard of education for our pluralistic society in social studies programmes and history programmes varies from school to school. Some schools are so monocultural it would be possible for a child to leave school with little exposure to New Zealand's indigenous culture. Such schools are mainly in the private sector though, and New Zealand state schools try very hard to give students an effective knowledge of Maori culture, Maori protocol and ritual (*kawa*) and of the constitutional significance of the Treaty of Waitangi as the founding document of the state. In line with this, these schools also have positive ESOL programmes and give curriculum time to highlight all members of the school community. This is particularly true of schools in the main centres, with Auckland schools having developed very positive programmes for the large Pacific Island communities.

In the teaching of foreign languages there has been a major swing to the languages of the Pacific Rim. French and German have disappeared in some schools with Mandarin-Chinese, Japanese and Cantonese taking over as the main foreign languages. In the last 20 years, Japanese has become a curriculum subject in most New Zealand schools.

At July 1995, there were 44,5174 students enrolled below form three. Of these, just over 1.5% (6,729 students) were learning Japanese and almost 1.5% (6,623 students) were learning French. Of the 23,3659 students enrolled in forms three to seven, more than 11.0% (26,486 students) were learning Japanese and almost 10.5% (24,511 students) were learning French.

Private and state schools also have fee-paying students who come from Asian countries, and the children of newly arrived immigrants. This has led schools to develop positive programmes that are welcoming to these students but that also assist other students to understand and appreciate the cultures of the new students. In 1996 there has been an anti-Asian immigrant campaign by one of the smaller parties wanting to make political capital out of a recent influx of Asian immigrants from Taiwan and Hong Kong. Many of these new settlers live in one Auckland suburb, Howick, and the political campaign has been very pointed.

Wellington currently has immigrants from Eastern Europe and whereas the focus was on Kampuchean (Cambodian) and Vietnamese new arrivals in the 1980s, this has now changed. Of the total school population (57,126 students), 8% come from non-English speaking backgrounds (July 1995 figures). This is an increase of more than 7.2% (3852 students) since July 1994.

Data on non-English speaking background students are collected by identifying students in five categories according to their competence in English. While the number of students from non-English speaking backgrounds needing no additional support (category 5) has decreased by 3.8% (559 students), the number of students unable to understand greetings, simple instructions and questions (category 1) has increased by 58.5% (1,620 students).

The usual criticism levelled at New Zealand schools by Maori activists and members of other ethnic communities is that of 'tokenism'. Schools are very often in a cleft stick: too little of a specific culture in the curriculum leads to criticism but too much may also lead to white flight. Schools fear the departure of white middle-class students; 1990 marked new policies in school management with more autonomy for schools and their Board of Trustees, and schools do not want to feel disempowered by losing articulate, wealthy and powerful parents. It is a very difficult line to tread and can result in major tensions in schools between management and Boards of Trustees and the staff of the school.

The humanities have tried to embrace a new Pacific orientation, with English offering the new writers of the Pacific in literature studies, art history focusing on its artists and the social sciences using New Zealand and Pacific case studies rather than European examples. This has not escaped criticism, and the Form 7 English curriculum changes were bitterly contested, with the arguments even attracting glossy magazine coverage. The traditionalists will not allow that Albert Wendt (Samoan novelist), Witi Ihimaera (Maori novelist) and Janet Frame (New Zealand novelist) can be studied alongside Shakespeare and Milton. The Eurocentrism of the colonial past is still very much alive and in many subjects there is an element of choice, so more traditional teachers can avoid looking at New Zealand or Pacific subjects. In art history at form 7 level, it is possible to select four papers that cover only Italian Renaissance art and many schools do this. Added to this conservatism is a reluctance by some teachers to enter into teaching citizenship or intercultural education.

A problem for teachers who do understand the need for positive citizenship and intercultural education programmes is that since the recession of the 1980s, New Zealand education has taken a decided turn toward a more utilitarian and functionalist approach. Subjects like economic studies and technology have come into the curriculum, and there is an emphasis on mathematics and the sciences. Traditional humanities subjects have taken a back seat, with history, geography and social studies having to reconstitute themselves to compete successfully. These are the subjects that would normally assist intercultural education and it is alarming to see them become less successful in fulfilling this important role. New Zealand does not have separate citizenship and civics education programmes as are found in some Australian schools. New Zealand's national pride and identity is low-key and rather understated. There is not the same effort made to induct new migrants as is made in Australia, and New Zealand does not have a languages policy (Lo Bianca, 1987) as there is in Australia. Government departments have adopted some bilingual signs and documents (Maori and English) but there is no overall coordinating programme and no requirement by law. The status of Maori language is guaranteed by the Treaty of Waitangi as it is one of the taonga or treasures which this Treaty guarantees, but it does not enjoy this status in many areas of the community. It is an idea rather than a reality and Maori language certainly enjoys less than 12% (the proportion of Maori people in the population) of the air-waves time on television and radio. Without a commitment to the language at an official level, efforts made in the education arena will always be peripheral.

Too often Maori education has been presented as 'a problem'. The many government reports like the Currie Report (1962) and the Hunn Report (1960) certainly reinforced beliefs about the 'problems' of Maori education. The research also focused on the deficit model. Maori homes were 'less visually and verbally complex and less consciously organised to provide a variety of experiences which will broaden and enrich the intellectual understandings of their children'; this attitude was typical of such early studies. It is only recently with the advent of the *kura kaupapa* Maori schools that educators have looked at the positive aspects inherent in traditional Maori education, which include:

| | |
|---|---|
| *Wairuatanga* | Spirituality |
| *Mana* | The child's uniqueness, individuality |
| *Mauri* | The characteristic spirit of all life forms |
| *nga taonga tuku iho na nga tipuna* | The heritage from the ancestors |
| *taha tinana* | The physical health of the body |
| *Whanaungatanga* | The extended family or communal life |
| *Whatumanawa* | Emotional sustenance |
| *Hinengaro* | The health of the mind, the source of all intellectual and emotional pursuits |
| *Waiora* | The well-being or wholeness of the individual. |

These aspects are still misunderstood by many New Zealand teachers and the situation could be made worse by the need to recruit over 1,000 primary teachers from overseas this year (1996) owing to a shortage in the primary sector. The government is recruiting in England and Scotland and there have been headteachers quoted in the local media who say they will refuse to have these overseas recruits because of the special character of their school (Maori and Pacific Island students). The race relations conciliator John Clark has already been asked to comment on this situation and may be asked to make a ruling on it should it come to an impasse. The headteachers quoted were *pakeha* teachers and have an awareness of the need to induct new teachers into the cultural needs of their student community.

The general monolingualism and monoculturalism of New Zealand society does need to be emphasized. A section of the population is still Eurocentric and xenophobic. Monolingualism equals civilization in this mind-set, as pointed out by D P Pattanayak, the Director of the Central Institute of Indian Languages, when commenting on this issue (Skutnabb-Kangas and Cummins, 1988). In this view a country with many languages is seen as under-developed and barbaric. However, as more New Zealanders have travelled since the 1960s, some of this mind-set inherited from our settler forebears with their middle-England, white, Protestant backgrounds has been modified, but there is still a strong colonial fear of militant Maori movements and of the 'outsider'. Some people see the Maori language as incapable of expressing the complex concepts of an advanced technological world. It is difficult to convince the average *pakeha* New Zealander that all languages are capable of expressing any idea in the universe and 'the vocabulary of any language can be expanded to include new words for new concepts'. The level of entrenched racism is of concern to teachers when trying to deal with cultural stereotypes and negative images in the classroom. Some of the ethnic communities have negative images themselves. One young Maori orator at a local speech competition said that while watching the TV programme 'Crime Watch' she often played 'spot the *pakeha*'. There is humour and good nature in such comments but also much sadness. Post-colonial New Zealand does have a widening gap between rich and poor, and Maori health statistics are indicative of their low-paid, low-status positioning in society. Their success in education is improving but there is still a poor retention rate of Maori students in our secondary schools and many Maori students still leave with no qualifications at all.

New Zealand education has undergone major change since 1989 when the first elections for Boards of Trustees were held as a result of a Labour policy paper called 'Tomorrow's Schools'. This was a result of the Picot task-force which advocated abolition of the old Education Boards and a greatly reduced Central Ministry. It also advocated that financial control be totally devolved to schools. Schools now have control of between 20 and 40% of their budgets, but teacher unions have strongly opposed the schools being responsible for teachers' salaries. Only 70% of schools have opted for what is referred to as 'bulk funding' which gives schools the control of teachers' salaries as well as the operational grant. Boards of Trustees are anxious about opting in to the new system for fear of becoming unpopular with the staff of their school and the teacher unions. The new system of educational administration was supposed to give more power to parents and lead to a better representation of racial minorities on Boards. It is questionable whether this has happened, and many Boards still have five European elected representatives and then have to co-opt members to truly represent their communities. If a Board of Trustees fails in its duties, a commissioner is appointed.

The administrative revolution with its managerial culture has been one of the most significant changes in the last decade, but this has been combined with the abolition of the old Inspectorate and its replacement with the ERO. Added to this, all students will be subject to a new curriculum from 1996, and assessment is changing from a norm-referenced system to one utilizing unit standards. This is a skills-based system involving a set of levels and it is claimed that it will benefit students formerly disadvantaged by the examination system. It is by no means certain, however, that the latter will disappear and New Zealand could be operating two parallel assessment systems with the unit standards system being relegated to second place in the eyes of employers.

In line with 'new Right' ideas emphasizing the market and how providers cater for it, some members of the government advocate the use of a voucher system where students in theory have a choice of school, as each is provided with a voucher to 'spend'. This is opposed by teacher unions who can foresee some schools in severely disadvantaged areas like South Auckland becoming more disadvantaged.

These changes do affect the role of schools in intercultural education, as it is often seen as an 'extra' in this climate where schools are nervous about their images and would rather spend money on a new computer system which will get favourable media coverage than on civics or citizenship education which is inclusive of the cultural groups and of the school. It is still possible for *pakeha* children to leave school with little knowledge of Maori language or any degree of understanding of the cultural traditions of their communities. The political structures of New Zealand society are not examined in any critical way in some schools. There was some attempt in 1990 to redress this lack of ideological depth and sense of a New Zealand identity. Schools had new literature, new assembly programmes and new discussion points, but then the fervour to examine ourselves critically was lost. 1995 was *Te Tau o te Reo Maori* (Maori Language year) but this impinged very little on the consciousness of the white majority. New Zealand needs a report similar to Britain's Swann Report to map out a way that we can move students to not only recognize the values they share but to commit themselves to examining their roles in a rational pluralistic society. New Zealand need only look at the developments in Eastern Europe to see the consequences of the lack of education for a pluralist democracy. Cohesion, order and freedom are worth drawing in to our much-trumpeted new curriculum, or fragmentation, repression and violent conflict could become hallmarks of our future society. Technology, economics, accounting and the sciences may build an infrastructure that assists this small democracy on the Pacific Rim to hold a place in the market, but this is all to little effect if the society is fragmented and divided. Students need to know what being a citizen of *Aotearoa* – New Zealand – means in a post-colonial age where the old icons have become outmoded. This is a politically naive society emerging with blinking eyes from a long sleep, woken up by the 1981 protest against the Springbok tour and Maori protests for land rights. We need to teach people to participate, argue, persuade and whistle-blow. The climate of the 1990s has not been conducive to this. There is a need to examine our commonality and our differences in order to challenge the racism in our society and thus strengthen our social order.

Teacher education in New Zealand competently teaches young teachers about cultures but does not teach them how to raise the difficult questions which may provoke serious discussion in a non-confrontational way. Social studies, which is taught from Primary School to Form 4, is the usual place for such education but there is still a tendency to give information about a topic and not ask wider questions. The recent visit of a replica of James Cook's (New Zealand's first British explorer, 1769) *Endeavour* led to a discussion of the ship and its layout in a class in an East Coast school, but there was no attempt by the teacher to cover the Maori protest that had resulted or any Maori perspective of history. The class was 50% Maori and one student had asked about the violent aspect of Cook's first encounters with local tribes (warriors were killed while presenting a *wero* or challenge, which was misunderstood by the British sailors).

New Zealand teachers still lack deep knowledge of local tribal histories. Colleges of Education feel they have contributed enough if the students have some Maori vocabulary, an understanding of *kawa* (Maori etiquette), a few *waiata* (Maori songs) and some *korero purakau* (legends). Teachers are ill-equipped and this leads to tokenism and superficial *taha Maori* programmes (programmes that highlight the Maori side of curriculum subjects). Teacher training must be a major thrust for succeeding governments, both in biculturalism and multiculturalism. There is also a need for more Maori and Pacific Island teachers who not only have language competency but competency in other curriculum subjects as well.

Teacher unions have highlighted issues of equity and criticized government ideas like the proposed voucher system. They are aware that the element of choice which voucher advocates claim also has a stratifying effect by race, social class and ethnicity. There would be administrative costs and transport costs that would be impossible for most parents. New Zealand education already provides much choice with its *kura kaupapa* Maori schools, bilingual schools, integrated schools (schools with a special character like religious schools which have opted to be partially state-funded), special education schools, intermediate schools (11–13-year-olds), senior schools (15–18-year-olds) and more recently middle schools (11–14-year-olds).

The 1990s are a critical time for intercultural education in New Zealand schools. There is a need for more funding to meet the needs of diverse services and to train teachers in a less superficial way so that the needs of an increasingly complex pluralistic society can be met. There are signs that middle New Zealand is becoming more xenophobic and racist as Maori demands have become more obvious. There is less acceptance of new migrant groups from Asia than might be assumed, and a tendency to dump the 'problems' of schools in terms of intercultural education on the ESOL teacher, the Maori language teacher or the social studies teacher. Citizenship education has taken a back seat in the new market-oriented education of the 1990s with its slick utilitarianism and 'no frills' approach. Multiculturalism is seen as a frill and biculturalism is tolerated only in so far as lip-service has to be paid to it under the obligations of the Treaty of Waitangi.

The New Zealand teacher has always had a sense of equity and fairness but this benign goodness is not enough to assist New Zealand students towards an ideology which will allow them to increase their political literacy in order to participate in a pluralistic society. New Zealand needs a languages policy which includes an official status for Maori, the language of its *tangata whenua* (indigenous people), and more ESOL teachers, but it also needs teachers trained to assist students to examine critically the features of the emergent New Zealand macro-culture with its bicultural heritage, and who can ensure that students have a knowledge of human rights, the law, decision-making and political skills. The ethnocentricity and assimilatory policies of the past need to be acknowledged and examined with students; New Zealand needs to be seen in its role as a small nation on the Pacific Rim with an interdependence on the other Pacific nations but also with historic ties with Europe and other countries. The rhetoric and gloss of the 1990 celebrations should not be lost, but New Zealand has yet to come to terms with the Treaty of Waitangi as it applies to education and social policy. In addition to bicultural issues, New Zealand needs more advanced language centres for its new migrants, the teaching of community languages and better teacher education programmes. As New Zealand faces the Republican debate, a new proportional representation parliament and major administrative and curriculum changes in education, it is the right time to be readmitting these issues in a dynamic way in the classroom, so that students can be aware of the polyethnic nature of our society and the complexities of allowing for equity for all its citizens whatever their cultural and linguistic backgrounds.

# References

Benton, R A (1981) *The Flight of the Amokura: Oceanic languages and formal education in the South Pacific*, Wellington: New Zealand Council for Education Research.

Benton, R A (1985) 'The evaluation of bilingual schooling in New Zealand', paper presented at the symposium on Language in a Multicultural Society, IEA General Assembly, Auckland.

Cummins, J (1986) 'Empowering minority students: A framework for intervention', *Harvard Education Review*, 56, 1, 18–36.

Cummins, J and Swain, M (1986) *Bilingualism in Education*, London: Longman.

Department of Education and Science and The Welsh Office (1990) *Modern Foreign Languages for Ages 11 to 16*, London: DES.

Freire, P (1970) *Pedagogy of the Oppressed*, New York: Herder and Herder.

Harker, R K (1978) 'Achievement, Ethnicity: Environment deprivation or cultural difference', *NZ Journal of Education Studies*, 13, 2.

Harker, R K and Nash, R (1990) 'Cultural reproduction and school achievement: A case for Kura Kaupapa Maori', paper presented at The NZARE Annual Conference, College of Education, Auckland.

Jacques, K (1991) *Community Contexts of Maori-English Bilingual Education: A Study of Six South Island Primary School Programmes*, Wellington: Department of Education.

Jeffrey, W (1992) *Aotearoa Speaking for Ourselves*, Wellington: Ministry of Education New Zealand.

Lo Bianca, J (1987) *National Policy on Languages*, Canberra: Australian Government Publishing Service.

Metge, J and Kinloch, P (1984) *Talking Past Each Other: Problems of cross cultural communication*, Wellington: Victoria University Press.

Ministry of Education (1984) *Developing Bilingual Schooling in New Zealand,* Wellington: National Advisory Committee on Maori/English Bilingual Education.

Ministry of Education (1989) *Maori Educational Statistics 1989,* Wellington: Research and Statistics Division, Ministry of Education.

Ministry of Education (1990) *National Summary of Primary Schools with Bilingual Education Units and Pupils,* Wellington: Ministry of Education.

Post Primary Teachers' Association (1988) 'Bicultural education and the disadvantaged child', *PPTA News,* 9, 9, 5.

Prendergast, L A (1990) 'Biculturalism: An Achievable Goal', *Speak up, Journal of New Zealand Federation of Business and Professional Women,* September.

Prendergast, L A (1992) 'Bilingual Education and the Maintenance of Minority Languages', unpublished M A Thesis, Institute of Education, University of London.

Skutnabb-Kangas, T (1981) *Bilingualism or Not: The education of minorities,* Clevedon: Multilingual Matters.

Skutnabb-Kangas, T and Cummins, J (1988) *Minority of Education: From Shame to Struggle,* Clevedon: Multilingual Matters.

Smith, G H (1990) 'The politics of reforming Maori education: the transforming potential of Kura Kaupapa Maori', in Lauder, H and Wylie, C (eds) *Towards Successful Schooling,* London: Falmer Press.

Spoonley, P (1990) 'Racism and ethnicity', in Spoonley, P *et al.* (eds) *New Zealand Society,* Palmerston North: Dunmore Press.

# 17. Minority Education in The People's Republic of China

Jianhong Dong

## Introduction

China is a unitary multinational state. In order to guarantee the lawful rights of minority ethnic groups, the state has developed positive policies and strategies for the political, socio-economic and cultural advancement of the ethnic minority groups throughout China since the founding of the People's Republic in 1949. Education is an important means for facilitating development in minority areas.

This chapter is mainly concerned with education for minority ethnic groups in China. It intends to examine the issue from the perspectives of national policies, strategies and practices concerning minority education. The chapter will first give a broad review of the state-of-the-art of political, socio-economic, cultural and educational development of minority areas in China; second, describe national policies, strategies and practices of minority education in China; and last, identify potential issues and problems in the development of minority education in China.

## General background information

In China, there are all together 56 ethnic groups speaking more than 90 languages. The majority group, Han, comprises 92% of the total population and the other 55 ethnic minority groups have a total population of about 100,000,000. The minority peoples are scattered in about two-thirds of the national territory and are mainly distributed in mountainous, nomadic and border areas in north-west and south-west China. At present, there are five autonomous regions, three minority populated provinces, 30 minority autonomous *zhou* (prefectures) and 142 minority autonomous counties or *qi* in China.

Great changes have taken place in minority populated areas since 1949. Politically, 14.7% of the representatives of the National People's Congress were from minority backgrounds in 1993, representing all the 55 ethnic minority groups of the country. In the Eighth National Political Consultative

Conference (1993), there were 243 minority members who made up 11.58% of the total. Economically, the gross output value of industry and agriculture in the minority autonomous areas in 1994 was 73.8% higher than that of 1990. The growth rate of gross national product in these areas also increased faster than that of the developed areas in recent years. The living conditions of minority peoples have been improved, the average annual salary per worker in the autonomous areas was 2,040 yuan in 1990 and increased to 2,970 yuan (equivalent to US$367) in 1994. The average net income per farmer was 546 yuan in 1990, raised to 944 yuan (equivalent to US$117) in 1994.

Due to historical and geographical differences, the socio-economic development in the minority areas is still lagging behind. Compared with the average national socio-economic indicators, most of the minority populated areas are underdeveloped. From 1979 to 1992, apart from Xinjiang Uigur Autonomous Region, Yunnan and Guizhou provinces, the average growth rate of gross national product in other areas was lower than that of the national average (9.0%). The average gross domestic product per capita in the autonomous areas falls in the lower or lower-middle income groups. Among the 592 poor counties of the country, 295 are located in the minority areas which take 49.8% of the total. In 1992, there were 80,000,000 people who were identified as living under the national poverty line, half of them within the minority population.

Minority education has played an important role in promoting socio-economic as well as cultural development and has become an indispensable part of the national system of education in China. It has achieved enormous progress since 1949. According to statistics of 1994, the number of minority students was 17.04 times higher than in 1949. There were altogether 99,160 primary schools, 11,888 secondary schools, 1,436 technical and vocational schools in 1994 and 117 higher education institutions (including 12 community colleges) in 1993 in minority areas. In addition, 25,037 of the primary schools, 2,889 of the secondary schools and 303 of the technical and vocational schools and around 40 higher education institutions have been set up solely for minority peoples. Among 589 counties which are densely populated by minority peoples, more than 200 have universalized primary education and the illiteracy and semi-illiteracy rate decreased from 80% in 1949 to 30.1% in 1993. In 1994, enrolment for girls at primary education stage reached 97.7%, which is 80 percentage points higher than in 1949. In some of the autonomous regions like Uigur, Inner Mongolia and Guangxi Zhuang, the illiteracy and semi-illiteracy rates are lower than that of the national average.

## National policies, strategies and education

Since 1949, the Chinese government has attached great importance to minority affairs and worked out a series of policies which give priority to the social and economic development of minority groups and the protection of minority cultures, languages and customs in national autonomous areas. The Constitution of the People's Republic of China declares that,

> All nationalities in the People's Republic of China are equal. The state protects the lawful rights and interests of the minority nationalities and upholds and develops the relationship of equality, unity and mutual assistance among all China's nationalities. Discrimination against and oppression of any nationality or instigation of their secession are prohibited.

In education, the state adopts a monosystem of multicultural education. Though the majority Han culture is the mainstream of education, priority is given to the educational development of all minority cultures which are taken as an indispensable component of the Chinese culture as a whole. Therefore, the Education Law of the People's Republic of China declares, 'The state shall, in accordance with the characteristics and needs of respective national minorities, provide assistance to the development of educational undertakings for each national minority'. Strategies and practices along the lines of the national policies have been implemented in administration and management, language of instruction, curriculum and teaching and the financing of minority education. The remainder of this chapter deals with each of these issues in turn and concludes by considering current difficulties and problems.

## Administration and management

According to the national policy, the minority autonomous areas are encouraged to develop their own education systems to cater to their own needs and local conditions. Provinces with a minority population of over 10% of the total are required to establish education divisions for minority education, and in those provinces with a minority population of less than 10%, full-time staff are appointed. At the national level, the Department of Minority Education has been set up in the State Education Commission.

Diversified delivery systems for minority peoples have been formulated. At the primary and secondary levels, boarding schools are the main body of the formal schooling system. At present, about 6,000 such schools with 1,000,000 minority children have been built in 18 provinces and autonomous regions throughout the country. The development of boarding schools has greatly helped to increase the enrolment rate of school-aged children and to improve the retention rate of school children in minority areas. According to the latest statistics, the enrolment rate of children in Tibet Autonomous Region has reached 63.2%, 2.8 percentage points higher than that of 1993.

Another form of minority education is the special minority schools and/or minority classes in regular schools. For instance, in Ningxia Hui (Muslim) Autonomous Region, primary and secondary schools and classes for Muslim children have been built up in areas where Muslim inhabitants are over 50% of the total local population.

In recent years, new attempts have been made to improve the access to and quality of basic education for minority children. For example, schools for minority children have been set up in economically developed areas: in 1993, schools or classes for Tibetan children in 26 cities and provinces. In addition, more than 330 classes and preparatory classes for minority students are organized in some key national universities or provincial colleges and universities, and preferential considerations are given to minority students at admission.

## Language of instruction

The encouragement of bilingual and trilingual teaching in minority areas is one of the national policies for the development of minority education. As early as the 1950s, at the First National Conference for Minority Education, it was decided that minority ethnic peoples who have their own languages, such as Mongolian, Korean, Tibetan and Uigur, should take their own language as the medium of instruction at primary and secondary levels of education. Those ethnic groups which have independent languages but with no written, or with incomplete written, forms are encouraged to create or reform their own written forms or adopt Mandarin as a means of instruction on a voluntary or temporary basis. This policy has been reaffirmed in the Constitution (1982) and the Education Law (1995). Among the 55 minority groups, only Muslims and Manchus have adopted Mandarin both in daily life and education. The other 53 minority groups speak more than 80 languages. Among these groups, 24 have more than 30 written forms of language and 20 of them share both oral and written language with people from the same ethnic groups abroad. At present, 11 minority groups, such as Tibetan, Mongolian, Uigurian and Korean have adopted their own language as the medium of instruction. Ten further minority written languages are being used for instruction on a trial basis.

Different patterns of bilingual instruction have been employed, according to the actual conditions of the ethnic areas. For example, schools at different levels in Xinjiang Uigur Autonomous Region have adopted six languages for instruction. In the Inner Mongolia Autonomous Region, the main medium of instruction is Mongolian at primary stage, while the Han language is taken as the second language of instruction. In Tibet, there are two major patterns of bilingual teaching. The first involves the use of the mother tongue (Tibetan) as the main medium of instruction. Mandarin is offered as an independent subject, while other courses are all taught in Tibetan. The practice is mainly adopted in areas which are inhabited solely by Tibetan people. The other pattern is to take the Han language as the main medium of instruction, while Tibetan is offered as the independent subject. This method is widely used in multi-ethnic areas where majority people use the Han language as a language of communication.

## Curricula and teaching-learning materials

The state has also stressed the development of teaching and learning materials for minority peoples. A national mechanism in this field has been formulated. At present, there are ten institutions which are responsible for translating and editing teaching and learning materials in minority languages; five institutions for reviewing and examining these materials and eight publishing houses for printing the materials. As a result, 30 kinds of materials in 21 minority languages have been developed and adopted at schools in 12 provinces and autonomous regions.

In higher education, the State Education Commission worked out a Teaching Plan for Preparatory Courses on Humanities and Sciences Instruction for Minority Students in Regular Higher Education Institutions in April 1993. In June of the same year, the State Education Commission released curricula of the preparatory courses in basic Mandarin, reading and writing, mathematics and foreign languages (English) for minority students in regular higher education institutions. In line with the teaching plan and curricula, an expert group has been formed from specialists and professors from all over the country. Eleven volumes of teaching materials have been developed and tried out in higher education institutions or classes for minority students.

The curricula and contents of teaching and learning materials for minority students are flexible. Take the subject Language and Literature as an example: 40–50% of the texts are adopted from common textbooks used nation-wide, and 50–60% are selected from the literatures of specific ethnic groups.

## Financing

In terms of educational finance, the Education Law of the People's Republic of China states that:

> The State Council and the people's governments, at or above the county level, shall set up a special education fund to be used mainly for the implementation of compulsory education in remote and poverty-stricken areas and areas inhabited by national minorities.

Apart from the regular allocation to all education institutions, the national government has established a special fund for minority education. In the meantime, local governments are required to allocate certain amounts of additional funds for minority education. These funds are mainly spent on the necessary learning and living demands of minority children at school: teaching facilities, equipment and aids; training of teachers; and private or community schools for minority people.

Another practice is to set up learning grants for minority students, especially those who are from remote rural and poor families. For instance, tuition, textbooks, lodging and boarding are provided for ethnic minority children at primary and secondary schools. Stipends or grants are also available to minority students at universities and colleges.

## Difficulties and problems

Due to historical and socio-economic as well as geographical constraints, education development in minority autonomous areas is highly disparate and is still relatively weak and backward on the whole. The 1993 statistics show that the national average enrolment rate is 97.72%, while in some minority autonomous areas the lowest rate is less than 8%, and the average rate is only 89%. The low enrolment and retention rates and high drop-out rate are still the major problems which hinder the process of universalizing basic education. For instance, in some minority areas, the enrolment, retention and success rates are 70, 50 and 20% respectively. As regards education for girls, there are still 1.3 million girls who are unable to go to school. In Guizhou province, the 1994 statistics show that the enrolment rate for girls was only 89.39% while the drop-out rate was 6.64%. Besides, the average literacy rate in some minority areas is also low, for example in Tibet it is 55.57%, the lowest in the country. The average educated years per person in Tibet is 1.81, which is also the lowest.

In order to find better solutions to the difficulties and problems of minority education, studies and research on such issues and problems are emphasized, and reform and innovations have been launched both at the national and grassroots levels. Initiatives such as introducing electrical audio-visual aids in minority education, setting up schools and classes for girls, training women teachers of minority ethnic origin, getting community and religious leaders involved in the management of schools and organizing twinning programmes between economically developed provinces or cities and minority autonomous regions or provinces have achieved good results.

In short, the state will maintain the policy which favours minority education in both human and material terms. Meanwhile a greater effort will be made to motivate minority people themselves to manage their own education. The joint effort will undoubtedly make a great contribution to the success of minority education in China.

## References

Anon (1995) 'The Progress of Human Rights in China', *Guangming Daily*, 28 December.

Department of Minority Education, State Education Commission (1993) *A Milestone for the Development and Reform of Minority Education in China: A Collection of Documents at the Fourth National Conference of Minority Education*, Beijing: Education Science Press.

Guo Fuchang and Wei Pengfei (eds) (1995) *A Selection of Working Documents of Minority Education in Cities, Provinces and Autonomous Regions*, Chengdu: Sichuan Ethnic Press.

Jin Chili (ed.) (1995) *Ethnic Unity*, Beijing: Beijing Ethnic Press.

People's Republic of China (1980) *Constitution of the People's Republic of China*, adopted on December 4, 1982 by the Fifth National People's Congress of the People's Republic of China at its Fifth Session, Beijing.

State Education Commission (1994a) *Yearbook of Education: 1994*, Beijing: People's Education Press.

State Education Commission (1994b) 'The Development and Reform of Education in China: 1993–1994', Country Report submitted to the 44th Session of International Conference on Education, Geneva.

State Education Commission (1995) *Education Law of the People's Republic of China*, Beijing.

Wang Rongxue (1995) 'Development of Ethnic-Nationality Education of China', paper presented at The Regional Workshop for Cultural Minorities in Asia and the Pacific, 11–15 December, Kunming.

Zhang Jian and Zhou Yuliang (eds) (1984) *Yearbook of Education in China: 1949–1981*, Beijing: China Encyclopaedia Publishing House.

# 18. Language and Education in South Africa

Zubeida Desai and Nick Taylor

In any society, language and education are both highly politicized issues, and their intersection doubly so. The last century of struggle for human rights in South Africa has manifested itself intensely in the domain of education, often around language issues. It is appropriate, therefore, that any attempt to understand questions of intercultural education as the country enters a new non-racial democratic era, should commence with an analysis of the subject of language in education.

## A brief history

Under successive British colonial governments, language was an explicit element of imperialism. Thus in 1903, Lord Milner, installed as British High Commissioner following the Boer War, declared that:

> It is perfectly well-known to be a fundamental principle of the educational policy of the government that the medium of instruction is, as a general rule, to be English. The principle of equality of the two languages has been consistently rejected by us from the first. (Quoted in Hartshorne, 1994, p.308)

The two languages referred to by Milner were English and Dutch. Afrikaans would only emerge as a significant force some quarter of a century later, while ignoring the African languages suited Milner's vision of perpetuating domination by English-speaking whites. There is a strong case for the view that this policy was a significant factor in fuelling the vehemence of Afrikaner nationalism for the better part of the century.

By 1910, negotiations between the four provinces had resulted in unification, the terms of which included the continued disenfranchisement of blacks – except for those with political rights in the Cape – and the equality of language between English and Dutch. English remained the medium of instruction for black pupils.

At this time, the majority of schools for blacks remained under the control of missionaries, who also took the lead in developing written forms of the African languages. By the mid-1930s, mother tongue was the language of instruction for black pupils during the early years of primary schooling, followed by one of the official languages, almost invariably English.

During the same period Afrikaans, which had replaced Dutch as an official language in 1925, became a central element in the struggle by the Purified Nationalists to win political control. After their election victory in 1948, the Nationalist government instituted school language policies even more drastic than the recommendations of their own Eiselen Commission. Mother tongue instruction was extended to cover the entire primary phase, and both English and Afrikaans became compulsory subjects at high school level, where both official languages were also to be used as mediums of instruction.

Mother tongue instruction became a key element in the Nationalist dream of 'purifying' the racial terrain and keeping the different 'peoples' of the country apart. The policy at high school level was an attempt to develop and entrench the position of Afrikaans. While the latter contributed significantly to the strength of Afrikaans as a national language, its longer-term effects were quite opposite to those intended. The Afrikaners could not have misread the lessons of their own opposition to Milner with more disastrous consequences. For it was this issue which sparked the Soweto student uprising on 16 June 1976, which in turn ignited the low grade civil war, which culminated ultimately in the first democratic elections on 27 April 1994.

## Emerging education policy

As our historical review shows, language in education policy (LIEP) in South Africa has two components: language as medium of instruction and language as subject. It is the first component that has been a major problem in South African education. The majority of learners in schools are currently learning through a language which is not their primary language. (We have used the term 'primary language' as opposed to 'home language', 'mother tongue' or 'first language' deliberately because it assumes that people's linguistic repertoires are not only determined at birth. There are choices involved, both circumstantial or individual. People's primary languages can change.)

LIEP in South Africa is currently being redrafted. In line with the language policy outlined in the Constitution, LIEP too has to move away from the official (Afrikaans and English) bilingualism of the past to a more additive multilingualism. The Draft Language Policy (Department of Education, 1996) defines additive multilingualism as 'the situation in which one or more languages are added to the learner's home language(s) without replacing the home language(s) or reducing its importance'. This is proving to be a slow process but, given the sensitivity of the issues and the failure of South Africans to find constructive policies in the past, the caution and thorough consultation which characterize the approach of the new government are appropriate.

The key elements of this debate are recorded in various government documents, commencing with the new constitution, both in its interim form

(RSA, 1993) and the draft bill (RSA, 1996a) due to come into effect when the present Government of National Unity is dissolved in 1999. Proposed language policies are most comprehensively detailed in the Draft Language Policy (Department of Education, 1996), but a great deal of texture is added through two Education White Papers (RSA, 1995; 1996b) and the Draft Schools Bill (Ministry of Education, 1996).

The Constitution provides the fundamental legislative framework within which language policy in education must be determined. Key language provisions from sections 3 and 32 of the interim constitution and chapters 1 and 2 of the draft bill are summarized below.

(a) Eleven South African languages are declared official at national level. These are, in alphabetical order: Afrikaans, English, isiNdebele, isiXhosa, isiZulu, Sepedi, Sesotho, Setswana, siSwati, Tshivenda and Xitsonga. It is declared that conditions shall be created for their development and the promotion of their equal use and enjoyment.

(b) Regional differentiation in relation to language policy and practice is permissible, subject to certain conditions.

(c) Legislation, as well as policy and practice, shall be subject to and based on the following principles:
  (i)   the creation of conditions for the development and promotion of equal use, status and enjoyment of all official South African languages;
  (ii)  the extension of those rights relating to languages which at the commencement of the constitution are restricted;
  (iii) the prevention of the use of any language for the purposes of exploitation, domination or division;
  (iv)  the promotion of multilingualism and the provision of translation facilities;
  (v)   the fostering of respect for languages spoken in the Republic other than the official languages and the encouragement of their use in appropriate circumstances; and
  (vi)  the non-diminution of rights relating to language and the status of languages existing at the commencement of the Constitution. (This clause does not feature in the 1996 Constitution Bill.)

(d) No person shall be unfairly discriminated against, directly or indirectly, on one or more of the following grounds: race, gender, sex, ethnic or social origin, colour, sexual orientation, age, disability, religion, conscience, belief, culture or language.

(e) Every person shall have the right:
  (i)   to receive education in the official language or languages of his or her choice in public educational institutions where that education is reasonably practicable;

(ii) to establish and maintain, at their own expense, independent educational institutions that do not discriminate on the basis of race,
are registered with the state and maintain standards that are not
inferior to standards at comparable public educational institutions.

An important addition to the Constitution Bill of 1996 is the provision for a
commission for the promotion and protection of the rights of cultural, religious and linguistic communities. The White Paper on Education and Training
(RSA, 1995) notes that while the constitution does not in itself define a
language policy for education, constitutionally entrenched language rights
and language policy principles must underpin such a policy at national and
provincial levels. National norms and standards in this regard must therefore
'aim positively at the promotion and development of all official languages, the
non-diminution of language rights existing when the Constitution came into
effect, equal respect for official languages, and multilingualism' (Chapter 7,
Paragraph 38).

Chapter 7, Paragraph 39 notes that 'Language in education policy must
accommodate the right to be instructed in a language chosen by the learner,
where this is reasonably practicable', and concludes: 'The Ministry of Education encourages schools which are willing and able to offer more than one
language medium in order to accommodate parental or learners' preferences
to do so in order to provide for the learner's right of choice of language
medium'.

The following paragraphs are taken from the Minister's introductory message in the Education White Paper on the Organisation, Governance and
Funding of Schools (RSA, 1996b).

My Ministry does not support language imperialism. We will not promote,
under any circumstances, the use of only one of the official languages as the
language of learning (medium of instruction) in all public schools. Language
policy in education cannot thrive in an atmosphere of coercion. No language
community should have reason to fear that the education system will be
used to suppress its mother tongue.

My Ministry is also vehemently opposed to the misuse of cultural and
linguistic distinctiveness as a pretext or camouflage for the perpetuation of
racial privilege in public school education. Any such attempt would be
repugnant to our democracy and false to our nation's history.

The Draft South African Schools Bill (Ministry of Education, 1996) reiterates
the constitutional prohibition of discrimination and prescribes the following
language policy for public schools.

(a) A learner in a public school shall have the right to instruction in the
language of his or her choice where this is reasonably practicable.

(b) The governing body of a public school may determine the language
policy of the school subject to:

(i)   the national policy determined by the Minister under the National Education Policy Act, 1996; and

(ii)  the provincial policy determined by the Member of the Executive Council; provided that no form of racial discrimination may be practised in exercising its policy.

We have outlined this framework within which LIEP is to be formulated in considerable detail so as to provide the reader with a clear picture of the political context within which LIEP is being drawn up. We are reminded of Hawes' (1979) observation that language policies for education are highly charged political issues and seldom, if ever, decided on educational grounds alone. Experience has shown us that those with technical expertise can attempt to influence the process but ultimately the decision is taken by the political actors. The grim history of LIEP in this country, as outlined in our historical introduction, is the spectre that haunts present attempts to formulate new policy. The Draft Language Policy (Department of Education, 1996) attempts to give content to the LIEP principles outlined above. The main proposals contained in the Draft are as follows.

(a)  The role of language in admission requirements. No public school shall apply admission requirements which discriminate on the grounds of language.

(b)  Languages of learning and teaching (LOLTs).
    (i)   A learner in a public school shall have the right to instruction in the language of his or her choice where this is reasonably practicable.
    (ii)  The governing body of a public school may determine the language policy of the school subject to:
    (iii) the national policy determined by the Minister under the National Education Policy Act 1996; and
    (iv)  the provincial policy determined by the Member of the Executive Council provided that no form of racial discrimination may be practised in exercising this policy.
    (v)   Schools shall provide for more than one language of teaching where the need arises.

(c)  Languages as subjects.
    (i)   All learners shall offer at least one approved language as a subject in Grade 1 and Grade 2.
    (ii)  All learners shall offer at least two approved languages, of which at least one shall be an official language, from Std 1 onwards.
    (iii) All language subjects shall receive equitable time and resource allocation.
    (iv)  The following promotion requirements apply to language subjects:
        (iv.i)   In Grade 1 to Grade 4 (Std 2) promotion is based on performance in one language and mathematics.

(iv.ii)  From Grade 5 (Std 3) onwards, one language must be passed.
(iv.iii) Subject to national norms and standards as determined by
         the Minister of Education, the level of achievement required
         for promotion shall be determined by the provincial educa-
         tion departments.

## Analysis

The aims of the policy proposal are designed to avoid the pitfalls of the past.
Broadly speaking, these aims are to facilitate learning and to promote communication and understanding between South Africans through the development of additive multilingualism. However, their effect might be to counter
both these aims. It is surprising to note that only one language is now
compulsory for promotion purposes. This could result in learners being less
multilingual than in the past. Also, the level of proficiency in a language is not
specified, so there is no guarantee that optimal language development, so
crucial in the learning process, will take place.

The assumption, as outlined in a note in the draft policy, seems to be that
such language development would take place in content subject teaching. But
given the very poor learning conditions existing at most schools and the virtual
non-existence of a language across the curriculum approach, the chances of
such language development happening are very slim indeed. Also, in the
present context, given the nature of many teachers' proficiency in the language of learning and teaching, and their general lack of awareness of the role
of language in learning, specialist language teachers will continue to play a
vital role in developing learners' language abilities. Dropping the requirement
to pass all languages learnt as subjects might work against such language
development processes, for there might not be sufficient incentive for learners
to apply their minds to acquiring additional languages.

## Issues arising

Although the Draft Language Policy is a serious attempt to address the
linguistic inequalities of the past, a number of implicit tensions run through
the document. These revolve around three issues.

### The choice factor

The Soweto uprising of 1976 is a grim reminder that no state can afford to
impose a language policy on learners. The drafters of the new LIEP obviously
have been mindful of this fact in providing learners with a fair degree of choice
with regard to the languages they learn. But it is precisely in the scope of this
choice that the problems arise.

Currently, most learners, after the fourth year at school, use either English or Afrikaans as a language of learning and teaching. For that choice to be extended to the nine other official languages involves much more than is acknowledged in the draft language policy. Currently, there are not many materials (textbooks, resources, worksheets, etc) in the nine African languages. These languages have also been confined to limited domains in greater South Africa. It is not likely, therefore, that many learners (and their parents) will voluntarily choose any one of them as their language of learning and teaching.

In addition, the history of LIEP under apartheid is still very fresh in people's memories. Promoting the use of African languages as languages of learning is often perceived as an attempt to 'ghettoize' African learners and deny them access to the mainstream of South African life. Unless such individual choice is accompanied by a public awareness campaign around language and learning issues, the prejudices of the past are likely to militate against individual learners choosing African languages as languages of learning. This might mean that the state would have to play more of an interventionary role in order to facilitate extending the use of African languages in domains other than the ones in which they are currently used. Afrikaans is a case in point. From humble origins it has developed into one of the most widely spoken languages in the country, through vigorous promotion by government and a host of civil society institutions. However, this occurred at enormous cost to the nation. The challenge in developing any language lies in avoiding promoting chauvinism on the part of its speakers, and resentment amongst non-speakers.

## Issues of access

There is also potential tension between the access of learners to the education system and their success within it. The first proposal in the Draft Policy states that no learner can be excluded from a school on the grounds of linguistic proficiency, presumably in any particular language. While such a policy will ensure that a learner is granted physical access to a particular institution, it cannot ensure 'epistemological access' (Morrow, 1993) for that learner if the language of learning and teaching is not his or her primary language. For learning to be facilitated in such a context, teachers who are proficient in the learner's primary language will also have to gain access to that institution. This would have obvious implications for teacher employment or redeployment – a factor that is not currently being mentioned in discussions on the rationalization of teachers.

## Promoting multilingualism

One of the aims of the Draft Policy is to establish additive multilingualism as an approach to language in education. Yet if one looks at the proposals on languages of learning and teaching and languages as subjects outlined above, it is not clear that additive multilingualism will necessarily follow. The constraints on exercising choice in the language of learning and teaching have already been mentioned. In addition, there is no guarantee that a learner will choose to study his or her home language as a subject. Also, it is not necessary for learners to pass their home language in order to be promoted to the next grade.

## Conclusion

Educationists in all multilingual countries face a very difficult choice in formulating and implementing language policy. The problem is particularly acute in South Africa with the legacy of social fragmentation, racial tension and huge disparities in wealth distribution left by 300 years of domination and exploitation.

The fundamental dilemma lies between the development of underprivileged languages on the one hand, and the promotion of a dominant language on the other. The former course is motivated by the need to develop a sense of cultural community and self-worth amongst the speakers of underprivileged languages and to ensure that the majority of South Africans are able to participate fully in the political, social and economic life of the country. The latter is driven by the need to facilitate communication, commerce and nation-building.

The two prongs of this dilemma are not mutually exclusive. Indeed, it can be argued that understanding across the various components of a diverse society would be best achieved through the development of all languages, together with the active promotion of multilingualism. But the reality of the matter is that, given finite resources, there will inevitably be a tipping of the balance one way or the other. How this issue is resolved will depend in large measure on the relative strengths of the different political protagonists.

## References

Department of Education (1996) *Draft Language Policy*, Pretoria, mimeograph.
Hartshorne, K (1994) 'Language Policy in African Education; A Background to the Future', in Mesthrie, R (ed.) *Language and Social History: Studies in South African Sociolinguistics*, Cape Town: David Philip.
Hawes, H (1979) *Curriculum and Reality in African Primary Schools*, London: Longman.
Ministry of Education (1996) 'Draft South African Schools Bill', *Sunday Times*, 9 June.
Morrow, W (1993) 'Epistemological Access in the University', in *AD Issues*, published by the Academic Development Centre, University of the Western Cape.
RSA (Republic of South Africa) (1993) *Constitution of the Republic of South Africa*. Act No. 200 of 1993, Government Printer.

RSA (1995) *White Paper on Education and Training,* Notice No. 196 of 1995, Government Printer.
RSA (1996a) *Constitution of the Republic of South Africa Bill,* Government Printer.
RSA (1996b) *Education White Paper on the Organisation, Governance and Funding of Schools,* Notice No. 130 of 1996, Government Printer.

# 19. Intercultural Education in the UK

Nigel Grant

## The United Kingdom of Great Britain and Northern Ireland

The UK is and always has been multicultural in population, despite perceptions that this has recently changed. This is partly because there is little understanding of the nature and origins of the state itself. We are frequently hearing of Britain 'becoming multicultural', as if it were culturally uniform until the first black Britons settled in the 1950s (Carter *et al.*, 1993; Grant, 1994). The intercultural composition of the population certainly changed over the centuries, but the state was already multinational, multilingual and multicultural right from the start.

This is not always widely recognized, as there still is a confusion of the terms 'the United Kingdom', 'Britain' (or 'Great Britain') and 'England', which are used as synonyms. This confusion is astonishingly common; the vast majority of football fans apparently think that the Union flag is the British or English flag, and we see English fans waving Union Flags, even when playing against Scotland. Indeed, the majority of fans seem to believe that this is the banner of Britain or England. At the risk of becoming pedantic, we need to sort this out, for these terms are not the same (Barrow, 1981).

The United Kingdom of Great Britain and Northern Ireland consists of four countries, in order of size: England, Scotland, Wales and Northern Ireland. They came together at different times and in different ways (Bell and Grant, 1977; Kee, 1976). They vary in population: England has about 50 million people, Scotland 5 million, Wales about 3 million and Northern Ireland about 1.5 million. They have at one time or another been joined with England. Wales was conquered, annexed and then incorporated in 1536. England tried to conquer Scotland, but was finally defeated in 1314 at Bannockburn; this was recognized by treaty in 1328. Scotland was joined to England by a union of the Crowns in 1603 and the parliaments were merged in 1707. Constitutionally, it was a union of two sovereign kingdoms, while Wales was a principality. Together, they make up Great Britain, the English and Scottish flags being combined to form the British flag. The 'Great' in Great Britain has never been a grandiloquent title, in spite of constant misunderstandings; it was simply to distinguish it from Little Britain (Brittany). The Union did not affect the churches of Scotland or England, which were and are still separate and both

178

established, or the legal systems, which are also separate.

In 1801, after the failure of the Irish Rising of 1798, the Protestant Parliament of Ireland was abolished and merged with the British (Kee, 1976). For the flag (the Union Flag) a new cross was invented to add to it. The cross of St Patrick, red diagonal on a white ground, was devised to lie alongside the Cross of St Andrew of Scotland, with an additional narrow white stripe to separate the red and the blue, thus saving the colour-scheme of red, white and blue for the overall effect, while producing a rather messy flag, which almost no one can draw accurately.

The English flag is a simple red cross on a white field; the Scottish flag is a white diagonal cross (a Saltire) on a blue field; the Irish flag was deemed to be a red diagonal cross on white (the modern Irish flag is a tricolour of green, white and orange, and is used in the Republic), and the Welsh flag was never incorporated at all, as Wales was not a kingdom but a principality, and anyway a green and white flag with a red dragon in the middle would not fit the colour-scheme. The Union Flag is not, and never was, the flag of Britain or England.

The last change in the country's name required no changes to banners, for it became the United Kingdom of Great Britain *and Northern Ireland*. Even here, there is some confusion. Northern Ireland is not British: it broke away from the rest of Ireland and stayed in the UK after 1921, having the area with a Protestant majority, six of the nine counties of the province of Ulster – not the whole of Ulster, but part of it. Three counties of Ulster are in the Republic, including Donegal, which contains the northern-most part of Ireland.

The other entities, aside from the Republic of Ireland, are the Isle of Man and the Channel Islands (more accurately, the Bailiwicks of Jersey and Guernsey, which are totally independent of each other). These are not in Britain or the United Kingdom at all; they are not subject to the Westminster Parliament. They are Crown Dependencies, and pay towards defence and foreign policy, which they leave to the UK government. All other powers are in the hands of the Tingwall (Man) and the States of Jersey and Guernsey. Their powers over education are limited in effect because of their scale and dependence on England for models and example, not for any lack of autonomy or legal control (Bell and Grant, 1977).

The various countries have their own languages. England has English, as do many other countries – the United States, Canada, Australia, New Zealand and the Caribbean and of course Scotland, Wales and Ireland, apart from any other languages that may be current. It is also widely used as a *lingua franca* in many other countries, including India, Pakistan, Bangladesh and much of Africa. All English-speakers use the language with their own pronunciations.

Scotland has two native tongues, apart from English. Gaelic is a Geodelic Celtic language; it is spoken by very few (some 60,000 according to the last census) though in some areas like the Western Isles it is spoken by about 80%. The majority of Gaels, however, live in the Lowlands of Scotland (Grant, 1985,

1987; Grannd, 1984; MacKinnon, 1974, 1991). The Scots language is a Germanic tongue, close to English; both developed from 'Anglo-Saxon' dialects. It created a rich literature, particularly in the 15th and 16th centuries, best known for the work of Burns in the late 18th century, by which time it was much penetrated and corrupted by English, which had taken over the role of the official and cultivated language (Kay, 1988). There are no census figures (unlike for Gaelic); many believe that they are speaking 'bad English', which many certainly are not, in spite of the repressive attitudes of many schools. It is widely said that Scots is 'just a dialect', but that is both ignorant and confuses similarity with dependency: Scots is a language *with* dialects, but developed from Anglian separately (McClure, 1986). Most Scots can and do speak English, often shading into Scots.

Welsh, a Brythonic Celtic language, is spoken more widely in Wales, by about 20% of the population, and is used in education, the churches and the media. The number of young speakers is rising, but the overall picture is of general decline, largely because of the influx of non-Welsh-speaking people. It is stronger in the north and centre than in the urbanized south, and immigration has been weakening the currency of Welsh, especially in the border areas. Most Welsh people nowadays speak only English (Bell and Grant, 1977). In Northern Ireland, most of the inhabitants are Anglophone.

The UK, therefore, is a multinational state, with different cultures and to some extent different languages. No other country is part of England (though Wales was for a while). It is not quite a unitary state, nor (so far) federal; it is an accretion that lacks any theoretical framework. The English are, of course, the vast majority, but they are not the whole of the UK. If the UK means anything, it will have to decide what kind of state it is, because it has now become more plural, 'racially' as well as linguistically. This is so not only of the original peoples in the Kingdom, but of others coming into it. This is also true of our European neighbours.

## Immigrant-descended groups in the UK

### European settlers

There have, of course, been settlers in the UK from many sources, but there have been certain patterns since the 19th century which still leave their marks. The first settlers in numbers were the Irish, at a time when the whole of Ireland was still part of the UK. The Great Hunger of the 1840s devastated the West of Ireland, and led to massive emigration from which Ireland is just now recovering (Kee, 1976). The potato blight killed about a million from starvation, and more fled for survival – to Glasgow, Liverpool, London, New York, Boston and many other parts of America, Australia – with marked effects on the populations of these countries. The language was allowed to die, as were some other cultural 'markers', but two were clung to: the Catholic Church and, more vaguely, an attachment to the values (or at least the rhetoric) of Irish Nationalism or, more minimally, support for radical causes. The immigrants were extremely poor, and had to work for what they could get. This led to strike-breaking and undercutting, which encouraged anti-Irish and anti-Catholic feeling for many years, which still can appear at times in the UK. Most of the Irish, however, do not now experience direct discrimination, though memories can be long.

The Italians began coming in the 19th century, at first as workers for the *padroni* (patrons, bosses), who organized seasonal workers to come to Britain for agricultural or unskilled manual work (Colpi, 1991). The earliest, according to the 1861 Census, came from the north and centre of Italy. Immigration expanded to develop in particular trades. The attachment to *campanilismo* (devotion to the region) reinforced the tendency for people from one region to favour one area. In 1871, when the population had come mostly from Central Italy, the earliest southerners settled, making up 20 per cent of the total. This tendency militated against the formation of a single Italian-language community, for there was very little mixing of people from different regions; at first, they kept to their own dialects, as in Italy too. *Padronismo*, which had begun about 1880, lasted until the 1920s. One successful development was in catering – restaurants, cafés, fish and chip and ice-cream shops. The Italians had successfully integrated into British society, and had also found a profitable gap in the market.

Then came the rise of Mussolini and Fascism, and the war. Up to 1940 there was already suspicion; some Italians were active Fascist supporters. At the outbreak of war, there was much action, official and informal, against them, and many were interned. All of the UK experienced anti-foreign sentiment, some of which is still obvious (Colpi, 1991). It took time, but the UK did recover from this episode of anti-Italian hysteria. By the 1960s, Italian cafés were once again reappearing, but with cappuccino and espresso coffee and restaurants deliberately emphasizing their Italianness. The *trattoria* was becoming popular; this has a great deal to do with the rise in popularity of foreign package holidays, and the growth in liking for foreign food. But the figures of Italian residents in the UK – just under 100,000 in 1981 – are almost certainly wildly inaccurate. The Census counted as Italian only those born in Italy: and the numbers of those who changed their names in the 1940s or after are, of course, not known. This applies to most 'immigrant' groups in the UK.

The early settlement of Europeans did not stop there. There were refugees from Eastern Europe, of Jews from Russia and the Baltic States and Poland. Most of them came in the 19th century, and some settled in identifiable 'Jewish' areas (Krausz, 1972). Many were in professions like banking, finance, jewellery; some were successful in academia or the media and publishing; but others were too poor or uneducated to enter these, and instead entered tailoring or the garment industry. Jews in the UK have assimilated to various degrees; most have let their languages fall out of use, and the extent to which they keep up their religion depends largely on their sect. Some arrived with nothing and had to make their own way, some successfully (Krausz, 1972; Wistrich, 1992). Their numbers were added to, slightly, by the Nazi *Endlosung*. Few escaped, fewer were admitted, but a handful of German and East European Jews, survivors of the Holocaust, did come here. They are mostly elderly by now, but some have children, some of whom still retain Jewish identity. There are also other groups of European origin, though most of them came later, after 1950.

## Later immigrant-descended groups in the UK

Most of the Poles came during and after the Second World War. They have not assumed any particular occupational pattern, but because of their military origin, they were nearly all men. Some have maintained their identity, and their children use complementary classes; the attitude of the wives ranges from supportiveness to rejection. Learning Polish can be a burden for a child; it is a complex language, and requires opportunities for practice, which a father is often not well-placed to supply. The absence of Polish-speaking mothers is a particular problem for UK Poles (Graham, 1989).

There was a further change in about the 1960s. One of the earliest records of Chinese immigrants dates from 1814; Hong Kong became a colony in 1843, has grown and prospered. The original immigrants to the UK were settled seamen, latterly overwhelmingly from Hong Kong. Occupational patterns tend, even now, to stress catering, attributable to the growing popularity of Chinese restaurants, in which the Hong Kong Chinese have established a dominance. The languages are mainly Cantonese and Hakka, but while Cantonese has social prestige among the Chinese, Hakka has not, and this tends to colour their own reporting. They learn Chinese characters of writing, but Chinese is essentially idiographic rather than phonetic; their pronunciation is radically unlike that of Putonghua or 'Mandarin'. Most are also fluent in English, especially the young (Chan, 1990; Pan, 1990)

The Afro-Caribbean or West Indian population is descended from slaves who, after liberation, formerly emigrated to the United States, but were stopped in 1952 by the US authorities, and switched their attention to the UK (Krausz, 1972). It seems hard to imagine now, but in the 1950s there was a shortage of labour, especially in jobs that the British were unwilling to do, such as public transport or nursing (Krausz, 1972). Practically all of the West Indians came from Jamaica, Barbados, Trinidad, Bermuda or Tobago, many from the islands where there is a strong British tradition but serious overcrowding, where almost everyone speaks English, where most are Christian, but where there is unemployment and poverty. There is also, in Jamaica for example, an acceptance of single parenthood. They have had to adapt to the realities of life in contemporary Britain, where there is no longer a surplus of jobs, and where racism can still be active. Not surprisingly, many find the social climate hostile, and education does little to improve things, no matter how successfully the children may try to cope with it. West Indians are not evenly distributed through the UK. There are very few, for example, in Scotland, and a large concentration in London. This is partly because they tend to settle in areas with links with their original areas. The host population tend to regard them simply as 'West Indians', to whom they are inclined to attach stereotypes, positive or negative. The Afro-Caribbeans, however, do not think of themselves as simply one undifferentiated group.

It is hard to be precise as to where those from the Indian sub-continent come from, as some of them came before Partition in 1947, and were reinforced when the East African Asians were forced out in 1967 (Khan, 1994). They come mainly from Gujarat and the Punjab (the latter both Indians and Pakistanis) and Bengal, particularly since the independence of Bangladesh in 1971. In fact, the Punjab is a major area for emigration to Scotland for both Indians and Pakistanis (Maan, 1992). Gujaratis are more common in England. They are often referred to as 'the Indian community', 'the Pakistani community' or even 'the Asian community'. These are misnomers, for they are not a single community in any real sense; they constitute several communities, varying hugely in nationality, religion (Hindu, Muslim and Sikh, again with varying degrees of observance and commitment) and in language (Gujarati, Punjabi, Bengali, Urdu, Hindi and several others).

There are other areas of uncertainly as well. The question of prestige applies here, as with the Chinese. Take the case of Punjabi, spoken by most of the Southern Asians in Scotland. Among Indians, especially Sikhs, Punjabi is a sacred and literary language, and therefore has high status. Among Pakistanis, it is not, unlike Urdu (which most Pakistanis speak to some extent). This can therefore colour the self-perception of Muslims, Hindus or Sikhs about their real or *aspired to* language, whatever their fluency may be. Another complication is the passing of time in the host country, for primary immigration has now almost stopped, while children continue to be born. Consequently, a majority of UK Asian children are locally-born, and grow up speaking English (and sometimes other tongues as well), often with unmistakable local pronunciation. This is true of other 'immigrant' groups in the UK as well. *Some* have learned about the home country from their parents' memories, which may describe things as they no longer are (Corner, 1984).

This is particularly obvious among Muslims, but not confined to them. The young people may well meet different sets of values among their contemporaries, and some may find them different from the traditional values of their home. There is a widespread belief that Asian girls will submit to arranged marriages; some do, but this is by no means guaranteed. This is a western perception. It is, in fact, a common occasion of generational conflict in some Asian families.

The extent to which children pursue their parents' values, languages and religion varies enormously. The use of complementary schools and language and religious schools, and the motivation for using them, are impossible to predict. Surveys have suggested that Muslims are the most likely to set a high value on religion, Sikhs least likely, but one has to be careful (Corner, 1984). Most Muslim children use the ordinary schools, though in Scotland, where there are Catholic schools within the public system, some Muslims use these, liking the religious emphasis, even if it is of the wrong kind. The low priority apparently given by Sikhs to religion, according to surveys, may be misleading as well. They are less likely than some Muslims to press for religious or language teaching, but that may be because they prefer to leave that to the *Gurdwara* rather than the school.

The occupation patterns of the Indian and Pakistani groups range from unemployment and unskilled work to professional careers, with a high demand for education. Asians tend to do quite well at school, and the support for education among parents is high (Corner, 1984). But they have also identified successfully a new slot in the market, namely catering. The first Indian settlers in the UK were seamen, who found that there was a demand for their cooking among their own countrymen, and like the Italians and the Chinese came to dominate a portion of the market. It has proved popular, partly because it is different and relatively cheap. These groups, like the Greeks (or at least the Cypriots) have noticed that the British have a habit that they have been able to profit by. In most cities, 'ethnic' food is more interesting without being expensive.

This has implications for young people in settled groups. There is a widespread belief that employment is taken care of: 'They can always go into the restaurant or shop'. Alas for this comforting belief, most young people have no intention of going into the catering or retail trade if there is anything else available; they may use this as a standby, but aspire to qualifications and a profession just as much as anyone else (Corner, 1984; Maan, 1992). Nor are they likely to accept a lower performance from the school. Some will expect the same chances as anyone else to compete with their compatriots, and are as likely as any to react negatively if this is denied them. Minority groups, whatever their achievements, are all too likely to find that the real problems of growing up are compounded by two factors – being part of a cultural minority, and widespread racism.

How many 'ethnic' people are there in the UK at present? The 1993 Census attempted to count the non-Europeans, and came to about three million, 5.5% of the population: about 840,000 Indians, 477,000 Pakistanis, 163,000 Bangladeshis, 157,000 Chinese, and some 891,000 'black groups', of whom 67,000 described themselves as 'black British'. It is largely a matter of self-definition. For one thing, the majority of 'adventitious' populations were born in the UK, and some of them have lost their own language, or have modified their cultural identity somewhat. Ethnic minority populations are found all over the UK, with concentrations in the south-east (about 10%, mostly in London), over 8% per cent in the West Midlands, almost 5% in the East Midlands, over 4% in Yorkshire, but fewer than 2% in Wales, Scotland and the North. This takes no account of the native and European populations, and relies entirely on self-reporting.

This gives us well over 100 languages spoken in the UK. They include Gujarati, Punjabi, Bengali, Hindi, Urdu, Polish, Italian, Portuguese, Greek, Turkish, Cantonese, Hakka, Chinese (Putonghua), and smaller groups speaking Arabic, Thai, Serbo-Croatian, Maltese, Welsh, Gaelic, Scots and Irish, and of course, the West Indian variants of English. All of these languages are to some extent being maintained. The 'native' population is, as has been pointed out, already multicultural. The tasks that this highly diverse population sets the UK are extremely complex. They have to cope with the availability of and access to the learning of their languages, and religion and cultural norms. Then there is racism, xenophobia and religious bigotry. There are many complications, and a great deal more research is needed.

## Problems

### *Language use and availability*

We do not yet know with any certainty about language maintenance among the various minority groups. We do not even know with any accuracy how many there are, both for reasons of distrust of official-seeming enquiries, and because some of the groups may have ambiguities about their own identities.

There are a great many studies of particular minorities, such as Terri Colpi on the Italians (Colpi, 1991) or Bashir Maan on the Scottish Asians (Maan, 1992) but very few studies covering several groups. There is *The Other Languages of England* by the Linguistic Minorities Project, based in London (Khan, 1985). It is a good study but, as the title suggests, it deals only with languages used in England. (It is like the ESRC Centre at the University of Coventry for research into ethnic affairs, which has a great deal of impressive documentation, based on England entirely, but designated as a *national* centre of excellence.) The case studies deal with London, Coventry and Bradford, thoroughly and extensively; but there are no studies of anywhere else in the UK, not in this study nor in the ESRC Centre. The picture is distorted in that no data take account of the multicultural nature of the indigenous population.

What we do learn from this study is the variety in the degree of language retention or switching, the variations in use between generations, something of language revival or decay, and the use of mother-tongue teaching in the schools or complementary classes. The complexity of the tasks is daunting, as this and other studies make clear, because English is the normal language of the UK. Many children still need some help with it, especially linguistic minorities, but not only these. There is little evidence that bilingualism carries a 'deficit' (Haugen *et al.*, 1981).

There is a need for the acceptance of the other languages – their own or someone else's – not just for conversation, but for study. This could take some time, for one of the reasons for scepticism on the part of some minority parents and pupils is the notion that their language will have no currency in society or in education. It also has to be available to children from other groups. There is no need for languages to compete against each other. Anyone can learn several languages. If the Dutch and the Danes can do it, so can the UK.

A basic problem is an assumption that languages are extremely difficult and that everyone speaks English anyway. Some believe that other languages will interfere with the command of English. There are teachers actually forbidding Asian children to speak their own languages to each other, or even mocking them. (This has happened with Welsh, Gaelic and Scots too.) There is at least one local authority which collects figures of children 'whose first language is not English', and sets them out in a way which suggests little understanding of languages or even of geography. This kind of reaction to bilingualism is not universal, but is still far too common. Intercultural education requires a major change in our attitude towards not only pedagogy but the curriculum, for everyone.

This is not to decry the work being done by many local authorities in mother-tongue teaching, and of course the immense difficulty of the tasks in terms of resources, teachers, materials and books. Much good work is being done, and in many schools the attitudes of teachers towards ethnic minorities cannot be faulted. But the negative attitudes survive, and some languages are marginalized. In Scotland, where Gaelic figures in examinations, it suffers in some schools from being offered only as an alternative to French (Grant, 1985) and the Scots language does not figure at all, except in some lessons in literature, usually under 'English' (Kay, 1988). Where is intercultural education in the 'National' Curriculum, or the 5–14 guidelines in Scotland, stated as urgent?

It has to be realized that the study of languages, religions, history and cultures cannot be left as a matter for the minorities. There can be no future for the country if intercultural education is viewed simply as an 'extra' course. Every child needs to be introduced at least to the cultures (languages and the rest) of the people among whom we live, and to develop cultural under-standing beyond this as well. Intercultural education has to be for *everyone*.

## Racism and xenophobia

Quite apart from the social analyses of racial discrimination, its effects on the people who suffer from it, the social waste, the potential for racist attitudes and actions to build up trouble and even danger, there is another basic objection. It is supremely irrational to discriminate against people on the grounds of 'race'. There were even racist 'schools of thought' in the 19th and early 20th centuries, which did a great deal to 'inform' colonial and domestic policy (Grant, 1992); as we celebrate the ending of Apartheid in South Africa, we are too early to rejoice at the relegation of racism to the dustbin of history. Apart from anywhere else, in the UK there are at least 140,000 racial attacks every year. Few (at any rate publicly) advocate 'scientific' racism, but the publications of Professor Richard Lynn of the University of Ulster are just one indication that attempts to generalize about the mental ability of blacks are not altogether gone (Grant, 1992; Lynn, 1972). Many members of minorities in the UK experience disproportionate unemployment, discrimination, insult, even physical attack. This is bound to militate against their chances of success in education. But it goes far beyond victimization of Afro-Caribbeans or Pakistanis. Racism is not all that precise in its selection of victims. This is why racism and xenophobia are linked, as the Jews in the Third Reich had cause to know. It very often is connected with conspicuous physical characteristics, but not necessarily. Essentially, the necessary characteristic is to be *perceived* as basically different (Evans, 1953).

Prejudice is insidious, and not confined to 'races'; women meet it quite often and so can working-class people. Just as Broca tried to justify racial discrimination by arguing from brain-size, he also used the same arguments to justify prejudice against women and the lower classes (Gould, 1984). Prejudice is much more widespread than most of us realize; it can distort relationships by adding curiosity, distaste, dislike, fear, contempt, hatred and so on to discrimination. Racism has been often defined as 'prejudice plus the power to discriminate'. This is incomplete as a definition, but power certainly reinforces prejudice, as happened in South Africa until recently.

The 'outgroup' may seem to be a threat, to the social structure or economically, to housing or jobs, or may simply be there and not subservient, and may actually demand attention to language or religious or cultural needs in education or anything else. If the outgroup is obviously different, it is easy to scapegoat them for all kinds of threat, whether there is any evidence or not. If they are not obviously different, it is still easy to generalize about 'character' (Grant, 1992). People of any 'race' can be racist, and so can the victims. Most people in the UK are 'white', and some of the depressed groups are black or brown; and the whites have most of the power (Ashrif, 1986). In the UK also, the majority have experience, if only vicariously, of being dominant and may react against threats to this with hostility. But to say that whites *must* be racist, and that blacks *must* be victims, is to take the whole argument beyond the exercise of reason, let alone free will. Education does not have an impressive record in shaping attitudes when the pressures in society are strong the other way. We can perhaps deal with the myths and superstitions, and we can do something to make children more familiar with other peoples. Familiarization is possibly a step towards international understanding.

But international understanding is not a specific against conflict. There is no way in which we can ensure that a child can be made to love his Pakistani classmate, but it is possible to get him to treat him right, or at least to avoid kicking or insulting him or her. The ultimate justification of intercultural education is a sense of fairness and justice. If need be, there are certain things we can present as unacceptable. Some attitudes are to be encouraged, and we know how they should seem. They may not be *internalized*, but at least the expectations will be known (Ashrif, 1986).

It is an illusion to expect that 'getting to know' other peoples will guarantee that all will then be well. Prejudice can be aggravated by ignorance, but is easy to forget how fragile knowledge can be. At present, the two communities in Europe who can be assumed to know each other well are in former Yugoslavia and Northern Ireland. They lived next to each other, even with each other, and have just stopped killing each other, at least for the time being. In neither case were the great majority involved, but the fear and the hatred exacerbated it and enabled the active forces to continue. 'Knowing' what the others were 'like' was open to distortion, and at least provided an acceptance of hostility.

All one can say is that it may help if all forces are pulling in the same way and at the same time. Education has to be broad-based, working together with social and political policies. Then something might be achieved, but it will be an uncertain process. Anti-racist, multicultural education cannot work as a mere addition to the curriculum. It cannot rely on having one panacea to solve the whole question of racism. It is an extremely complex phenomenon, and will need complex solutions.

The prospects of effective anti-racist or multicultural education (essentially the same thing) are not great, for the forces behind racism are deep-seated in our society. This is one reason why some authorities tend to marginalize the whole issue as 'trouble'. But it is about accepting peoples' right to be themselves, as themselves, as valuable in their own right, however different they may be in the way they look or the way they speak. It will be a fearsome job, but we have to try (Advisory Council for the Arts in Scotland, 1989).

## Concluding note

The UK is already, and always has been, multicultural in composition, and the peoples that compose it have their own needs and demands as equals. It is also part of the European Union, which is also essentially intercultural. We all, majorities and minorities alike, have to start thinking more plurally. If the EU is important to us, we have to remember that *all of us are minorities now*. Some are not used to this. We do not know our neighbours well enough, and make few attempts to adjust our way of thinking to the fact that the world has changed and we are no longer a world power.

The plurality of the population of the UK is an actual potential advantage. The non-English nations have several hundred years' experience of being a neglected minority, and the English have a great deal to learn about being in a similar position in Europe. This can cut both ways. They can learn what it is like to be in this position – the Danes, for example, know this already – and what it is like to be *distinctive* and maintain self-respect, in language or anything else (Rordam, 1972). Dealing with this is an enormous task for the *whole* curriculum, not just as an add-on. One childhood will not be enough to deal with the necessary lifelong attitudes and skills.

# References

Advisory Council for the Arts in Scotland (1989) *Scottish Education: A Declaration of Principle*, Edinburgh: Scottish Centre for Economic and Social Research.

Ashrif, S (1986) Paper presented to In-service Teachers' Course, Strathclyde Region, November 1986 (Mimeo).

Barrow, G W S (1981) *Kingship and Unity: Scotland 1000–1306*, London: Edward Arnold.

Bell R E and Grant N D C (1977) *Patterns of Education in the British Isles*, London: Allen and Unwin.

Carter, B, Green, M, and Sondhi, R (1993) 'The one difference that "makes all the difference"? Schooling and the politics of identity in the UK'. *European Journal of Intercultural Studies*, 3, 2/3 81–7.

Chan, A (1990) *The Chinese Community in Britain*, Glasgow: Glasgow University Department of Education.

Colpi, T (1991) *The Italian Factor: The Italian Community in Great Britain*, Edinburgh: Mainstream.

Corner, T (1984) *The TEEM Project*, Glasgow: Glasgow University Education Department.

Dutto, M (ed.) (1986) *Fli Italiani in Scozia: la loro cultura e la loro lingua*, Edinburgh: Consulato Generale d'Italia in Scozia.

Evans, B (1953) *The Natural History of Nonsense*, London: Michael Joseph.

Ferguson, J (ed. and commentary) (1320) *The Declaration of Arbroath 1320*, Edinburgh: Edinburgh University Press.

Fryer, P (1995) *Staying Power: The History of Black People in Britain*, London: Pluto Press.

Gould, S J (1984) *The Mismeasure of Man*, Harmondsworth: Penguin.

Graham, Y (1989) 'The Polish Community in Scotland', University of Glasgow MEd thesis.

Grannd, N (1984) 'A Ghaidhlig agus foghlam aur a Ghaidhealtachd's a'Ghalldachd an Alba', *Gairm*, 127, an Samhradh, pp.205–11.

Grant, N (1994) 'Multicultural societies in the European Community – the odd case of Scotland', *European Journal of Intercultural Studies*, 5, 1, 51–9.

Grant, N C D (1985) 'Gaelic in education: needs and possibilities', *Modern Languages in Scotland*, 25 January, 141–50.

Grant, N C D (1987) 'The education of linguistic minorities in Scotland', *Aspects of Education*, 36, 35–52.

Grant, N C D (1992) '"Scientific" racism – what price objectivity?', *Scottish Educational Review*, 24, 1, 24–31.

Haugen, E *et al.* (eds) (1981) *Minority Languages Today*, Edinburgh: Edinburgh University Press.

Hiro, D (1995) *Black British, White British – A History of Race Relations in Britain*, London: HarperCollins.

Kay, B (1988) *Scots – The Mither Tongue*, Edinburgh: Mainstream.

Kee, R (1976) *The Green Flag*, London: Quartet.

Khan, S (1994) 'Bilingualism and the Curriculum', *Multicultural Teaching*, 13, 1.

Khan, VS (ed) (1985) *The Other Languages of England*, London: Routledge and Kegan Paul.

Krausz, E (1972) *Ethnic Minorities in Britain*, London: Paladin.

Kuper, L (1981) *Genocide*, Harmondsworth: Penguin.

Lynn, R (1972) 'Intelligence in Black and White', *The Daily Telegraph*, 20 May, p.14.

Maan, B (1992) *The New Scots*, Edinburgh: John Donald.

MacKinnon, K (1974) *The Lion's Tongue*, Inverness: Club Leabhar.

MacKinnon, K (1991) *Gaelic: A Past and Future Prospect*, Edinburgh: Saltire.

McClure, JD (1986) *Why Scots Matter*, Edinburgh: Saltire.

Modgill, S *et al.* (eds) (1986) *Multicultural Education: The Interminable Debate*, London: Falmer.

Pan Lynn (1990) *Sons of the Yellow Emperor*, London: Mandarin.

Prebble, J (1993) *The Lion in the North*, Harmondsworth: Penguin.

Rordam, T (1972) *Schools and Education in Denmark*, Copenhagen: Det Danske Selskab.

Wistrich, RS (1992) *Anti-Semitism*, London: Mandarin.

# 20. Struggling for Continuity: Ethnic Identities and Language in the United States

William B Thomas and Kevin J Moran

## Introduction

Renewed calls for federal and state laws declaring English the official language of the United States have prompted national debates among scholars, politicians, educators and diverse citizen groups. Champions of 'official English' statutes argue that bilingual programmes are divisive. They threaten national cohesiveness and undermine the unifying role which public schools have historically assumed. In addition to contributing to 'a loss of shared culture' (Porter, 1990, p.214), critics continue, bilingual educational programmes segregate schools and their pupils along ethnic and racial lines. They isolate from the dominant culture those minority communities with the least amount of social power.

Bilingualism opponents have buttressed their national campaign with an ideology that there is greater value in socializing new immigrant groups to prevailing norms than in perpetuating cultural differences, which may foster ethnic pluralism. As an antidote to threats of pluralism, therefore, bilingualism critics prescribe early learning of English to afford newcomers opportunities to assimilate into the mainstream.

At the seat of the controversy over bilingualism is the role of government and public institutions as perpetuators of ethnic group pluralism. Given their views that pluralism is divisive, 'official English' proponents resist spending tax dollars to print thousands of government documents in a hundred or more different languages in order to cater to or validate ethnic differences.

Contrary to National Education Association contentions (Trasvina, 1988), these outcries are not limited to those of right-wing extremist groups. Instead, proponents of 'official English' policies have comprised, over time, US Supreme Court Justices, federal and state legislators, scholars, clergy and assimilated immigrants who were themselves products of Americanization programmes. Columbia University historian Diane Ravitch (1985) sums up the position of the 'official English' proponents. She asserts that these programmes are political tools by which groups promote the maintenance of distinct ethnic communities, each with its own cultural heritage and language.

In her view, most bilingual programmes are neither educationally sound nor grounded in solid research.

Defenders of bilingualism, on the other hand, regard their opponents' perspectives as isolationist. Attitudes which underpin the 'official English' position, they argue, adversely affect foreign relations and commerce, while promoting ethnic tensions. They embrace a view that bilingual classes are useful for preserving the language and culture of diverse ethnic groups. They perceive them as tools for enhancing the learner's self-concept and their school success. To these advocates, forcing minority status groups to relinquish their own language is a mark of oppression, tantamount to cultural genocide. These groups fear that when school-aged immigrant children learn English without receiving instruction in their native tongues, their ethnic groups are probably destined to lose within three generations their ability to converse in the mother language. By forcing students away from their heritage, therefore, teachers may alienate them from their parents, while intensifying parental opposition to the school culture. Champions of bilingualism further maintain that children learn concepts of the host society best in their native language. After a while, these children learn English as they become acclimatized to their new environments.

Bilingualism proponents gained significant political ground and federal support in the 1974 *Lau v. Nichols* case. The US Supreme Court found that San Francisco, California, had denied 1,800 Chinese students equal opportunities through monolingual educational programmes. It decreed:

> There is no equality of treatment merely by providing students with the same facilities, textbooks, teachers, and curriculum; for students who do not understand English are effectively foreclosed from any meaningful education. Basic English skills are at the very core of what these public schools teach. Imposition of a requirement that, before a child can effectively participate in the educational program, he must already have acquired those basic skills is to make a mockery of public education. We know that those who do not understand English are certain to find their classroom experiences wholly incomprehensible and in no way meaningful. (*Lau v. Nichols*, 1974: 566)

Since this decision, the US continues on a trajectory of ethnic and linguistic diversity. The 1990 national census reports that more than 31.8 million people (14% of the nation) speak a language in their homes other than English, compared with 23.1 million in 1980. Moreover, increasing numbers of immigrants are people of colour, some of whom are establishing viable ethnic communities after resettlement. For example, in 1990 there were 355,000 Arabic speakers in US homes, a 57% increase from 227,000 in 1980. Dearborn, Michigan, a community adjacent to Detroit, is the home of the largest Arab population in any US city; their numbers (14,114) comprise 15.8% of this community's total population.

In their book *Multiculturalism and Education*, La Belle and Ward (1994) assert that ethnic groups represent a common ancestry, hold memories of their historical past, or share ways of behaving which help to define members as a distinct population:

> While a group may or may not objectively describe itself, it may also be assigned valid and invalid characteristics by others... The interplay of cultural self perception and perceptions by others combine to provide a foundation for an ethnic group's internal relationships, as well as for its relationship to other groups in society.

Today, as in the past, ethnic groups in the US continue to demand that public institutions accommodate their differences. Some groups have successfully lobbied to have voting ballots issued in a second language. As the largest non-English speaking group in the US, Hispanics have led the charge for bilingualism. These groups are acutely sensitive to anti-bilingual legislation, such as the 'official English' position. They believe that these laws are directed especially at them. Given recent physical attacks upon illegal immigrants arriving from Mexico, these claims are possibly based more upon fact than upon perception.

Opponents of bilingualism have advocated legislation forbidding the publication of voting ballots in Spanish (Barron, 1990; Crawford, 1992). Unlike New Mexico, which allows instruction in languages other than English, California (1986), Arizona (1988), and Florida (1988) have all adopted 'official English' legislation. Large numbers of Hispanics cluster in these four states. To exacerbate Hispanic anxieties, some residents worry, in general, about giving rights and privileges to illegal immigrants, reflected in recent California legislative propositions. These referendums deny public assistance and education to illegal immigrants to the US. Concerned about a redistribution of political power, other citizen groups are fearful of potential Hispanic domination of congressional voting districts.

These clamours for a national language, however, are not recent phenomena. Rather, they are recurring demands arising whenever large waves of minority status ethnic groups immigrate to the US and in some significant way threaten national accord or the status quo. In the wake of World War I hysteria, Nebraska legislators passed laws that were the first of their kind in the US. In 1919, they required all school instruction to be conducted in English, allowing foreign language teaching only after the eighth grade. Additionally, lawmakers mandated that all public meetings be held in English. They then repealed laws that had required that all public documents be printed in German, Swedish and Bohemian newspapers. In 1921, these laws not only became part of the Nebraska state constitution, but legislators also declared English the state's official language (Tatalovich, 1995, pp.33–62).

In the light of these contemporary and historical developments, the remainder of this chapter presents a socio-historical illustration of the enduring conflicts over ethnic group identity and language diversity in the US. We focus on late-19th and early-20th century Polish immigrants to Buffalo, New York, highlighting their struggles against bureaucratic Americanization school programmes. At that time, educational policy-makers developed strategies to eradicate the language of Poles and their ethnic identity. This was an era when agents of public schools exerted their strongest and broadest political initiatives to unify the country through a national language programme.

This chapter will show that with Americanization victories in some Polish communities, contemporary Polish-Americans now experience a sense of lost ethnic identity through their assimilation, contributing to a resurgence of Polish consciousness among their group. Today, third and fourth generation Polish-Americans have rekindled a historic passion for Polish language instruction in public schools. The Polish-American experience has relevance to contemporary debates over bilingualism and ethnic identity. Parallel to this ethnic group's experiences, non-native English speaking ethnic groups immigrating to the US will likely become embroiled in similar political battles over the eradication or preservation of their language and ethnic identities.

## Polish quests for new opportunities

Polish immigrants came to the US in large waves between 1881 and 1930. During the 1921–30 decade alone, 227,734 Poles immigrated, the largest single group of 95,089 arriving in 1921. Of this population, 31,406 settled in Buffalo, New York, by 1920 (Moran, 1993). Second to Chicago, Illinois, Buffalo was the largest resettlement area for Poles in the US.

Several factors contributed to the large exodus of Poles from their homeland. In addition to war and political unrest, economic conditions for Poles and their quest for freedom after years of oppression affected immigration decisions. As an agrarian society, Poland had become overly populated with a peasant class. Agricultural methods were primitive on small farms, which produced meagre crop returns. Insufficient industrial development, depressed wages and high taxes compounded the economic problems of Poles in their homeland.

Despite these conditions, some Polish immigrants to the US later returned to Europe. Anti-immigrant sentiment aimed at southern and eastern Europeans gave rise to concerns about assimilation. Writing about their immigration to Buffalo, John S Curtiss (1931, p.16) noted that migration:

> was no longer made up largely of people from Western Europe. Instead, we find that great numbers came in from Russia, Poland, Italy, Greece, and the Slavic parts of Austria-Hungary. And as men watched this great flood pour in, year after year, they began to doubt whether it was a good thing and to ask if the Melting Pot would work with this vast influx of raw materials or

whether there perhaps would come out a new product, imperfectly mixed, and so a weakened and less useful one.

Other conditions contributing to Polish emigration included prohibition laws, which interfered with their customs of meeting at favourite taverns for social discourse, and unpleasant relationships in certain Polish parishes where Americanization movements thwarted the teaching of Polish in schools (*Foreign-Born*, 1920a, p.21).

New York State legislators debated other anti-immigrant legislation, such as bills forbidding the publication, circulation, or possession of a newspaper written in a language other than English, unless a full English translation accompanied the text. A second bill prohibited the teaching of any foreign language in the public schools other than Greek, Latin, French and Spanish. A third bill banned speech-making about the government in any language other than English (*Foreign-Born*, 1920b, p.5; 1921a, p.173; 1921b, p.217).

At that time, ethnic identity among some Poles ran high. They fervently resisted assimilation, tenaciously held onto their language and remained devoted to memories of a past in their native Poland. Poles feared what journalist Henry Sienkiewicz (cited in Bochenek, 1981, p.11) described as the effects of late 19th and early 20th century assimilation. Commenting on the threats to Polish ethnicity, he criticized

> the strong influence of the American life style and the English language on the conduct and speech of Polish immigrants. Young Poles were marrying women of non-Polish nationality. Polish speech was being corrupted by Anglicisms and falling into disuse among children of immigrants.

Polish anti-assimilation attitudes are best understood in the context of a history of oppression against their group. In Europe, Poles had lived in a divided state under conquering, repressive regimes. They were not permitted to study their language in Russian-dominated sectors of Poland. Prussians tolerated only German language instruction in their schools. Although Austrian-dominated Poland allowed instruction in Polish, educational opportunities for Poles in that sector were greatly limited (Fox, 1970, pp.44–5).

## Coping with ethnic prejudice in the workplace

Sociologist Niles Carpenter of the University of Buffalo found that Poles perceived themselves victims of an unusual amount of antagonism from members of other ethnic groups from the Old World, as well as from American-born citizens. Language differences were in part at the root of much of this enmity. By 1925, Poles were mostly working class, employed as operatives on the docks and in railroad and heavy steel industries. Employer attitudes stereotyping them as 'husky', 'easily influenced by radical labour agitators', and 'difficult to handle' helped to determine employment patterns among

Poles (Carpenter, 1927, p.108). Many of these workers did not understand English. This fact made them the brunt of pranks and jokes from co-workers and validated negative stereotypes of their ethnic group as 'dumb'. German foremen were habitual abusers of their Polish subordinates. However, when Poles learned English through their night schools, communications seemed to have improved, and they were able to ward off much of the verbal taunting (Carpenter, 1927, pp.125–8).

Poles undoubtedly had been sensitive to nativists' rebuffs of their culture, to ethnic jokes, and to pressures to become Americanized and assimilated. Nevertheless, some resisted Americanization efforts. Poles attempted to preserve their ethnic heritage through their churches, parochial and public schools, and newspapers. When threatened by ethnic assimilation initiatives, their clergy declared that the teaching of the Polish language and religion would continue. A 1920 editorial published in Buffalo's *Dziennik dla Wszystkich* (Everybody's Daily) urged its readers:

> Poles! Do not deny your mother tongue and use English only. It is deplorable that so many Americans object so much to foreign customs. It smacks decidedly of Prussianism, and it is not at all in accordance with American ideals of freedom. (Hartmann, 1948, p.256)

The hue and cry of anti-Americanization among Poles was widespread, coming from some of the eminent citizens of Poland. Concert pianist Jan Paderewski echoed these sentiments, proclaiming: 'The Poles in America do not need any Americanization. It is superfluous to explain to them what are the ideals of America. They know them well for they have been theirs for a thousand years' (*The Survey*, 1918).

## Stripping away Polish identity in public schools

In *The Polish Peasant in Europe and America*, sociologists Thomas and Znaniecki (1984, pp.252–3) described the significance of Chicago's parochial schools to Polish identity. These schools were a 'necessary expression of the tendency of the immigrant community to self-preservation and self-development'. They preserved in the younger generation the language and cultural traditions of the old country, while promoting social unity through successive generations. In contrast, these scholars observed that public school children were becoming estranged from their immigrant parents, due to school efforts to acculturate immigrant children.

Poles in Buffalo, like those in Chicago, had to rely upon their parochial schools for the perpetuation of their ethnic identity and religion. When they did so, judicial authorities chided parochial schools for their seeming inability to control the rising crime among their pupils. One judge charged that these schools were retarding the Americanization of Polish children by promoting the Polish language, implying that the language contributed to crime. A vigilant Catholic Church, incensed over these allegations, refuted them in its newspaper, the *Catholic Union and Times* (1921).

At this time, some Anglo-Americans feared that poverty among the foreign-born bred not only delinquency, but social and political revolution as well. To them, Americanization of immigrant adults and the socialization of first-generation Polish-American children were antidotes to threats of radicalism and a deteriorating urban society. George E Smith, Deputy Superintendent and Americanization Director of the Buffalo public schools, defended his programme:

> a polyglot citizenry is a potential danger; illiteracy is a disgrace to a community; the inability of the foreign born to speak the language of the child is a primary factor in the amount of crime... [and] if we are to continue to be a united country, we must provide in some way to afford educational opportunity to and in our Little Italys, Polands, and Ghettos and make our foreign born partners in the U.S. and Co. (*Buffalo School Board Minutes*, 1921)

Reflecting the political tenor of the US, Smith woefully predicted, 'Verily, we are on the way not upward toward enlightenment, but downward to Bolshevism and chaos' (Vogt, 1921, p.222).

Throughout the 1920s, public schools continued to direct their Americanization efforts at recalcitrant parents, through the patriotic values schools transmitted to their children. For example, teachers in a Polish-dominated school contended that immigrants' 'customs and manners belong to the old country; it is therefore our duty to correct and change them to those practiced in our country' (ARB, 1928; Schreiber and Ortney, 1922). Sometimes teachers instructed pupils who had no knowledge of English or American customs. They used this opportunity to teach patriotism as early as pre-kindergarten. They believed that as children began to learn the new language and to converse with friends in it, their parents would sense the need to acquire the language of their adopted country along with the children. In turn, parents would seek language instruction at night school or in Americanization classes (Hopkins, 1921).

Working-class schools for Polish youth used other methods to eradicate Polishness within the pupils. Hoping to supplant foreign language usage through a book reading campaign, teachers tried to permeate immigrant homes with English. They trusted that other family members would read the books their children brought home. A result might be to use 'American ideas and ideals [to] conquer foreign prejudices and [to] bring about the Americanization of some who never could have been reached by other means' (Parkhurst, 1922).

Another strategy for eradicating all traces of ethnic identity in Polish schools and communities entailed lessons that directly accentuated the Americanization effort. Aware that her pupils were of Polish parentage, one teacher developed her language classes around the following theme:

I am an American. I want to become a good American citizen. Every American citizen should be able to speak good English. The school is the place where I can learn to speak good English. I pledge myself to use only the English language in school and on the school grounds (Parkhurst, 1922).

Noting an additional value of this emphasis on English, she believed that by using English at home, the child helped the parents to learn it. So, when pupils returned to school, teachers deluged them with slogans and mottoes such as: 'America! Speak English'; 'Speak the language of your flag'; 'One flag – One language'; and 'Say it in English' (Parkhurst, 1922).

## Fighting teachers' ethnic prejudices

Some administrators objected to practices aimed at transforming immigrant pupils into 'good American citizens' at the expense of their ethnic heritage. John Walsh, principal at a Polish-dominated school, was sympathetic to the Polish child attending public schools. He was critical that some co-workers seemed impervious to the heritage of their pupils. Some even resisted learning to pronounce their pupils' names. To correct this ethnic slight, Walsh chastised 'teachers in the Polish sections of Buffalo [who] often exclaim quite disparagingly that Polish names are impossible to pronounce.' He understood that the practice of changing pupils' names 'to some phonetic spelling or an abbreviated form for the convenience of the teachers' was an assault upon the Polish child's ethnicity. In addition, this practice created problems for children when they sought their school records, citizenship papers, and other documents. He charged:

it is the indisputable right of every child to say how his name shall be spelled and pronounced... a tactful teacher may learn readily from her own pupils how to pronounce their names correctly; and thereby retain that high estimate in the child's judgment that she knows everything or at least is able to learn anything. She gradually inculcates in her pupils that feeling of individuality and self-respect which underlies good character. A failure of any kind is always disheartening. (Walsh, 1921)

Walsh recommended that once teachers were definitely assigned to a school in the Polish district, they ought to study Polish names, their correct spelling and pronunciation. He offered a phonetic guide of Polish sounds, and then reassured teachers that Polish names were easily pronounced, advising them that 'the easiest way of doing anything is the right way of doing it'.

Indeed, ethnic denigration was not limited to Polish youth in Buffalo. In Pittsburgh, Pennsylvania, teacher attitudes toward Polish youth compounded some parental pressures that encouraged some pupils to drop out of school and seek employment instead. One high school student recounted that he left school because his teacher continually made him self-conscious and uncomfortable by mispronouncing his name. He recalled: 'That was the one thing that bothered me and caused me the hell to drop out' (Bodnar *et al.*, 1982, p.43).

Undoubtedly, teachers were overwhelmed by having to instruct pupils from a wide assortment of social, economic and ethnic backgrounds. At times, elementary teachers in the immigrant school districts wrestled with problems of low-achieving pupils. Coming from Poland, children often had little or no schooling experience in their native land. This fact placed additional burdens upon teachers who themselves were not adequately equipped to teach pupils in a second language or were from non-American homes. Typically, language was the greatest barrier between home and school. Some American-born pupils had learned to speak English in homes where Polish was their parents' first language and English their second. When these pupils entered public schools, they spoke English using incorrect grammatical forms.

Teacher concern for proper speech played an important role in forming their perceptions about pupils' character. Emphasizing the necessity for attacking the problems of poor speech at an early age, when the child's mind was plastic, teachers pointed to factors contributing to poor speech. One attributed some pupils' mispronunciation to sociological factors and to other physiological causes, including i) the carry over of foreign linguistic characteristics from the Old World; ii) the influence of the street; iii) carelessness and indifference to proper speech; iv) the wrong position of speech organs; and v) the absence of teeth and thickness of tongue (*School Magazine*, 1922).

As a consequence of problems which pupils brought to school, much of the pedagogy to eradicate errors in speech was routine drill work, involving much repetition. When all else failed, school authorities examined pupils with intelligence tests and sent them off to special classes (Davidson, 1926). Of these classes, 50% were located in Polish-dominated schools. Some parents resisted this policy; school officials reported that 'the idea of placing children in a special class was not taken too kindly by the parents of such children'. In response, special class teachers launched a public relations campaign to sell the idea to their co-workers and to the public (Donnelly, 1929).

## Polish-American teacher responses to ethnic prejudices

Despite these kinds of bureaucratic responses to the foreign-born, there were teachers who spoke out against ethnic prejudices. Some of them were of Polish extraction, although public schools employed only a few such teachers in the 1920s. At these schools, teachers taught pupils about the lives of Polish classical musicians, such as Chopin and Paderewski. One teacher believed that studying these artists 'gives the children a sense of pride in these sons of a race from which their parents also sprang' (Shantz, 1928).

Among this corps of teachers and administrators, Marta Mazurowska was one of the most outspoken advocates for immigrant pupils and their families.

As a seminal figure in the Polish community, she was sensitive to factors which seemed to impinge upon the schooling experiences of Polish children. One factor was teacher attitude. She asserted: 'Some teachers are disposed to consider teaching in the foreign section of our city very difficult and undesirable. This is a mistaken idea' (Mazurowska, 1921). She called for teachers to change their perceptions about teaching in immigrant communities and their schools. Her administration of a multiethnic elementary school, comprising children from 32 ethnic groups, provided her with the opportunity to validate the heritages of her school's diverse pupil population. Aware of the negative ethnic stereotypes prevalent in the US, she taught her pupils about an assortment of classical composers, whose music the bourgeoisie would term 'high culture'. She selected Chopin, Strauss, Dvorak, Gounod, Grieg, Liszt, Saint-Saens and MacDowell, not to inspire ethnocentrism, but rather to 'establish a bond of sympathy which welded together a multitude of difference in language, race, and tradition' (Mazurowska, 1927).

Bureaucratic practices of tracking pupils into school programmes in response to their social behaviour, ethnic backgrounds, or educational problems was anathema to Mazurowska. She illustrated how the annual transfer of 90 fourth and fifth graders from Polish parochial schools to her school affected its programme. She was aware that many of these newcomers had never been in the public school system and that they all knew some English but had learned it as a second language. These pupils had spoken Polish at home. When they took intelligence tests, there were extreme highs and lows in their scores. She believed that the tests measured not only intelligence, but the language abilities of the pupils. So, she administered two intelligence tests (Otis Primary Group Intelligence Test, Form B) to her Polish pupils to consider the effects of language upon their performance. One test was given in English during one week, and the other in Polish the following week.

Mazurowska found evidence that the test was culturally biased in favour of native English speakers. Test items, including teddy bear (named for Theodore Roosevelt), and the lack of fine distinctions between abstract concepts, such as 'justice', 'deceived' and 'capture', proved problematic for the Polish child. There were no teddy bears in Poland. The meaning of adages, such as 'a stitch in time saves nine' had no Polish equivalent. When Mazurowska re-tested these pupils in their native language, two-thirds improved their scores from one to 27 points. This meant that 21 out of 42 pupils would have been misplaced in their grade level assignments and categorized as over-age and retarded. Although her translations compromised the test's validity, she demonstrated that intelligence test items and their meanings were socially constructed. Her findings called into question unfair practices of labelling and tracking Polish pupils on the bases of their comprehending English (Mazurowska, 1922).

This administrator's campaign to rectify the misplacement of Polish youth in special classes had important ramifications for public misperception of this ethnic group as a whole. In an era when people believed that intelligence tests were indicators of 'native mental abilities', they inferred that those who scored poorly on these tests were inherently 'stupid'. For some people, these tests gave credence to ethnic prejudices and negative stereotypes of Poles. Moreover, mental tests helped to legitimize positioning ethnic and racial groups in a social and economic hierarchy in which Poles and other minority status groups were often relegated to the lower end (Thomas, 1986).

## Campaigning for Polish language instruction

In addition to their struggle to overcome teacher prejudices, Poles fought to have Polish language instruction in public schools to preserve their language and as a validation of their ethnic identity. Their struggle differed somewhat from that of German immigrants, who had preceded them to the US. As early settlers in Buffalo, Germans also tried to use schools to promote their ethnic heritage. They viewed German language instruction as the linkage to their ethnic historical past. When school officials denied their petition in 1859 for bilingual instruction in German, they established their own private, parochial schools. However, as Germans began to occupy positions of power in city government, school authorities later acquiesced to petitions to install German as the only foreign language to be taught in elementary schools. With the institution of German instruction (not instruction in German), their children now had a medium through which to communicate with their non-English speaking parents and grandparents (Seller, 1979).

Some Poles, as immigrants, did not see the desirability of adopting English as their language. In lieu of becoming Anglo-Americans, which Americanization programmes implied, they opted to remain Polish or to become Polish-American citizens. As such, they hoped to avoid the risk of total ethnic eradication. Poles were not as successful as Germans in winning a place for their language on the public school horizon.

The outcomes of their struggles demonstrate how ideas about language take on meaning in the political context in which they are used. The meanings may change at any time to suit the interest of groups attempting to gain or to maintain power and control. Illustratively, in 1896, Poles appealed to school authorities to offer their language as a medium for learning English, a concept which the superintendent of education endorsed. Under the weight of negative stereotypes, the Polish language had to vie against images of being the tongue of former peasants and of the working class. Anglo-Saxon public remonstrances successfully squelched their requests. According to University of Buffalo Professor Maxine Seller (1979), German politicians who controlled the public schools at that time opposed any plans to adopt Polish language instruction in schools. Having successfully argued for publicly funded German instruction for their group, ironically, German members of the political body governing public education now contended that teaching Polish was 'un-American'.

## Rekindling the embers of ethnic identity

Despite Polish resistance against their immediate assimilation, public school authorities succeeded in imposing upon the Polish community a bureaucratic, anti-immigrant Americanization programme at the expense of their Polish heritage. After several generations, many Poles would come to embrace the American way of life, succumbing to politicians, public school officials, and public and familial pressures in this battle over Polish language and ethnic identity. Brownie T, a Polish-American living in Buffalo, recalled in a 1996 interview how his father discouraged his children from learning Polish:

> My father said, 'I don't want you to have an accent.' So, whatever was Polish was belittled. Whatever was American was proudly welcomed. So that we couldn't speak Polish, couldn't sing Polish songs, that we learned the Irish holidays and we learned to sing 'When Irish Eyes Are Smiling,' and that made us American. Because no matter what you do, you are going to follow this process of acculturation... The Poles lived in their little community, and they had to acculturate. They had to speak English; they had to know everything there was except Polish.

With much of their group having assimilated over time, Polish-Americans addressed members of their ethnic group in Buffalo in the 1980s. They bemoaned the fact that cultural assimilation had taken its toll on Polish language and identity. Leonard Walentynowicz (1981), a local attorney, reminded the group:

> We must remember we are living in an America where for the last 80 or 90 years we have been told to assimilate ourselves, to reduce, deny and suppress our ethnic identity.

Alfred E Bochenek, a professional engineer and President of the American Council of Polish Cultural Clubs, chastised the Polish community because:

> Polish parishes, the strongholds of Polishness have been decimated... Polish youth of the past, as Polish youth is [sic] doing today, opted for success in the American market place. Priority was given to the English language and the American way of life. Successive generations have departed from parish and neighbourhoods, forgetting the Polish language and eradicating from their speech the residuum of Polish accent. (Bochenek, 1981, p.4)

As political contentions rekindled over English as the national language in the US, Polish ethnic identity surfaced once again. Writing in the *Polish-American Journal*, Eugene Obidinski pointed out the inherent irony of a national language policy in a country that is as ethnically diverse as the US has become.

In a conversation with his newspaper editor, he satirized the apparent redundancy of English becoming official:

> E.O.: 'Have you heard that some of the political candidates want English to be the official language of the United States?'
> Editor: 'Surely after all these years it must be official since everyone uses it everyday... Some Polish Americans feel they can use Polish in their conversations.'
> E.O.: 'If English is mandatory, what will happen to such conversations?'
> Editor: 'Probably it will survive. We have free speech in this country. And when freedom of speech was approved, no language requirement was attached to it'. (Obidinski, 1995)

Responding to this national language issue, and in an attempt to generate enthusiasm for and dispel further passivity among Poles toward a revitalized Polonia in the US, Polish-Americans continue to press for reforms. Throughout the years since immigration, Polish petitions to the Buffalo school board for instruction in their language have been intermittent. Contemporary Polish-Americans now desire to return to a relationship which highlights their ethnic group's historical importance. They seek to create a Polish language magnet school as a reaction to the total assimilation of third and fourth generation Poles and threats to Polish ethnic perpetuity in the US. One Polish-American cultural activist views this opportunity to reinstitute Polish language instruction as a means to preserve the heritage of their ancestors, 'instilling in the Pole a sense of worth and a feeling that they represent the offspring of generations of highly intelligent, highly capable people'. In addition to serving as an intergenerational bridge, he maintains, knowledge of the Polish language provides access to the information published in that language. Andrew G, a fellow critic of public school responses to Polish culture in Buffalo, observed ways in which, even today, teachers denigrate Polish language and culture. He asserts in a 1996 interview:

> Many Polish-Americans are ashamed of their heritage, mainly because they are ignorant of it and exposed to the negative propaganda. Polish is intentionally discouraged by the Buffalo Board of Education by being forced on low achieving students and denied to high achievers interested in it. Guidance counsellors would encourage a student to take French or Spanish but discourage them against Polish by stating it is only taught in the worst schools in the district... We should have Polish language and Polish language studies for students who are losing their identity. We are doing to white Americans what slavery did to black Americans. We are killing their sense of continuity in this world.

Several factors may contribute to contemporary Polish-Americans becoming more comfortable with an ethnic consciousness and their seeking to rekindle a self-ascribed ethnic identity. First, public sentiment has become somewhat less hostile toward and suspicious of Poles. Reduction in social distance has modified historic fears, prejudice and stereotyping of this ethnic group. Second, for some Poles, ethnic identity is probably a defence mechanism against any residual prejudice some Poles continue to encounter in stereotypic anecdotes about their group or in the estrangement which results from the unattained promises of their society. Still others may find comfort in their ethnic identity, given the increase in the numbers of their group who have achieved international and national prominence, including Lech Walesa, Pope John Paul II, and US presidential contender Senator Edmund Muskie. Finally, there are those Polish-Americans who, according to Marcus Hansen's three-generation hypothesis, seek an ethnic resurgence as a consequence of an interest in their ethnic heritage. Hansen's much-debated hypothesis claims that the third generation, once secure in its status attainment, becomes interested in its ethnic heritage which the second generation had eschewed earlier to avoid ethnic stereotyping and prejudice.

As were some of his forebears, Buffalo educator Michael Z is an outspoken opponent of past and current efforts to Anglicize ethnic groups in the interest of a notion that the US is a 'melting pot'. In a 1996 interview, he stated that he favours the pluralist or 'salad bowl' concept, which highlights unique features of each ethnic group living in a diverse society. On the issue of Polish language instruction in public schools, he notes that Hispanics in Buffalo have a strong lobby to garner funding for bilingual programmes in schools which they attend. Polish-American youth should have similar opportunities to learn their language at public expense. Similarly, in a 1996 interview, Leonard W views the issue of ethnic perpetuity as political. He comments that:

> if the ethnic language you are pushing for is not one of the fashionable languages, then it is like hell to get the language studied. We talk multicultural pluralism but we are not in action. Whoever is in power at the time will say where the funding goes.

## Analysis and conclusion

Issues relative to assimilation into the mainstream American culture are complex. It is clear, however, that ethnic identity and language perpetuity remain primary targets at which assimilationists have directed much of their attention. In the US, as in other parts of the world, conflicts over whose ethnic identity and language will prevail in public education are a recurring theme that is likely to resound well into the 21st century. As we approach the next millennium, public schools will continue to grapple with questions about their roles and responsibilities to new ethnic groups immigrating to the US. Can a nation founded on the principle of *e pluribus unum* tolerate in its public schools the diversity in language and ethnic identities which some groups aspire to preserve? Should schools be the appropriate place to perpetuate or to eradicate ethnic differences, and with whom should these decisions lie?

These questions and the events in this case suggest that issues relating to language and ethnic diversity are more of a political consideration than an educational concern. La Belle and Ward (1994) maintain that it is the dominant group in a society which tends to set the agenda and the long-range goals for both the subordinate group and for itself. As such, educational policies and their implementation – even in multicultural settings – are oftentimes the monopoly of the dominant group. 'The results', these scholars further assert, 'demonstrate the extent to which the dominant group values homogeneity or is willing to tolerate differences' (p.58).

Languages of minority status groups are markers of their ethnic identity. Under these terms, bilingualism issues are much more than concerns about lost employment opportunities for immigrants who resist learning the English language. Rather, these issues undergird an ongoing oppositional discourse about language, pandering to public apprehensions about the national economy and social stability. Considering the experiences of Poles in this country, contemporary immigrants, especially members of subaltern classes, may learn painful lessons from the Polish experience in the US. Some immigrants, with their unique cultural attributes, will face an uphill struggle against negative stereotypes directed at their group, in much the same manner as Polish and other southern and eastern European immigrants faced the ridicule and social stigma of their peasant and working-class backgrounds. This time, however, colour will likely become an added obstacle in any struggles arising over control of language and ethnic group identity in public schools.

Irrespective of the outcomes of imminent conflicts over language preservation and ethnic identities, concerns for the well-being of children, whether immigrant or assimilated, must remain paramount. Until these issues are resolved, intractable politicians and policy-makers, at odds with groups favouring rigid, insulating ethnic boundaries, will continue to limit possibilities of identifying and developing the full range of talent needed in any society.

## Acknowledgements

We wish to acknowledge the financial support of the University of Pittsburgh's Canter for Russian and East European Studies and the University's School of Education Faculty–Student Research Fund. We also acknowledge the research assistance of Nancy M Hilligas, graduate student at the University of Pittsburgh.

## References

ARB (1928) 'Character Building Through Poster Work', *School Magazine*, 10, 263.
Barron, D (1990) *The English-Only Question: An Official Language for Americans?* New Haven, CT: Yale University Press.

Bochenek, A (1981) 'The Assimilated Polish-Americans', in Bochenek, A (ed.) *American Polonia: The Cultural Issues*, Detroit, MI: American Council of Polish Cultural Clubs.
Bodnar, J, Simon, R and Weber, M P (1982) *Lives of Their Own: Blacks, Italians, and Poles in Pittsburgh, 1900–1960*, Urbana, IL: University of Illinois Press.
*Buffalo School Board Minutes* (1921) Letter from Smith, G E to Emerson, E D, Chairman, Board of Education (March 21) 1892–1894, Buffalo, NY.
Carpenter, N (1927) *Nationality, Colour, and Economic Opportunity in the City of Buffalo*, Buffalo, NY: University of Buffalo.
*Catholic Union and Times* (1921) 'Can't He Change the Tune?' January 20.
Crawford, J (1992) *Hold Your Tongue: Bilingualism and the Politics of 'English Only'*, Binghampton, NY: Addison-Wesley.
Curtiss, J S (1931) *Our Local Community: Buffalo and Erie County*. Buffalo, NY: Grotzka Press.
Davidson, A C (1926) 'The Problem Child', *School Magazine*, 8, 460.
Donnelly, F (1929) 'Sub-Normal Delinquency', *School Magazine*, 11, 464–5.
*Foreign-Born* (1920a) 'Foreign-Language Press Comments', 1, 7, 19–27.
*Foreign-Born* (1920b) 'Recent Legislation Affecting the Foreign-Born', 1, 4, 2–7.
*Foreign-Born* (1921a) 'Recent Legislation Affecting the Foreign-Born', 2, 5, 169–73.
*Foreign-Born* (1921b) 'Recent Legislation Affecting the Foreign-Born', 2, 7, 215–18.
Fox, P (1970) *The Poles in America*, New York: Arno Press.
Hansen, M L (1966) 'The Third Generation', in Handlin, O (ed.) *Children of the Uprooted*, New York: Harper and Row.
Hartmann, E G (1948) *The Movement to Americanize the Immigrant*, New York: Columbia University Press.
Hopkins, F M (1921) 'Kindergarten and Americanization', *School Magazine*, 3, 150.
La Belle, T J and Ward, C R (1994) *Multiculturalism and Education: Diversity and its Impact on School and Society*, Albany, NY: SUNY Press.
*Lau v. Nichols* (1974) 414 US 563.
Mazurowska, M (1921) 'An Invitation', *School Magazine*, 4, 41.
Mazurowska, M (1922) 'An Experiment with Otis Group Intelligence Scale', *School Magazine*, 4, 270–72.
Mazurowska, M (1927) 'Music Appreciation Lessons', *School Magazine*, 10, 126–7.
Moran, K J (1993) 'School Knowledge Differentiation in Selected Elementary Schools of Buffalo, New York, 1918–1932', unpublished doctoral dissertation, University of Pittsburgh.
Obidinski, E (1995) 'Pride, Prejudice, and the 'P' Word', *Polish-American Journal*, 84, 11, 2.
Parkhurst, J (1922) 'Project – Making an "English" Poster', *School Magazine*, 14, 221–2.
Porter, R P (1990) *Forked Tongue: The Politics of Bilingual Education*, New York: Basic Books.
Ravitch, D (1985) 'Politicization and the Schools: The Case of Bilingual Education', *Proceedings of the American Philosophical Society*, 129, 2.
*School Magazine* (1922) 'Correct Enunciation and Pronunciation in the Primary Grades', 4, 136–7.
Schreiber, H and Ortney, H (1922) 'The Foreigners as Seen in the Homemaking Class at School No. 42', *School Magazine*, 4, 151.
Seller, M S (1979) *Ethnic Communities and Education in Buffalo, New York Politics, Power, and Group Identity, 1838–1979*, Occasional Paper #1, Buffalo, NY: State University of New York at Buffalo.
Shantz, A E (1928) 'English for Special Classes', *School Magazine*, 10, 460–61.
*The Survey* (1918) 'The Spirit of Poles in America', 40, 721.
Tatalovich, R (1995) *Nativism Reborn? The Official English Language Movement and the American States*, Lexington, KY: University of Kentucky Press.
Thomas, W B (1986) 'Mental Testing and Tracking for the Social Adjustment of an Urban Underclass, 1920–1930', *Journal of Education*, 168, 9–30.

Thomas, W I and Znaniecki, F (1984) *The Polish Peasant in Europe and America,* Urbana, IL: University of Illinois Press.

Trasvina, T (1988) *Official English/English Only,* Washington, DC: National Education Association.

Vogt, J M (1921) 'Field Notes', *Foreign-Born,* 2, 7, 221–2.

Walentynowicz, L (1981) 'The Polish-American Professionals', in Bochenek, A (ed.) *American Polonia: The Cultural Issues,* Detroit, MI: American Council of Polish Cultural Clubs.

Walsh, J J (1921) 'Polish Names', *School Magazine,* 3, 192–3.

# Section IV:
# Afterword

## 21. The Way Forward

Jagdish Gundara

The present century has left a legacy of intolerance and hatred but the dominant voice of the new millennium has to be in relation to systems of reconciliation, equity and the strengthening of the civic domain. The replacement of class struggles, despite vast levels of destitution, by religious, ethnic and cultural conflicts, heralds even deeper divides – a new barbarism.

Human societies will require the pooling of all their ingenuity, resources and technologies to obviate some of the conflicts, exclusions and deep cleavages that may occur. Intercultural education can assist this process, particularly in building a civic culture in the context of a civil society. Such a process can help in the socialization of groups of people, and in developing a common shared value system and social cohesion in diverse communities.

This volume on intercultural education contributes to this process by outlining some of the problems, inhibiting factors, possibilities and developments in this field. Educational communities in the new millennium are likely to be diverse by definition. These diverse communities ought to become increasingly democratic by constructing participatory processes which assist in resolving conflicts through dialogue.

The negative way in which social exclusion has reinforced the marginalized or poverty status of many groups not only inhibits the development of equity but also leads to the fragmentation of communities. The growth of bigotry, fundamentalism, brutal child labour and the feminization of poverty in many parts of the world have thus exacerbated intercultural relations. In general, exclusionary educational practices have helped break up what were previously integrated and diverse communities which, in turn, have destabilized polities. Unless more inclusionary policies can be activated this decomposition of solidarities will increase. Nevertheless, inclusionary and exclusionary educational policies and practices are not themselves static. Societal diversities are reflected by historically marginalized groups like Amer-Indians, Inuits, Abo-

208

rigines, and travelling communities like the Masai, Tuereg and Gypsies. Their educational needs and demands can be markedly different from those of European colonizers in the southern hemisphere, or immigrants and refugees from the southern hemispheres who now live in Europe and America.

The assumption in most parts of the world is that nation states are homogeneous, but these are an exception to the rule. Attempts by dominant ethnicities to impose their versions of the nation on others raises conflict. The abominations of 'ethnic cleansing', in Yugoslavia, have revisited Europe 50 years after their seeming eradication. The normalization of this appalling concept has occurred in other contexts in Europe, with events in Northern Ireland in July 1996 having similar consequences. States, *per se*, can only demand loyalty to the civil society if it is based on a shared value system and public culture. In complex societies, attempts to erase autonomous and distinctive cultures, religions, languages, beliefs and ways of life, not only violate human rights but do not enhance national unity. Education systems in such complex situations confront contradictory, paradoxical and divergent demands. The challenges that such complex systems represent have been analysed in many of the chapters in this volume. Education systems will increasingly have to come to grips with these questions and devise flexible and imaginative policies to deal with them. This requires analysis of the whole educational system, the substance of the curricula and formal education systems as well as teacher competencies and pedagogies in order to establish new intercultural educational practices.

Development of new paradigms are critical for the stability of societies in the future. Such educational initiatives ought to obviate the xenophobic and narrow identities which lead to the fragmentation of localities, communities and societies, particularly if these are democratic, rational and egalitarian in principle.

The complex challenge for intercultural education in the next millennium is therefore how to protect the narrow or local identities of groups at one level, while at another developing a broader policy for more democratic civic cultures in which every citizen's human rights are protected and in which all groups have a stake. Intercultural discourses are by definition complex, particularly if they are to engage with substantive education questions. The field cannot respond with simple solutions to complex problems nor can it point to simple truths, which its critics and detractors have tried to assert. In short, there is no simple truth but complex truths and these are politically, economically and socially constructed. It is this complexity that educators will have to unpick during the new millennium. A key element in this complexity is the dominance of exclusionist and supremacist European discourses.

These hegemonic understandings have been informed by the imperialism which led to the powerful intellectual traditions of Eurocentric knowledge. As Edward Said writes:

Without significant exception the universalising discourses of modern Europe and the United States assume the silence, willing or otherwise, of the non-European world. There is incorporation; there is inclusion; there is direct rule; there is coercion. But there is only infrequently an acknowledgement that the colonising people should be heard from, their ideas known. (Said, 1993, p.58)

As a result of this imperial enterprise, not only is Europe in the world but the world is in Europe. Ostensibly this has profound implications for the multilateral, bilateral and intercultural transfer of systems of knowledge. The current reality is that the modes of classification and transfer of knowledge are primarily one way. Discourses from the colonized peripheries are still treated as being marginal in contemporary Europe and America. This, in its wake, has led to reactions which define other civilizations narrowly, which is not an appropriate response where intercultural discourses need to be developed.

In the United States, William Bennett, previously Secretary of State for Education, and Lynne Cheney, who followed him at the National Endowment of the Humanities, reaffirm each other's understanding of western supremacism. Others argue that a multicultural future is already here and that non-culturally supremacist voices dominate the field. They argue that the term multicultural is redundant because culture, like Bakhtin's conception of language, is a socially plural construct. The role of intercultural education in the context of such multicultural realities is to develop new ways of seeing and mapping knowledge at all levels.

Cultures therefore can be construed as signs, sign systems, systems of meaning. They are also a collective positioning, frameworks for giving order and coherence, and ways of thinking and understanding. In particular, for future analysis, culture cannot be restricted to definitions of cultural groups – a substitute for the term 'ethnic' or 'minority'. Every society consists of diverse cultural groups and in that sense every society is constituted of different cultures and, indeed, different languages.

Cultures are also linked to identities and identities inevitably mean differences. We define by defining against each other. If we then argue that there is a continual process of marking out between different cultural groups and attitudes, then all relations, within all societies, are undoubtedly intercultural. Future analysis, research and discourses ought to inform the directions and development of a culture of intercultural relations in the educational domain.

If culture is a system of meanings, then it is essential that we understand the meaning of difference and work to construct a culture which relates to better inter-group relations, so that educators can see it as being a positive aspect which does not threaten any constituency in society.

Democratic processes are deficient but necessary. Discussions therefore ought to be about the educated and educative and about participatory democracy. Majoritarian democracy does not always constitute good governance, particularly if it constructs itself against minority groups of all kinds, including cultural, linguistic and racial minorities. The fact that terms and concepts are ambivalent, or that there are disagreements about some of their meanings, should not lead to their surrender, as there is a continuing power struggle over meanings within and between languages and cultural systems.

Educational rights in intercultural terms not only have to be legally and constitutionally binding but have to have elements like skills and employment, as well as lifelong learning. Such measures of continuing education would help ensure that the citizens remain dynamic and part of intercultural learning and working communities, rather than remain chauvinist and static.

This book has explored a broad range of intercultural educational issues, including issues and questions which need to be explored further. At regional or continental levels it can be argued that intercultural education raises issues which have a different time-span. The European and American discourses in the field arise at a time when these societies assume that they are integrated states. However, the issues as they impinge on Asian and African contexts come at a time when many societies are in the process of constituting their national identities. These are obvious continental and regional differences and disparities.

The processes of modernization and technological change have been successfully accomplished in many East Asian contexts, while the African continent has singularly failed to modernize its indigenous cultural and linguistic systems. Colonialism, Christianity and Islam have all played a role in inhibiting the African elites from engaging seriously and in a positive way with the modernization and integration of African languages, cultures and inter-ethnic relations and with scientific and technological discourses. The processes of ethnicization of Africa may not only be exacerbated by certain financially corrupt African elites but also by the heavy debts owed to the World Bank and the International Monetary Fund. The lack of an educational intervention which engages with African peoples and cultures, places African educationalists and intellectuals in an extremely difficult position. The 'afro-pessimism' of the African middle class is not shared by the younger African educators and intellectuals. Their contribution to intercultural education requires serious consideration to broaden our understanding of problems and potentials for intercultural relations in that vital part of the world.

Intercultural education is a relatively new field and at the present time has not developed a critical and rigorous analytical perspective in a systematic manner, nor are there coherent practices within mainstream education systems. These developments have to take place in and into the new millennium to ensure that education systems can play a proper and fuller role in developing cohesive communities.

## Reference

Said, E (1993) *Culture and Imperialism*, London: Chatto & Windus.

# Index